The Echo of God:

A Commentary for Beginners on
St. Louis Marie Grignion
de Montfort's *True Devotion to Mary.*

Fr. Lance W. Harlow

Nihil Obstat
Reverend Richard L. VanderWeel, S.S.E.
Censor Librorum of the Diocese of Burlington
July 9, 2006

Scripture references are from the:

New American Bible (NAB)
St. Joseph Edition
Catholic Book Publishing Co, 1970

Catholic Family Edition of the Holy Bible (CCD/Douay)
Confraternity of Christian Doctrine Text
Challoner-Douay Text
New York: John J. Crawley & Co., Inc., 1953.

"We have not yet praised, exalted, honored, loved and served Mary as we ought."
— *St. Louis Marie Grignion de Montfort*

De Maria numquam satis

Dedicated to those who taught me true devotion.

Table of Contents

Part II
Perfect Devotion to the Blessed Virgin Mary

Chapter IV. Particular Practices of This Devotion

Introduction

In his Apostolic Letter <u>Rosarium Virginis Mariae,</u> His Holiness Pope John Paul II exhorts the world to "contemplate with Mary the face of Christ." He encourages us further to "contemplate the face of Christ in union with, and at the school of, His Most Holy Mother."[1] The Holy Father presents the Rosary as the means of contemplating Jesus through Mary's eyes.

It is well-known that the Pope's love for Mary was particularly stimulated by his reading of <u>True Devotion</u> while a young man in Poland. He comments in his book <u>Gift and Mystery</u>:

> At the same time I was greatly helped by a book by Saint Louis Marie Grignion de Montfort entitled <u>Treatise of True Devotion to the Blessed Virgin</u>. There I found the answers to my questions. Yes, Mary does bring us closer to Christ; she does lead us to him, provided that we live her mystery in Christ. This treatise by Saint Louis Marie Grignion de Montfort can be a bit disconcerting, given its rather florid and baroque style, but the essential theological truths which it contains are undeniable. The author was an outstanding theologian. His Mariological thought is rooted in the mystery of the Trinity and in the truth of the Incarnation of the Word of God.[2]

This present work is an attempt to respond to the Holy Father's appeal to contemplate Jesus through Mary by making St. Louis de Montfort's <u>True Devotion</u> accessible to the modern reader by explaining some of St. Louis' ideas.

How to Use this Book

<u>The Echo of God</u> incorporates Fr. Frederick William Faber's 19th Century translation of St. Louis de Montfort's <u>True Devotion</u>. Father Faber remarks that the mystery of true devotion to Jesus through Mary continues to reveal itself even after repeated readings and much study of St. Louis' work. He states in the preface to his 1862 translation that:

> I have translated the whole treatise myself, and have taken great pains with it, and have been scrupulously faithful. At the same time, I would venture to warn the reader that one perusal will be very far from making him master of it. If I may dare to say so, there is a growing feeling of something inspired and supernatural about it, as we go on studying it; and with that we cannot help experiencing, after repeated readings of it, that its novelty never seems to wear off, nor its fullness to be diminished, nor the fresh fragrance and sensible fire of its unction ever to abate.[3]

The text of <u>True Devotion</u> appears in *italics* throughout the book.

The purpose of this book is to offer a paragraph by paragraph commentary on what St. Louis is describing. The commentary is not intended to be too theological or academic, but practical and simple enough for the average reader to get the gist of the theological opinions being expressed. There are brief and extended sections of commentary depending upon what is being discussed in order that the reader may understand some principles of spirituality for growth in virtue. Also, the Scripture citations St. Louis refers to have been written out in full both in the New American Bible translation and the older Challoner-Douay translation. Any reader of the <u>True Devotion</u> realizes that the modern English translations don't "match" with what St. Louis is using. In a couple of cases the Latin Vulgate has been included when the English translation doesn't correspond at all to St. Louis'.

In addition there is a "Who's Who?" commentary that explains different saints, theologians, writers and other people St. Louis mentions in his work. This commentary is not an extensive biographical resource, but simply a biographical synopsis to situate the person within history and within some kind of Mariological context if possible.

The last feature of this book includes "Questions for Application" at the end of major sections. The purpose of these questions is to aid the reader in stopping to consider how he or she can live the lifestyle of true devotion.

Audience

This book is intended for beginners in the way of true devotion. Because this book is a commentary and aid to living the lifestyle of true devotion it is essentially a study text. It can be used for individual study or for group study in prayer and discussion groups. It can be incorporated in the making of one's annual renewal of consecration or first-time consecration to Jesus through Mary.

One of the "graces" of studying the <u>True Devotion</u> is that one never arrives at knowing it all. This book is not intended to be an exhaustive commentary on St. Louis' work, but a primer for beginners in the way of true devotion. This is not a book through which one races, but rather is one that ought to be studied, discussed and meditated upon so that the seeds of St. Louis' insights may be deeply rooted in souls.

It is the author's hope that this work will lead many people to Jesus through Mary. Through the intercession of St. Louis de Montfort, and His Holiness Pope John Paul II, may the new springtime of evangelization and the formation of the apostles of the latter times begin to blossom in our lifetime.

Fr. Lance W. Harlow
St. Charles Parish
Bellows Falls, VT
Solemnity of the Annunciation
March 25, 2006

Baptismal Promises and Act of Consecration

Frequently throughout the True Devotion, St. Louis speaks about the perfect renewal of one's baptismal promises. These promises are renewed annually at the Easter Vigil and Easter Sunday Masses. The renewal of promises includes the 3-fold rejection of Satan and the 3-fold Profession of Faith. This baptismal renewal is included below for the reader to keep in mind the essential aspects of our faith in Christ. St. Louis maintains that the lifestyle of true devotion is essentially the renewal of these baptismal promises and that by means of the perfect consecration to Jesus through Mary we are better equipped by Mary's intercession to live out those promises.

Also included below is the formula for the consecration to Jesus through Mary. The consecration is not found in the True Devotion, but in another work entitled the Secret of Mary. For those who use the TAN translation, this formula is found in the back of the book in the collection of prayers. The Montfort Fathers have published a more modern translation that lends itself more to the modern ear. The long form of the consecration is included below with the "core" of the consecration in italics. It is this core that can be renewed daily. Keep in mind the baptismal promises and consecration formula while studying the True Devotion which form the backbone to St. Louis' text and to which he constantly refers.

Baptismal Promises

Do you reject Satan?
And all his works?
And all his empty promises?

(Respond to each question: "I do")

Do you believe in God the Father almighty, creator of heaven and earth?
Do you believe in Jesus Christ, his only Son, Our Lord, who was born of the Virgin Mary, was crucified, died and was buried, rose from the dead, and is now seated at the right hand of the Father?
Do you believe in the Holy Spirit, the holy catholic Church, the communion of saints, the forgiveness of sins, the resurrection of the body, and life everlasting?

(Respond to each question: "I do")

The Act of Consecration

O Eternal and Incarnate Wisdom! O sweetest and most adorable Jesus! True God and true man, only Son of the Eternal Father, and of Mary, always virgin! I adore Thee profoundly in the bosom and splendors of Thy Father during eternity; and I adore Thee also in the virginal bosom of Mary, Thy most worthy Mother, in the time of Thine Incarnation.

I give Thee thanks for that Thou hast annihilated Thyself, taking the form of a slave in order to rescue me from the cruel slavery of the devil. I praise and glorify Thee for that Thou has been pleased to submit Thyself to Mary, thy holy Mother, in all things, in order to make me Thy faithful slave through her. But, alas! Ungrateful and faithless as I have been, I have not kept the promises which I made so solemnly to Thee in my Baptism; I have not fulfilled my obligations; I do not deserve to be called Thy child, nor yet Thy slave; and as there is nothing in me which does not merit Thine anger and Thy repulse, I dare not come by myself before thy most holy and august Majesty. It is on this account that I have recourse to the intercession of Thy most holy Mother, whom Thou has given me for a mediatrix with Thee. It is through her that I hope to obtain of Thee contrition, the pardon of my sins, and the acquisition and preservation of wisdom.

Hail, then, O Immaculate Mary, living tabernacle of the Divinity, where the Eternal Wisdom willed to be hidden and to be adored by angels and by men! Hail, O Queen of Heaven and earth, to whose empire everything is subject which is under God. Hail, O sure refuge of sinners, whose mercy fails no one. Hear the desires which I have of the Divine Wisdom; and for that end receive the vows and offerings which in my lowliness I present to thee.

> *I, (Name), a faithless sinner, renew and ratify today in thy hands the vows of my Baptism; I renounce forever Satan, his pomps and works; and I give myself entirely to Jesus Christ, the Incarnate Wisdom, to carry my cross after Him all the days of my life, and to be more faithful to Him than I have ever been before.*
>
> *In the presence of all the heavenly court I choose thee this day for my Mother and Mistress. I deliver and consecrate to thee, as thy slave, my body and soul, my goods, both interior and exterior, and even the value of all my good actions, past, present and future; leaving to thee the entire and full right of disposing of me, and all that belongs to me, without exception, according to thy good pleasure, for the greater glory of God, in time and in eternity.*

Receive, O benignant Virgin, this little offering of my slavery, in honor of, and in union with, that subjection which the Eternal Wisdom deigned to have to thy maternity, in homage to the power which both of you have over this poor sinner, and in thanksgiving for the privileges with which the Holy Trinity has favored thee. I declare that I wish henceforth, as thy true slave, to seek thy honor and to obey thee in all things.

O admirable Mother, present me to thy dear Son as His eternal slave, so that as He has redeemed me by thee, by thee He may receive me! O Mother of mercy, grant me the grace to obtain the true Wisdom of God; and for that end receive me among these whom thou lovest and teachest, whom thou leadest, nourishest and protectest as thy children and thy slaves.

O faithful Virgin, make me in all things so perfect a disciple, imitator and slave of the Incarnate Wisdom, Jesus Christ thy Son, that I may attain, by thine intercession and by thine example, to the fullness of His age on earth and of His glory in Heaven. Amen.

True Devotion to Mary
Preliminary Remarks

These preliminary remarks are directed to leading the reader into the study and life of true devotion in order to excite devotion to Mary. Devotion to Mary leads directly and quickly into knowledge of Jesus Christ. Once one knows and loves Him there is a greater zeal for evangelization.

>*1. It was through the most holy Virgin Mary that Jesus came into the world and it is also through her that He has to reign in the world.*

St. Louis begins his preliminary remarks to the true devotion to Jesus through Mary by introducing the role of the Virgin Mother as a means. She is the means by which Jesus came into the world by virtue of the Incarnation and Nativity. And she is the means by which Jesus continues to reign in this world. Another English translation[1] states that He "must reign" (from the French: "doit régner.") That is, she must continue to give birth to Him in a mystical sense as she gives Him to the world. Her maternity must continue because His majesty continues.

>*2. Mary was singularly hidden during her life. It is on this account that the Holy Spirit and the Church call her Alma Mater—"Mother secret and hidden." Her humility was so profound that she had no inclination on earth more powerful or more constant than that of hiding herself from herself as well as from every other creature, so as to be known to God only.*

Two recurrent virtues ascribed to Mary throughout <u>True Devotion</u> are her hiddenness and humility. St. Louis cites St. Jerome's translation of the Hebrew word 'almah' as 'hidden and unknown' (as does Bérulle). St. Louis maintains that Mary's humility was so extensive that there was not even a trace of self-complacency or self-love. There was no self-consciousness. Perfect humility hides itself. Mary, with deepest humility, remained hidden in the sight of men and women and ardently desired that obscurity. Only God knows the depths of her humility. Mary fulfills in the most perfect way St. Paul's dictum: "It is no longer I who live, but Christ who lives in me."[2]

>*3. He heard her prayers when she begged to be hidden, to be humbled and to be treated as in all respects poor and of no account. He took pleasure in hiding her from all human creatures, in her conception, in her birth, in her life, in her mysteries, and in her resurrection and assumption. Even her parents did not know her, and the*

angels often asked one another: "Who is that?" (Cant. 3:6; 8:5) because the Most High either had hidden her from them, or if He did reveal anything, it was nothing compared to what He kept undisclosed.

<u>Scriptures</u>

Song of Songs 3:6 and 8:5 NAB: "What is this coming up from the desert?," and "Who is this coming up from the desert?" St. Louis cites this passage in order to stress wonder at such an elegant and beautiful creature who emerges from the obscurity of the "desert." This perfect creature is none other than the Virgin Mary. The text lends mystery to the arrival of the woman coming from the obscurity of the desert of humility.

St. Louis continues to treat of her hiddenness and humility as being divinely willed by God. Not even the angels understand the sublimity of this particular creature and certainly no human being fully understands her.

> *4.   God the Father consented that she should work no miracle, at least no public one, during her life, although He had given her the power to do so. God the Son consented that she should hardly ever speak, though He had communicated His wisdom to her. God the Holy Spirit, though she was His faithful spouse, consented that His Apostles and Evangelists should speak very little of her, and no more than was necessary to make Jesus Christ known.*

True Devotion is very theocentric and Trinitarian. That is, it always refers to God (Father, Son and Holy Spirit) and takes its source from God. Mary has reference to each person of the Blessed Trinity. St. Louis states that it was God's will that Mary perform no public miracle although she was full of grace and charisms. Think of what charismatic gifts Mary possessed yet refrained from exercising them! Jesus, the Son, the Word-made-Flesh, wills that she who was full of the "Word" not preach from the fullness of these word gifts—prophecy, knowledge, understanding and wisdom. And the Holy Spirit who inspired the Apostles and Evangelists wills that Mary remain unknown by history—except for that which pertains to her Son and to making Him known. The will of the Trinity then, during Mary's life on earth, was that she remain obscure, silent and unknown by men. This dimension of charismatic, personal and worldly silence finds its source in her profound humility. Pope Paul VI comments on the Trinitarian dimension of Marian devotion when he states:

> In the first place it is supremely fitting that exercises of piety directed towards the Virgin Mary should clearly express the Trinitarian and Christological note that is intrinsic and essential to them. Christian worship in fact is of itself worship offered to the Father and to the Son and to the Holy Spirit, or, as the liturgy puts it, to the Father through Christ in the Spirit…In the Virgin Mary

everything is relative to Christ and dependent upon Him. It was with a view to Christ that God the Father from all eternity chose her to be the all-holy Mother and adorned her with gifts of the Spirit granted to no one else. Certainly genuine Christian piety has never failed to highlight the indissoluble link and essential relationship of the Virgin to the divine Savior.[3]

5. Mary is the excellent masterpiece of the Most High, the knowledge and possession of which He has reserved to Himself. Mary is the admirable Mother of the Son, who took pleasure in humbling and concealing her during her life in order to favor her humility, calling her by the name of "woman" (Jn. 2:4; 19:26), as if she were a stranger, although in His heart He esteemed and loved her above all angels and all men. Mary is the "sealed fountain" (Canticles 4:12), the faithful spouse of the Holy Spirit, to whom He alone has entrance. Mary is the sanctuary and the repose of the Holy Trinity, where God dwells more magnificently and more divinely than in any other place in the universe, not excepting His dwelling between the Cherubim and Seraphim. Nor is any creature, no matter how pure, allowed to enter into the sanctuary except by a great and special privilege.

Scriptures

Canticles 4:12 Douay: "My sister, my spouse, is a garden enclosed, a garden enclosed, a fountain sealed up."

Song of Songs 4:12 NAB: "You are an enclosed garden, my sister, my bride, an enclosed garden, a fountain sealed."

In this love song from the Song of Songs, St. Louis alludes to the Virgin Mary who is reserved solely for her Spouse, the Holy Spirit. The "enclosed garden" and "fountain sealed" imply both her virginity and her exclusive relationship to the Holy Spirit. From their relationship of Divine love the Incarnation of Jesus the Eternal Word results. St. Louis states that Mary becomes the "sanctuary" (a holy dwelling place) of the Trinity whereby God occupies "space" in this world.

Again, St. Louis follows the three-fold Trinitarian exposition of Mary in relation to the Father, Son and Holy Spirit. As a creature, she is the Father's greatest work of creation. (Jesus, of course, is one with the Father, and is not one of His creatures). Jesus, protects his mother's humility by continuing to conceal her from the world of men. St. Louis goes so far as to say that this concealment gives the appearance that she is "a stranger" to her own Son, as He refers to her simply as "woman" at the wedding feast of Cana (Jn 2:4) and at the Crucifixion (Jn19:26) in John's Gospel. The latter is a reference to the word "woman" in the Book of

Genesis. This title bestows upon Mary the designation as the new mother of the living in the life of the Church. It is she who will be fruitful and multiply in the lives of souls.

Pope Paul VI explains in Marialis Cultus the Virgin's unique relationship with the Holy Spirit:

> Reflecting on the Gospel texts— (Lk. 1:35), (Mt. 1:18,20)— ["Fathers and writers of the Church"] saw in the Spirit's intervention an action that consecrated and made fruitful Mary's virginity and transformed her into the "Abode of the King" or "Bridal Chamber of the Word" the "Temple" or "Tabernacle of the Lord" the "Ark of the Covenant" or "The Ark of Holiness," titles rich in biblical echoes. Examining more deeply still the mystery of the Incarnation, they saw in the mysterious relationship between the Spirit and Mary an aspect redolent of marriage, poetically portrayed by Prudentius: "The unwed Virgin espoused the Spirit" and they called her the "Temple of the Holy Spirit" an expression that emphasized the sacred character of the Virgin, now the permanent dwelling of the Spirit of God.[4]

St. Louis furthermore reveals that admission to this sanctuary –the Immaculate Heart of Mary—is God's gift to those who practice true devotion; a point on which he will elaborate further.

> *6. I say with the saints, the divine Mary is the terrestrial paradise of the New Adam, where He was made flesh by the operation of the Holy Spirit, in order to work there incomprehensible marvels. She is the grand and divine world of God, where there are beauties and treasures unspeakable. She is the magnificence of the Most High, where He hid as in her bosom, His only Son, and in Him all that is most excellent and most precious. Oh, what grand and hidden things that mighty God has wrought in this admirable creature, as she herself had to acknowledge, in spite of her profound humility: "He that is mighty hath done great things to me." (LK 1:49). The world knows them not, because it is both incapable and unworthy of such knowledge.*

<u>Scriptures</u>

Luke 1:49 NAB: "The Mighty One has done great things for me, and holy is his name."

This verse is part of Mary's Canticle in which she proclaims the greatness of the Lord. Despite Mary's profound humility, she admits for generations to come the wonders that God has worked in her. Only those who know Mary and abide in her Immaculate Heart will begin to know and appreciate the depths of these wonders and graces.

In this paragraph St. Louis speaks about Mary as the new paradise on earth in which is located the New Adam—Jesus. From Mary's womb even Jesus works miracles as one notices in the scene of the Visitation where John the Baptist leaps in the womb of his mother, Elizabeth. The use of the adjective "divine" to describe Mary does not imply that she is a deity. It is simply an attribute of perfection or excellence, in as much as one would say that "the meal was divine."[5] Mary is a perfect creature, but she is not God.

An interesting point of contrast that St. Louis makes early in his preliminary remarks is the opposition between "the world" and Mary. The world, meaning those who do not have the Holy Spirit and are opposed to God, cannot understand the beauty and mystery of Mary and her role as the Mother of God. Nor does the Lord give to those who reject Him an understanding into this mystery for "they look but do not see and hear but do not listen or understand" (Matthew 13:13).

> 7. *The saints have said admirable things of this holy city of God; and, as they themselves avow, they were never more eloquent and more content than when they spoke of her. Yet, after all they have said, they cry out that the height of her merits, which she has raised up to the throne of the Divinity, cannot be fully seen; that the breadth of her charity, which is broader than the earth, is in truth immeasurable; that the length of her power, which she exercises even over God Himself, is incomprehensible; and finally, that the depth of her humility, and of all her virtues and graces, is an abyss which never can be sounded. O height incomprehensible! O breadth unspeakable! O length immeasurable! O abyss impenetrable!*

The holy city of God now refers to Mary. Biblically it is Jerusalem. Mary becomes in a sense the new Jerusalem, the new Temple, in which dwells the holy of holies, Jesus. St. Louis extols four particular aspects of her virtues: namely, her merits, charity, power and humility. The contemplation and meditation upon these four virtues provide joy to the saints and to the Church. In living true devotion one has access to Mary's merits, charity, power and humility. The more we desire to possess them, the more she grants them to us.

> 8. *Every day, from one end of the earth to the other, in the highest heights of the heavens and in the profoundest depths of the abysses, everything preaches, everything publishes, the admirable Mary! The nine choirs of angels, men of all ages, sexes, conditions and religions, the good and the bad, nay, even the devils themselves, willingly or unwillingly, are compelled by the force*

of truth to call her "Blessed." St. Bonaventure tells us that all the angels in heaven cry out incessantly to her: "Holy, holy, holy Mary Mother of God and Virgin"; and that they offer to her, millions and millions of times a day, the Angelic Salutation, Ave Maria, prostrating themselves before her, and begging of her in her graciousness to honor them with some of her commands. Even St. Michael, as St. Augustine says, although the prince of the heavenly court, is the most zealous in honoring her and causing her to be honored, and is always anxiously awaiting the honor of going at her bidding to render service to some one of her servants.

Who's Who?

St. Bonaventure was a Franciscan and professor of theology at the University of Paris as well as Minister General of the Friars Minor. He lived from 1221-1274 and was greatly influenced by St. Bernard. His writings on Mary appear in commentaries on the Gospels of Luke and John, conferences on the gifts of the Holy Spirit and in twenty-four sermons specifically treating the Blessed Virgin Mary.[6] St. Bonaventure speaks about Mary's containing all the perfections of the saints. He develops devotion to Mary emphasizing her maternal relationship with us her children, her spiritual motherhood, mediation and a devotion to the Eucharistic Jesus through her hands.[7]

St. Augustine of Hippo, North Africa was a Bishop and Doctor of the Church. He lived from 354-430. A brilliant theologian he wrote on various theological topics. His writings on the Virgin Mary occur especially in his Christmas sermons and in some exegetical works on Scripture. He writes on her being without sin and on her faith.[8] St. Augustine writes about Mary in relation to her Son and to the Church. He examines theologically her role in the Incarnation, her virginity and cooperation with God's plan and her preeminent place as a member of the Church.[9]

All of creation recognizes the irrefutable truth that the Blessed Virgin Mary is God's masterpiece. The invisible world of the angels must acknowledge her blessedness as well as the visible world of mankind. St. Louis states that they are "compelled by the force of truth to call her 'Blessed.'" In this we find, of course, an echo of Mary's Magnificat: "All generations will call me blessed." (Lk. 1:48) The nine choirs of angels include: angels, archangels, powers, virtues, principalities, thrones, dominions, cherubim, and seraphim. The angels recognize her as the Queen of Angels and honor her with her title as "full of grace." These angels await assignments from Mary to go to earth. A close ally of Mary is the archangel St. Michael. He is associated with honoring her, causing her to be honored and tending to her devotees on earth. St. Michael is the ally of all those who make the true devotion and should be called upon to promote true devotion and to acquire the grace to live it. We grow in our love for Mary and in our fidelity to the practice of true devotion by earnestly seeking St. Michael's intercession and protection.

9. The whole earth is full of her glory, especially among Christians, by whom she is taken as the protectress of many kingdoms, provinces, dioceses and cities. Many cathedrals are consecrated to God under her name. There is not a church without an altar in her honor, not a country nor a canton where there are not some miraculous images where all sorts of evils are cured and all sorts of good gifts obtained. Who can count the confraternities and congregations in her honor? How many religious orders have been founded in her name and under her protection? How many members in these confraternities, and how many religious men and women in all these orders, who publish her praises and confess her mercies! There is not a little child who, as it lisps the Hail Mary, does not praise her. There is scarcely a sinner who, even in his obduracy, has not some spark of confidence in her. Nay, the very devils in hell respect her while they fear her.

The universality of Mary's presence in the Church is evident. Her influence exists not only in churches named after her and after the events in her lifetime, but also there are a great number of religious orders founded under her patronage. Ancillary to religious orders are confraternities and lay apostolates. From the purest and most innocent child to the most notorious sinner all find refuge in Mary. Even the demons recognize her and the graces God has given her.

Now there begins three "After that's" (French: "après cela"). Having demonstrated the universal importance of Mary in the life of the Church, St. Louis draws the following three conclusions. (1) Mary deserves more of our attention; (2) Her full dignity remains a secret to us; and, (3) Her holiness can only be revealed to us by grace.

10. After that, we must cry out with the saints: "De Maria numquam satis"—"Of Mary there is never enough." We have not yet praised, exalted, honored, loved and served Mary as we ought. She deserves still more praise, still more respect, still more love, and still more service.

The first "after that" is for us to have the zeal of the saints in doing more for Mary. St. Louis exhorts us first to praise, respect, love and serve her more--in imitation of the angels in heaven and of the generations of men and women on earth. As we live out the true devotion over the years we have to ask ourselves how do we praise, love, respect and serve Mary more and more. The occasion of her feast days is a good time to make this examination of conscience; so is the annual renewal of our consecration.

11. After that, we must say with the Holy Spirit: "All the glory of the King's daughter is within" (Ps. 44:14). The outward glory which Heaven and earth rival each other in laying at her feet is as nothing in comparison with that which she receives within from the Creator and which is not known by creatures, who in their littleness are unable to penetrate the secret of secrets of the King.

<u>Scripture</u>

Psalm 44:14 Douay: "All glorious is the king's daughter as she enters; her raiment is threaded with spun gold."

Psalm 45:14-15 NAB: "All glorious is the king's daughter as she enters, her raiment threaded with gold; in embroidered apparel she is led to the king. The maids of her train are presented to the king. They are led in with glad and joyous acclaim; they enter the palace of the king."

The gold here symbolizes the dignity, purity and glory of such a woman. Mary is the daughter of the King of Heaven. Her interior beauty remains hidden to all but the Blessed Trinity, despite the breathtaking outward adornment. There is a further allusion to Ezekiel 16:10-13, notably in verse 13 in which the prophet reminds Israel that God the Father has chosen her: "Thus you were adorned with gold and silver; your garments were of fine linen, silk, and embroidered cloth…You were exceedingly beautiful, with the dignity of a queen." Israel however, fell into disgrace because of her sins; Mary is preserved from sin and retains her queenly dignity.

Mary's being chosen by the Father to be the Queen of Heaven is much more notable than the attention she receives from men and angels. The Father's reasons for choosing Mary are so far beyond our understanding that we will never penetrate the mystery of His election. It remains a secret. For St. Louis this notion of secret implies three things. First, is that Mary's role in the economy of salvation is not fully understood. Secondly, each of us needs a special grace from the Holy Spirit to truly understand this lifestyle of true devotion. And thirdly, the secret remains in the inner life of the individual who lives the true devotion, because as St. Louis will state further on, the essence of this devotion consists of the interior life.[10]

> 12. *After that, we must cry out with the Apostle, 'Eye has not seen, nor ear heard, nor man's heart comprehended' (1 Cor. 2:9) the beauties, the grandeurs, the excellences of Mary—the miracle of the miracles of grace, of nature and of glory. "If you wish to comprehend the Mother," says a saint, "comprehend the Son; for she is the worthy Mother of God." "Here let every tongue be mute."*

<u>Scriptures</u>

1 Corinthians 2:9-10 NAB: "'But as it is written: What eye has not seen, and ear has not heard, and what has not entered the human heart, what God has prepared for those who love him,' this God has revealed to us through the Spirit. For the Spirit scrutinizes everything, even the depths of God."

13

St. Louis adapts this passage from 1st Corinthians to emphasize that the human imagination and senses cannot penetrate Mary's beauty and dignity. It remains the role of the Holy Spirit to reveal to us the mystery of salvation and how Mary participates in that plan of salvation. Just as St. Paul desires to communicate the wisdom of God through the Holy Spirit to the church at Corinth, so too does St. Louis stress that the secret and wisdom of God about Mary must be revealed through the same Holy Spirit. The notion of divine secret continues the thread of "secret" that St. Louis begins in the preceding paragraph.

Who's Who?

The "saint" quoted is St. Eucherius, a 5th Century bishop, who after the death of his wife, lived as a hermit in France in imitation of the great Egyptian desert hermits. Elected Bishop of Lyons around 434 he authored various letters and homilies. He died around the year 449.[11]

Three types of "miracles" are also mentioned in this paragraph. The miracle of grace refers to Mary's unique position as a creature being "full of grace." The miracle of nature refers to her position as having a perfect human nature without the stain of original or actual sin. And, finally, the miracle of glory refers to her assumption body and soul into heaven—one of the first fruits after her Son, Jesus, of what we shall be.

> 13. *It is with a particular joy that my heart has dictated what I have just written, in order to show that the divine Mary has been up to this time unknown, and that this is one of the reasons that Jesus Christ is not known as He ought to be. If then, as is certain, the knowledge and the kingdom of Jesus Christ are to come into the world, they will be but a necessary consequence of the knowledge and the kingdom of the most holy Virgin Mary, who brought Him into the world for the first time, and will make His second advent full of splendor.*

St. Louis emphasizes as he concludes his preliminary remarks that the world has not known Mary well enough and as a result neither has it known her Son, Jesus. If she reveals Him to the world and brings Him into the world (as indicated by the two advents) then to make her better known, would imply making Jesus better known, also. Hence the consequent goal of evangelization—one of the end results of the lifestyle of true devotion is that it leads to the revelation of Jesus Christ as Lord. While the first advent was in the silence of a cave; the second advent will be "full of splendor." For each advent, Mary is necessary. How this second advent will occur remains a mystery.

Application of the Lifestyle of True Devotion

1. Is my relationship with Jesus the most important of all my relationships?
2. How does Mary maintain my relationship with her Son?
3. How do I pray to be humble and hidden from the world?
4. How do I practice silence both internally and externally?
5. When do I pray for the grace every day to enter into the Immaculate Heart of Mary?
6. Do I pray to be in the world but not of the world? How do I practice that distinction?
7. Do I have a devotion to, or at least pray to, St. Michael the Archangel to know Mary?
8. What religious orders, cities, churches, or groups do I know who are named after Mary?
9. How can I show more respect, honor, love and service to Our Lady?
10. How am I evangelizing and leading people to Jesus through Mary?

Chapter 1

Necessity of the Blessed Virgin and of Devotion to Her

*14. I avow, with all the Church, that Mary, being a mere crea-
ture that has come from the very hands of the Most High, is in
comparison with His Infinite majesty less than an atom; or rather,
she is nothing at all, because only He is "He who is" (Exod. 3:14);
consequently that grand Lord, always independent and sufficient
to Himself, never had, and has not now, any absolute need of the
holy Virgin for the accomplishment of His will and for the manifes-
tation of His glory. He has but to will in order to do everything.*

Scriptures

Exodus 3:14 NAB: "God replied, "I am who am." Then he added, "This is
what you shall tell the Israelites: I AM sent me to you."

St. Louis alludes to Exodus 3:14 in which God reveals His name to Moses at
the burning bush. God the Father is not dependent upon His creatures for anything
and exists independently of them. He manifests Himself and reveals His plan of
salvation over time, beginning with Moses and culminating with Jesus, "born of
a woman, born under the Law, to redeem those under the law, so that we might
receive adoption as sons" (Galatians 4:4). But Mary is not God, she is a creature.
In this presentation on "necessity," St. Louis makes it clear that God's choice of
this "mere creature" is not of an absolute necessity (meaning that He had no other
choice or alternative). God is not dependent upon any creature to bring about His
will. God can do without Mary. The essential point is that the Almighty God
chooses this creature out of His love for her in order to bring about His great plan
of salvation through the Incarnation of His Son.

*15. Nevertheless, I say that, things being as they are now—that
is, God having willed to commence and to complete His greatest
works by the most holy Virgin ever since He created her—we may
well think He will not change His conduct in the eternal ages; for
He is God, and He changes not, either in His sentiments or in His
conduct.*

St. Louis continues by speaking about the immutability of God or the un-
changeability of God. God doesn't move from a lesser degree of perfection to
a greater degree. Everything that He does is perfect. Having already chosen the
most perfect means—that is, choosing Mary to be the mother of Jesus—He will
not discontinue His perfect work with her, nor find a better means. At this point
St. Louis introduces three articles illustrating the necessity of God's choice of the

Virgin Mary and he defines how that "necessity" is not absolute, but hypothetical. These articles include necessity for the Incarnation, in the sanctification of souls, and her role in the latter times. He presents in article two, two major consequences derived from Mary's role in the sanctification of souls.

Article One
Mary was Necessary to God in the Incarnation of the Word

In this article St. Louis presents reasons why Mary's role in the Incarnation is essential. He states that God needs Mary for the Incarnation, not out of an absolute necessity meaning that He is powerless to do it any other way, but out of a hypothetical necessity, meaning that He could have done it another way, but chose her as the most perfect means for the Incarnation.

> *16. It was only through Mary that God the Father gave His Only-begotten to the world. Whatever sighs the patriarchs may have sent forth, whatever prayers the prophets and the saints of the old Law may have offered up to obtain this treasure for full four thousand years, it was only Mary who merited it and found grace before God (Lk. 1:30) by the force of her prayers and the eminence of her virtues. The world was unworthy, says St. Augustine, to receive the Son of God directly from the Father's hands. He gave Him to Mary in order that the world might receive Him through her. The Son of God became man for our salvation; but it was in Mary and by Mary. God the Holy Spirit formed Jesus Christ in Mary; but it was only after having asked her consent by one of the first ministers of His court.*

Scriptures

Luke 1:30 NAB: "Do not be afraid Mary, you have found favor with God."

Who's Who?

St. Augustine (see above in #8)

In the entire plan of salvation history there was only one human being destined to find "favor with God." Despite the many great, holy and heroic men and women of the Old Testament era, Mary is the one who would be the Mother of the Messiah. This "favor" or grace is so important it even deserves a special, divine pronouncement, coming forth from the archangel Gabriel for her benefit and for all generations to remember. The dialogue of the Annunciation in Luke 1:26-38 also reveals the necessity of Mary's free co-operation with God's plan. She freely accepts her role in God's plan.

> *17. God the Father communicated to Mary His fruitfulness, inasmuch as a mere creature was capable of it, in order that He might give her the power to produce His Son and all the members of His mystical Body.*

Mary receives two types of fruitful motherhood from God: (1) She is the mother of His only-begotten Son; (2) She is the mother of the Church—the mystical body of Christ. As mother of the mystical body she becomes the mother of each individual son and daughter of God. This motherhood fulfills her vocation and brings about many fruits or graces in the lives of every individual; and in a special way, extraordinary graces for those consecrated to her by means of the lifestyle of true devotion.

> 18. *God the Son descended into her virginal womb as the New Adam into His terrestrial paradise, to take His pleasure there, and to work in secret marvels of grace. God made Man found His liberty in seeing Himself imprisoned in her womb. He made His omnipotence shine forth in letting Himself be carried by that humble maiden. He found His glory and His Father's in hiding His splendors from all creatures here below, and revealing them to Mary only. He glorified His independence and His majesty in depending on that sweet Virgin in His conception, in his birth, in His presentation in the temple, in His hidden life of thirty years, and even in His death, where she was to be present in order that He might make with her but one same sacrifice and be immolated to the Eternal Father by her consent, just as Isaac of old was offered by Abraham's consent to the will of God. It is she who nourished Him, supported Him, brought Him up and then sacrificed Him for us.*

> *Oh, admirable and incomprehensible dependence of God, which the Holy Spirit could not pass over in silence in the Gospel, although He has hidden from us nearly all the admirable things which the Incarnate Wisdom did in His hidden life—as if He would enable us by His revelation of that at least, to understand something of its excellence and infinite glory! Jesus Christ gave more glory to God the Father by submission to His Mother during those thirty years than He would have given Him in converting the whole world by the working of the most stupendous miracles. Oh, how highly we glorify God when, to please Him, we submit ourselves to Mary, after the example of Jesus Christ, our sole Exemplar!*

Jesus is the new Adam. While He is not formed "of the earth," His human nature is formed from the body of Mary. And while the Father does not breathe life into Him, Jesus is Life itself—"I am the Way, the Truth and the Life" (John 14:6). "I lay down my life in order to take it up again" (John 10:17). Mary's womb is analogous to the garden of Eden which is protected by another righteous servant, St. Joseph, who takes Mary and the Child in her womb into his home and protects them from their murderous enemies, e.g., King Herod.

St. Louis highlights two aspects of Jesus' gestation. It is in her womb that He experiences His first pleasure as a human being and it is also there that He performs His first miracle of grace—as we see in the scene of the Visitation.

There is a divine paradox between "imprisonment/liberty" and "pleasure" in her womb. It is truly the locus of contemplation where all external activity is momentarily suspended. There Jesus is nourished by His mother. St. Louis reprises the theme of hiddenness as he describes the hiddenness of Jesus in Mary's womb as the glory of the Father. Jesus' hiddenness is an aspect of the cross in its most embryonic stage where He first lays down His life in obedience to the Father's will. The splendor of His Divinity is hidden from other creatures.

His independence and royal majesty is reduced to dependence on a mother and foster father. His dependence on His mother is further emphasized at Calvary whereby she silently acquiesces to God's will at the foot of the Cross.

St. Louis stresses that Jesus gave more glory to God by submitting His "hidden life" to Mary for thirty years than He would have had He performed great miracles instead. By way of imitation of Jesus, then, St. Louis exhorts us to submit ourselves to Mary also which in turn will glorify the Father.

> *19. If we examine closely the rest of our Blessed Lord's life, we shall see that it was His will to begin His miracles by Mary. He sanctified St. John in the womb of his mother, St. Elizabeth, but it was by Mary's word. No sooner had she spoken than John was sanctified; and this was His first miracle of grace. At the marriage in Cana He changed the water into wine, but it was at Mary's humble prayer; and this was His first miracle of nature. He began and continued His miracles by Mary, and He will continue them to the end of ages by Mary.*

It is by Mary that Jesus begins His miracles. St. Louis remarks that at the Visitation Mary's greeting to Elizabeth sparks Jesus' first miracle of grace so that John the Baptist leaps in the womb of his old mother. (See Luke 1:30 ff.) The first miracle of nature is the changing of the water into wine at the wedding feast of Cana. (See John 2:1-12) This is also a miracle of self-manifestation. This miracle occurs at the prompting of his mother's intercession for the newly married couple who find themselves in dire straits. Of interest concerning this miracle is whether the couple actually know that they have no more wine or if only Mary and the wine steward know. In any event, one could surmise that Mary now continues to perform many acts of intercession with her Son on our behalf without our knowledge.

Commenting on the miracle at Cana, which Pope John Paul II has elevated to a luminous mystery of the Rosary, the Holy Father states:

> Another mystery of light is the first of the signs given at Cana when Christ changes water into wine and opens the hearts of the disciples to faith, thanks to the intervention of Mary, the first among believers…the role she assumed at Cana in some way accompanies Christ throughout his ministry. The revelation made directly by the Father at the Baptism in the Jordan and echoed by John the Baptist is placed upon Mary's lips at Cana, and it becomes the great maternal counsel which Mary addresses to the Church of every age: "Do whatever he tells you" (Jn. 2:5) This counsel is a fitting introduction to the words and signs of Christ's public ministry and it forms the Marian foundation of all the 'mysteries of light.'[12]

Mary opens the hearts of the disciples to faith and by the lifestyle of true devotion to Jesus through Mary, we see the gradual opening of our own soul to greater faith through her constant intercession. We may never know in this life how constant her intercession has been for each of us.

> *20. God, the Holy Spirit, being barren in God—that is to say, not producing another Divine Person—is become fruitful by Mary, whom He has espoused. It was with her, in her, and of her that He produced His Masterpiece, which is God made Man, and that He goes on producing daily, to the end of the world, the predestinate and the members of the body of that adorable Head. This is the reason why He, the Holy Spirit, the more He finds Mary, His dear and inseparable spouse, in any soul, the more active and mighty He becomes in producing Jesus Christ in that soul, and that soul in Jesus Christ.*

The relationship of the Holy Spirit and Mary is one of fruitfulness. The joint operation of the Holy Spirit and Mary producing Jesus foreshadows Mary's co-operation in the working of the Holy Spirit in individual souls. The Holy Spirit continues to work with Mary in "new Christs"—that is, Christians. And in one of his most insightful remarks, St. Louis observes the inseparability of the Holy Spirit and Mary. The more a soul is devoted to Mary, the more the Holy Spirit will operate in that soul, recognizing therein His spouse. What a wonderful charismatic dimension to this lifestyle of true devotion.

Pope Paul VI comments on the role of Mary who calls down the Holy Spirit to form Jesus in souls when he states in Marialis Cultus:

Considering finally, the presence of the Mother of Jesus in the Upper Room, where the Spirit came down upon the infant Church (cf. Acts 1;12-14:2:1-4) they enriched with new developments the ancient theme of Mary and the Church. Above all they had recourse to the Virgin's intercession in order to obtain from the Spirit the capacity for engendering Christ in their own soul, as is attested to by Saint Ildephonsus in a prayer of supplication, amazing in its doctrine and prayerful power: 'I beg you, holy Virgin, that I may have Jesus from the Holy Spirit, by whom you brought Jesus forth. May my soul receive Jesus through the Holy Spirit by whom your flesh conceived Jesus…May I love Jesus in the Holy Spirit in whom you adore Jesus as Lord and gaze upon Him as your Son.'[13]

Clearly the more one is devoted to Mary the more one receives the Holy Spirit and His gifts. A soul can grow more steadily in the virtues and charismatic gifts when the Spirit and the Bride are operating together. When we live the true devotion we have a special devotion to the Holy Spirit and should frequently pray to Him for an outpouring of His gifts.

21. It is not that we mean that our Blessed Lady gives the Holy Spirit His fruitfulness, as if He had it not Himself. For inasmuch as He is God, He has the same fruitfulness or capacity of producing as the Father and the Son; only He does not bring it into action, as He does not produce another Divine Person. But what we mean is that the Holy Spirit chose to make use of our Blessed Lady, though He had no absolute need of her, to bring His fruitfulness into action, by producing in her and by her Jesus Christ and His members—a mystery of grace unknown to even the wisest and most spiritual among Christians.

Mary brings the fruitfulness of the Holy Spirit into action. The Holy Spirit who is "Lord and Giver of Life" brings about new life both in the Incarnation of Jesus and in the sanctification of the members of the Church. St. Louis reiterates that this is not an absolute necessity, but one of divine predilection and love. In many respects how this works still remains a mystery.

<u>Application of the Lifestyle of True Devotion</u>

1. How do I recognize Mary's role in salvation history concealed in the prophetic books of the Bible? How do I see it especially in the readings at Mass during Advent and Christmas? On feast days of Our Lady?
2. How does my devotion to Mary lead me to a greater dependence upon God the Father?

3. How is my submitting to Mary giving more glory to God than if I did not submit? How do I submit every day?
4. Do I trust Mary or do I feel I have to make a "name for myself" on my own?
5. Have I thanked Our Lady for blessings she has obtained for me that still remain unknown to me?
6. How has my devotion to Mary increased my love for the Holy Spirit her Spouse? Have I tried to separate my devotion to her from my devotion to the Holy Spirit?
7. Do I invoke the Holy Spirit, through Mary's intercession, for an outpouring of graces?

Article Two
Mary is Necessary to God in the Sanctification of Souls

22. The conduct which the Three Persons of the Most Holy Trinity have deigned to pursue in the Incarnation and the first coming of Jesus Christ, They still pursue daily, in an invisible manner, throughout the whole Church; and They will still pursue it even to the consummation of ages in the last coming of Jesus Christ.

The work of the Holy Trinity continues in the lives of every baptized soul until the Second Coming of Christ. This work of the Trinity includes Mary's participation just as it did originally at the Incarnation. This is a mystery of God's operation in the world. St. Louis is continuing his idea of necessity. He will examine in the next three paragraphs each Person of the Trinity and His relationship to Mary.

Lumen Gentium, the Second Vatican Council's document on the Church, concerning the continuing role of Mary's maternity in the world, states:

This maternity of Mary in the order of grace began with the consent which she gave in faith at the Annunciation and which she sustained without wavering beneath the cross. This maternity will last without interruption until the eternal fulfillment of all the elect. For, taken up to heaven, she did not lay aside this saving role, but by her manifold acts of intercession continues to win for us gifts of eternal salvation.[14]

23. God the Father made an assemblage of all the waters and He named it the sea (mare). He made an assemblage of all His graces and he called it Mary (Maria). This great God has a most rich treasury in which He has laid up all that He has of beauty and splendor, of rarity and preciousness, including even His own Son;

and this immense treasury is none other than Mary, whom the saints have named the Treasure of the Lord, out of whose plenitude all men are made rich.

St. Louis alludes to the act of creation in Genesis by which God creates the waters (mare) necessary to provide for life on earth. In a similar way He creates Mary who will also bring about new life on earth through the birth of Jesus. Just as He gathered the physical elements together to form water, so too does He "gather together" the fullness of graces and virtues in the creation of Mary. Water leads to the sustenance of natural life. Mary leads to the sustenance of supernatural life by grace (in Christ Jesus) through the waters of Baptism.

> *24. God the Son has communicated to His Mother all that He acquired by His life and His death, His infinite merits and His admirable virtues; and He has made her the treasurer of all that His Father gave Him for His inheritance. It is by her that He applies His merits to His members, and that He communicates His virtues, and distributes His graces. She is His mysterious canal; she is His aqueduct, through which He makes His mercies flow gently and abundantly.*

Mary is a unique creature because she receives in advance all the graces of Jesus' death and resurrection before He is born. Pope John Paul II states:

> In Mary the Holy Spirit descends and acts—chronologically speaking—even before the Incarnation, that is, from the moment of her Immaculate Conception. But that happens in view of Christ, her Son, in the extra-temporal sphere of the mystery of the Incarnation. For her the Immaculate Conception constitutes, in advance, a participation in the benefits of the Incarnation and Redemption, as the highpoint and fullness of the "self-gift" which God makes to man. And this is accomplished by the power of the Holy Spirit.[15]

The reception of these graces enables her to be conceived without original sin. Pope Pius IX declared solemnly that: "The most Blessed Virgin Mary was, from the first moment of her conception, by a singular grace and privilege of almighty God and by virtue of the merits of Jesus Christ, Savior of the human race, preserved immune from all stain of original sin."[16]

Because Mary is without sin, she continues to be the pure vehicle through which Jesus' graces flow into the souls of men and women. What Jesus "acquired" by His death and resurrection was victory over sin. The lifestyle of true devotion is an habitual way of life for those who participate in Jesus' victory over sin, striving to live in a state of grace and avoid sin. They accomplish this especially through the renewal of their baptismal promises and the cultivation of virtue through Mary's aid and protection.

> *25. To Mary, His faithful spouse, God the Holy Spirit has communicated His unspeakable gifts; and He has chosen her to be the dispenser of all He possesses, in such wise that she distributes to whom she wills, as much as she wills, as she wills and when she wills, all His gifts and graces. The Holy Spirit gives no heavenly gift to men which He does not have pass through her virginal hands. Such has been the will of God, who has willed that we should have everything through Mary; so that she who, impoverished, humbled, and who hid herself even unto the abyss of nothingness by her profound humility her whole life long, should now be enriched and exalted and honored by the Most High. Such are the sentiments of the Church and the holy Fathers.*

Mary has received all the gifts of the Holy Spirit. And as the Spouse of the Holy Spirit she is entrusted with the " right" and "permission" to dispense of these gifts by her own choosing. According to St. Louis, all the charismatic gifts pass through Mary's hands. This heavenly privilege --dispenser of grace—is the fruit of the humility God found in Mary.

Pope John Paul II states that:

> The apostolic community [at Pentecost] had need of [Mary's] presence and of that devotedness to prayer together with her, the Mother of the Lord. It may be said that in that prayer "with Mary", one perceives her special mediation deriving from the fullness of the gifts of the Holy Spirit. As His mystical spouse, Mary implores His coming upon the Church born from the pierced side of Christ on the cross, and now about to be revealed to the world.[17]

We can seek those same charismatic gifts through her intercession according to the will of God for each one of us.

> *26. If I were speaking to the freethinkers of these times, I would prove what I have said so simply here, drawing it out more at length, and confirming it by the Holy Scriptures and the Fathers, quoting the original passages, and adducing various solid reasons, which may be seen at length in the book of Father Poiré,_ La Triple Couronne de la Sainte Vierge. But as I speak particularly to the poor and simple, who being of good will, and having more faith than the common run of scholars, believe more sim-*

ply and more meritoriously, I content myself with stating the truth quite plainly, without stopping to quote the Latin passages, which they would not understand. Nevertheless, without making much research, I shall not fail to bring forward some of them from time to time. But now let us go on with our subject.

St. Louis has drawn from many sources, one of which is the above-mentioned book whose full title is: <u>The Triple Crown of the Blessed Virgin Mary Mother of God Woven From Her Principal Grandeurs of Excellence, Power and Goodness, and Enriched with Multiple New Ways of Loving, Honoring and Serving Her</u>, written by Fr. François Poiré in Paris in 1639.[18] Many of St. Louis' references in <u>True Devotion</u> remain obscure to the modern reader, but perhaps one of the main points in this paragraph is the identification of his audience as the "poor and simple." The best motivation for, and perseverance in, the lifestyle of true devotion is love. An intellectual analysis of true devotion focusing on theological debate and scrutiny will bear little fruit. There appears to be a certain weariness in St. Louis' tone concerning these scholars. We make progress in the lifestyle of true devotion to the degree ultimately that we make progress in love.

> *27. Inasmuch as grace perfects nature, and glory perfects grace, it is certain that Our Lord is still, in Heaven, as much the Son of Mary as He was on earth; and that, consequently, He has retained the obedience and submission of the most perfect child toward the best of all mothers. But we must take great pains not to conceive this dependence as any abasement or imperfection in Jesus Christ. For Mary is infinitely below her Son, who is God, and therefore she does not command Him as a mother here below would command her child who is below her. Mary, being altogether transformed into God by grace and by the glory which transforms all the saints into Him, asks nothing, wishes nothing, does nothing contrary to the eternal and immutable will of God. When we read then in the writings of Sts. Bernard, Bernardine, Bonaventure and others that in Heaven and on earth everything, even God Himself, is subject to the Blessed Virgin, they mean that the authority which God has been well pleased to give her is so great that it seems as if she had the same power as God; and that her prayers and petitions are so powerful with God that they always pass for commandments with His majesty, who never resists the prayer of His dear Mother, because she is always humble and conformed to His will.*
>
> *If Moses, by the force of his prayer stayed the anger of God against the Israelites in a manner so powerful that the most high and infinitely merciful Lord, being unable to resist him, told him to*

let Him alone that He might be angry with and punish that rebel-
lious people, what must we not, with much greater reason, think of
the prayer of the humble Mary, that worthy Mother of God, which is
more powerful with His Majesty than the prayers and intercessions
of all the angels and saints both in heaven and on earth?

<u>Who's Who?</u>

St. Bernard of Clairvaux, France, a Benedictine/Cistercian and founder of the Clairvaux Monastery lived from 1090-1153. He is one of the great medieval theologians and writers on Mary. He has been called the "Champion and Singer of Mary."[19] St. Bernard uses the image of the "aqueduct" which St. Louis de Montfort will repeat throughout <u>True Devotion</u>. He wrote specifically Four Sermons "In Praise of the Virgin Mother," sermons for liturgical feasts and the sermon entitled the "Aqueduct." He also speaks about Mary as the mediator[20] with her Son the Mediator between God and men, an idea which St. Louis will use repeatedly as well. Another aspect of St. Bernard's understanding of Mary is the importance of devotion to her intercession because of her role in salvation history. While not developing many new ideas on Mary, he expresses himself with a mystical and contemplative depth heretofore unknown.

St. Bernardine of Siena, Italy lived from 1380-1444. He was a Franciscan reformer whose preaching mission throughout Italy consisted, among other things, of devotion to Mary. The focus of these missionary sermons was to call people back to the practice of their Christian lives and to promote devotion to Mary as Mother of God.[21] His collected sermons on Mary form the "Treatise on the Blessed Virgin." St. Bernardine develops the idea of Mary as the spouse of God and as the highest of all his creatures (ideas which St. Louis de Montfort will also use). St. Bernardine speaks as well about Mary's universal mediation.[22]

St. Bonaventure (see above in #8)

In this paragraph St. Louis states that because Mary is always obedient to God's will and neither asks for anything nor wishes anything contrary to His will, He always answers her prayers. In that respect, she fulfills most perfectly that which Jesus describes for His disciples who ask Him to teach them how to pray when He states in the Our Father: "Thy will be done on earth as it is in Heaven." Mary as a faithful disciple prays in perfect conformity to God's will. In living the true devotion, we learn to seek God's will above all other things and to find joy in His will even when there are crosses.

28. In the Heavens Mary commands the angels and the blessed.
As a recompense for her profound humility, God has empowered
her and commissioned her to fill with saints the empty thrones
from which the apostate angels fell by pride. The will of the Most
High, who exalts the humble (Lk. 1:52), is that Heaven, earth and
Hell bend, with good will or bad will, to the commandments of the

humble Mary, whom He has made sovereign of heaven and earth, general of His armies, treasurer of His treasures, dispenser of His graces, worker of His greatest marvels, restorer of the human race, Mediatrix of men, the exterminator of the enemies of God, and the faithful companion of His grandeurs and triumphs.

Scriptures

Luke 1:52 NAB: "He has thrown down the rulers from their thrones, but lifted up the lowly."

St. Louis provides a broad interpretation within this same Magnificat where Mary states that "all generations will call me blessed" (Lk.1:48) extending it to all souls in Heaven, on earth and in Hell. The souls of both the saved and the damned must acknowledge her blessedness.

The Marian praises ("sovereign", "general", "treasurer", etc.) are the titles of various stars from Fr. Poiré's book, Crown of Power. St. Louis notes that there is a progression in the spiritual life, as embodied by Mary, demonstrating that humility leads to empowerment. Empowerment needs to be "em-powered" by somebody, who, of course, is God. Humility empties the soul of self-conceit and self-preoccupation in order for the soul to be filled with grace. St. Louis referring to Luke 1:52 alludes to God's empowering or lifting up the lowly and humble--all those who imitate Mary's virtues in the lifestyle of true devotion. As we live this lifestyle we seek daily to be humble and to accept humiliations as part of our formation in sanctity—that God may empower us with His grace.

29. God the Father wishes to have children by Mary till the consummation of the world; and He speaks to her these words: "Dwell in Jacob" (Ecclesiasticus 24:13), that is to say: Make your dwelling and residence in My predestined children, prefigured by Jacob, and not in the reprobate children of the devil, prefigured by Esau.

Scriptures

Sirach 24:8 NAB: "Then the Creator of all gave me his command, and he who formed me chose the spot for my tent, saying, 'In Jacob make your dwelling, in Israel your inheritance.'"

These verses in Chapter 24 which speak of the praise of Wisdom are applied to Mary. St. Louis extends this meaning to indicate that through the lifestyle of true devotion Mary takes up her residence in the souls of the predestined, the "Jacobs"; that is, those children devoted to her. The "Esaus" are those who are damned. His discussion of the Jacob/ Esau metaphor will continue later.

While the Holy Spirit is most often identified as Mary's Spouse, St. Louis here mentions God the Father as desiring to create new children by Mary's "spiritual maternity." These children are formed in the spiritual life of those consecrated to her.

30. Just as in the natural and corporal generation of children there are a father and a mother, so in the supernatural and spiritual generation there are a Father, who is God, and a Mother, who is Mary. All the true children of God, the predestinate, have God for their Father and Mary for their Mother. He who has not Mary for his Mother has not God for his Father. This is the reason why the reprobate, such as heretics, schismatics and others, who hate our Blessed Lady or regard her with contempt and indifference, have not God for their Father, however much they boast of it, simply because they have not Mary for their Mother. For if they had her for their mother, they would love and honor her as a true child naturally loves and honors the mother who has given him life.

The most infallible and indubitable sign by which we may distinguish a heretic, a man of bad doctrine, a reprobate, from one of the predestinate, is that the heretic and the reprobate have nothing but contempt and indifference for Our Lady, endeavoring by their words and examples to diminish the worship and love of her, openly or hiddenly, and sometimes by misrepresentation. Alas! God the Father has not told Mary to dwell in them, for they are Esaus.

Here St. Louis draws a parallel between natural and supernatural motherhood confirming the need for both a mother and father in both types of generation—biological and spiritual. The absence of the mother leads to children with various maladjustments, both within a family and within one's own spiritual life.

The rejection of Mary as mother breaks up God's plan for the family and ultimately distorts or corrupts the relationship with the individual and God the Father.

Vocabulary

A heretic is one who is baptized and denies a divine truth which must be believed.

A schismatic is one who refuses to submit to the Holy Father and cuts himself off from the Church.[23]

Predestinate means those who respond to God's call and have heaven in their future.

Reprobate are those who refuse God's call and have hell as their future.[24]

One of the means of discernment for the identification of heretics is to determine their rejection of Mary as mother by their open contempt and detraction of her role in salvation history.

31. God the Son wishes to form Himself, and, so to speak, to incarnate Himself in His members every day, by his dear Mother, and He says to her: "Take Israel for your inheritance." (Ecclus. 24:13). It is as if He had said: God the Father has given Me for an inheritance all the nations of the earth, all men, good and bad, predestinate and reprobate. The ones I will lead with a rod of gold, and the others with a rod of iron. Of the ones, I will be the Father and the Advocate; of the others, the Just Punisher; and of all, the Judge. But as for you, My dear Mother, you shall have for your heritage and possession only the predestinate, prefigured by Israel; and as their Mother, you shall bring them forth and take care of them; and as their sovereign, you shall conduct them, govern them and defend them.

Scriptures

Ecclesiasticus 24:13 Douay: "And he said to me: Let thy dwelling be in Jacob, and thy inheritance in Israel, and take root in my elect."

Sirach 24:8 NAB: "'Then the Creator of all gave me his command, and he who formed me chose the spot for my tent, saying, 'In Jacob make your dwelling, in Israel your inheritance.'"

Jesus wants to become incarnate in souls by means of His mother. By divine decree Jesus provides for Mary chosen children; that is, those who cooperate with and respond to grace. As mother, Mary will give these children spiritual life. As queen, she will lead them along the narrow path that leads them to the Kingdom of God, govern them in the observance of the commandments of the Lord and defend them from the Evil One.

32. "This man and that man is born in her" (Ps. 86:5) says the Holy Spirit through the Royal Psalmist. According to the explanation of some of the Fathers, the first man that is born in Mary is the Man-God, Jesus Christ; the second is a mere man, the child of God and Mary by adoption. If Jesus Christ, the Head of men, is born in her, then the predestinate, who are the members of that Head, ought also to be born in her, by a necessary consequence. One and the same mother does not bring forth into the world the head without the members, or the members without the head; for this would be a monster of nature. So in like manner, in the order of grace, the head and the members are born of one and the same Mother; and if a member of the mystical Body of Jesus Christ—that is to say, one of the predestinate—were born of any other mother than Mary, who has produced the Head, he would not be one of the predestinate, nor a member of Jesus Christ, but simply a monster in the order of grace.

Psalm 86:5-7 CCD: "And of Sion they shall say: "One and all were born in her; And he who has established her is the Most High Lord."

Psalm 87:5-7 NAB: "But of Zion it must be said: 'They all were born here.' The Most High confirms this; the Lord notes in the register of the peoples; 'This one was born here.' So all sing in their festive dance: 'Within you is my true home.'"

The metaphor applies to Mary who is recognized as daughter Zion. The predestinate are those who are "born" of her, their true home. The lifestyle of true devotion should be one of great joy and festive dance because one recognizes that one is no longer in a land of exile but has come home to his "motherland."

St. Louis continues with the birth analogy he began in the preceding paragraph surmising that because Jesus as head of the Church is born of Mary, then the members of the Church must also be born of Mary. The head and its parts (one and all) must be born together coming from the same mother. If Mary is not their mother then they are born of something else—they are deformed.

> *33. Besides, this, Jesus being at present as much as ever the fruit of Mary—as Heaven and earth repeat thousands and thousands of times a day, "and blessed is the fruit of thy womb, Jesus"—it is certain that Jesus Christ is, for each man in particular who possesses Him, as truly the fruit and the work of Mary as He is for the whole world in general; so that if any one of the faithful has Jesus Christ formed in his heart, he can say boldly, "All thanks be to Mary! What I possess is her effect and her fruit, and without her I should never have had it." We can apply to her more than St. Paul applied to himself the words: "I am in labor again with all the children of God, until Jesus Christ my Son be formed in them in the fullness of His age." (Cf. Gal.4:19).*
>
> *St. Augustine, surpassing himself, and going beyond all I have yet said, affirms that all the predestinate, in order to be conformed to the image of the Son of God, are in this world hidden in the womb of the most holy Virgin, where they are guarded, nourished, brought up and made to grow by that good Mother until she has brought them forth to glory after death, which is properly the day of their birth, as the Church calls the death of the just. O mystery of grace, unknown to the reprobate, and but little known even to the predestinate!*

Scriptures

Galatians 4:19 NAB: "My children, for whom I am again in labor until Christ be formed in you!"

St. Louis places these words of St. Paul on Mary's lips. She desires with even greater fervor than the great apostle St. Paul that Christ should be formed in men's hearts.

In the repetition of Hail Mary's throughout the world, one constantly acknowledges that Jesus is the fruit of Mary's womb. He becomes fruitful in the soul of him who prays that prayer. We ought to thank Mary therefore for producing that fruit (Jesus) within our soul.

Borrowing from St. Augustine, St. Louis states that in order for us to be conformed to Christ we are in this world hidden in the womb of Mary where she:

--Guards us from Satan-
--Nourishes us on the Word of God-
--Brings us up in the practice of the Virtues-
--Makes us grow through the Sacraments—especially Reconciliation; and finally,
--Brings us home to glory at the hour of our death.

> 34. *God the Holy Spirit wishes to form elect for Himself in her and by her, and He says to her: "Strike the roots," My Well-beloved and My Spouse, "of all your virtues in My elect" (Ecclus. 24:13) in order that they may grow from virtue to virtue and from grace to grace. I took so much complacence in you when you lived on earth in the practice of the most sublime virtues, that I desire still to find you on earth, without your ceasing to be in Heaven. For this end, reproduce yourself in My elect, that I may behold in them with complacence the roots of your invincible faith, of your profound humility, of your universal mortification, of your sublime prayer, of your ardent charity, of your firm hope and of all your virtues. You are always My spouse, as faithful, as pure and as fruitful as ever. Let your faith give Me My faithful, your purity, My virgins, and your fertility, My temples and My elect.*

Scriptures

Ecclesiasticus 24:13 in Douay reads: "And he said to me: Let thy dwelling be in Jacob, and thy inheritance in Israel, and take root in my elect."

St. Louis paraphrases Sirach 24:12 NAB which states: "I have struck root among the glorious people, in the portion of the Lord, his heritage."

In Sirach the author speaks about Wisdom being rooted in Israel, the Chosen people. Here St. Louis places these words on the lips of the Holy Spirit who speaks to His Spouse, Mary, telling her to be rooted in the new Chosen people—His elect; those who are formed by her; the new predestined and chosen people.

The Holy Spirit wants Mary to form chosen souls and He aids her in that formation process. Mary leads the soul in virtue and holiness. The Holy Spirit searching for her "presence" on earth, finds her in those souls who practice her virtues, especially those of faith, humility, mortification, prayer, charity and hope. Mary's virtues are reproduced in chosen souls so that her faith gives birth to Christians. Her purity gives birth to virgins and religious vocations. Her fertility gives birth to churches and those children whom she forms through the lifestyle of true devotion.

> *35. When Mary has struck her roots in a soul, she produces there marvels of grace, which she alone can produce, because she alone is the fruitful Virgin who never has had, and never will have, her equal in purity and in fruitfulness.*
>
> *Mary has produced, together with the Holy Spirit, the greatest thing which has been or ever will be—a God-Man; and she will consequently produce the greatest saints that there will be in the end of time. The formation and the education of the great saints who shall come at the end of the world are reserved for her. For it is only that singular and miraculous Virgin who can produce, in union with the Holy Spirit, singular and extraordinary things.*

Once Mary's roots (virtues) are planted within a soul, great graces occur due to her own purity and fruitfulness operating within that soul. The cooperation between Mary and the Holy Spirit, after having formed Jesus in human history, is now to form us into saints. St. Louis states that her special mission in the Church is to form saints and to teach them the ways of the interior life which leads to sanctity. How much we have to learn in the school of Mary, whose textbook is the life of Jesus Himself!

> *36. When the Holy Spirit, her Spouse, has found Mary in a soul, He flies there. He enters there in His fullness; He communicates Himself to that soul abundantly, and to the full extent to which it makes room for His spouse, Nay, one of the greatest reasons why the Holy Spirit does not now do startling wonders in our souls is because He does not find there a sufficiently great union with His faithful and inseparable spouse. I say "inseparable" spouse, because since that Substantial Love of the Father and the Son has espoused Mary, in order to produce Jesus Christ, the Head of the elect, and Jesus Christ in the elect, He has never repudiated her, because she has always been fruitful and faithful.*

When the Holy Spirit finds in a man's or woman's soul Mary's virtues and a devotion to her, He communicates His gifts to that soul in the measure to which that person is devoted to her. The more that one is devoted to Mary, the more the Holy Spirit will overshadow that soul with charisms and graces.

St. Louis states that the union of Mary and the Holy Spirit in a soul produces the greatest outpouring of the charismatic gifts. The Holy Spirit has never "divorced" Mary after the Incarnation. Theirs is an indissoluble union. Our lifestyle of true devotion brings us into the heart of their spousal relationship and the bonds of their love.

Application of the Lifestyle of True Devotion

1. How has Mary been the "Treasure of the Lord" in my life?
2. What gifts of the Holy Spirit have I asked through Mary's hands?
3. What is the relationship between Moses and Mary as intercessors with God the Father? Why is my intercession by, with, in and through Mary so powerful?
4. How does God the Father reward humility?
5. What do I do with those who show contempt for Our Lady or for my devotion to her?
6. How do I thank God the Father for giving me such a good mother?
7. If Mary is my "true mother" who gives me life in Christ, who have been the "false mothers" of the world who have tried to give me birth unto sin?
8. From what temptations does Mary need to protect me? How does she nourish me on the Word of God? Of which of her virtues am I in most need? How does she inspire me to go to Confession? How do I trust that she will be with me "now and at the hour of my death"?
9. How do I allow Mary to form and educate me in the ways of holiness?
10. How am I growing in my lifestyle of true devotion?

Consequences

I. Mary is Queen of All Hearts

37. We may evidently conclude, then, from what I have said, first of all, that Mary has received from God a great domination over the souls of the elect; for she cannot make her residence in them as God the Father ordered her to do, and, as their mother, form, nourish and bring them forth to eternal life, and have them as her inheritance and portion, and form them in Jesus Christ and Jesus Christ in them, and strike the roots of her virtues in their hearts and be the inseparable companion of the Holy Spirit in all His works of grace—she cannot, I say, do all these things unless she has a right and a domination over their souls by a singular grace of the Most High, who, having given her power over His only and natural Son, has given it also to her over His adopted children, not only as to their bodies, which would be but a small matter, but also as to their souls.

God has given Mary the right and sovereignty over all men and women. He gave her authority over His own Son, and all His adopted children. She has rights to their bodies and souls by divine decree.

38. Mary is the Queen of heaven and earth by grace, as Jesus is the King of them by nature and by conquest. Now, as the kingdom of Jesus Christ consists principally in the heart or the interior of man—according to the words, "The kingdom of God is within you" (LK. 17:21)—in like manner the kingdom of our Blessed Lady is principally in the interior of man; that is to say, his soul. And it is principally in souls that she is more glorified with her Son than in all visible creatures, and so we can call her, as the saints do, the Queen of All Hearts.

Scriptures

St. Louis refers to Luke 17:20-21 NAB: "Asked by the Pharisees when the kingdom of God would come, he said in reply, "the coming of the kingdom of God cannot be observed, and no one will announce, "Look, here it is," or, "There it is." For behold, the kingdom of God is among you.""

St. Louis cites this Scripture to emphasize the interiority of Mary's influence. She exercises her dominion as Queen over the interior life of the soul. St. Louis will stress that the interior devotions form the core of the lifestyle of true devotion.

II Mary is Necessary to Men.

39. In the second place we must conclude that, the most holy Virgin being necessary to God by a necessity which we call "hypothetical," in consequence of His will, she is far more necessary to men, in order that they may attain their last end. We must not confuse devotion to the Blessed Virgin with devotions to the other saints, as if devotion to her were not far more necessary than devotion to them, and as if devotion to her were a matter of supererogation.

Vocabulary

Supererogation—(From the Latin super-erogare=to pay out more than is due). This term means to do more than is required by duty; to go over and above what is necessary. St. Louis uses the term to mean that it is not just something nice to have an extra devotion to Mary. It is necessary to have a devotion to her because of her status and role in salvation history.

There are three classic levels of devotion in the Church. Dulia –which is a devotion directed to the saints. Hyperdulia—which is a higher devotion directed to Mary. And, latria—which is adoration directed to God alone. Devotion to Mary then is higher than the saints and lower than adoration due to God. God wills that men and women have this devotion to her since He willed to make her necessary in the order of salvation.

The consequence of this devotion is that Mary has become Queen of the interior life as deemed by God by a hypothetical necessity.

§1. Necessary to all men to attain salvation

40. The learned and pious Jesuit, Suarez, the erudite and devout Justus Lipsius, doctor of Louvain, and many others have proved invincibly, from the sentiments of the Fathers (among others, St. Augustine, St. Ephrem, deacon of Edessa, St. Cyril of Jerusalem, St. Germanus of Constantinople, St. John Damascene, St. Anselm, St. Bernard, St. Bernardine, St. Thomas and St. Bonaventure), that devotion to our Blessed Lady is necessary to salvation, and that (even in the opinion of Oecolampadius and some other heretics) it is an infallible mark of predestination to be entirely and truly devoted to her.

Who's Who?

Francis Suarez, S.J. was a Spanish theologian who lived from 1548-1617. He is the founder of the systematic study of Mary and wrote on her being conceived without original sin, her merits and graces, her relationship to her Son and continues the thought of many of the Fathers of the Church including Augustine and Bernard, and her unique mediation. Yet in all of this theological reflection, he keeps the relationship of Mary truly in subordination to Jesus.[25]

Justus Lipsius who lived from 1547-1606 was a Dutch philologian and humanist who studied classical Latin texts. He was Catholic, became Lutheran and then Catholic again. He wrote two works on the veneration of Mary, but is known mostly as a Latin scholar.[26]

St. Augustine (see above in #8)

St. Ephrem of Syria lived from 306-373. He is called "the Harp of the Holy Spirit" and the "Marian Doctor." His writings are theological and poetic and express sentiments of love and devotion to Mary.[27] He is an early supporter of the Immaculate Conception. He writes on the Mary-Eve parallel and he is one of the first writers to call Mary the bride of Christ. With Mary as the perfect model he exalts virginity and writes on Mary's relationship to her Son in the Eucharist.[28]

Of St. Ephrem, Pope John Paul II states in Redemptoris Mater: "The poetic genius of St. Ephrem the Syrian, called 'the lyre of the Holy Spirit,' tirelessly sang of Mary, leaving a still living mark on the whole tradition of the Syriac Church."[29]

St. Cyril of Jerusalem was Bishop of Jerusalem from 349 until his death in 387. The date of his birth is unknown. He is another Doctor of the Church. He treats of Mary in one of his Catecheses or lectures for those preparing for baptism. In these catecheses he defends Mary's virginal conception of Jesus, defends her descent from the line of David, her vocation as mother of God, the Eve-Mary parallel and Mary as the model of virgins.[30]

St. Germanus of Constantinople was born somewhere around 631-649 and died in 733. He was a famous 8th Century Byzantine Marian theologian and bishop. He wrote on the Assumption of Mary into heaven, her purity, and her role as mediatrix. He calls himself a slave of Mary and describes how through her intercession the city of Constantinople was saved. He defends the representation of Mary in icons during the period of iconoclasm in the East.[31]

St. John Damascene was born around 676 and died around 750. He was the last and greatest of the Greek Fathers of the Church. His writings on Mary are found in homilies, texts, a treatise on the orthodox faith, poetry and hymns. He speaks of Mary as Mother of God, he defends her perpetual virginity and her Assumption. He also describes her as a spouse of God the Father and her role as mediatrix. He treats of her predestination and the Old Testament prophecies foreshadowing her. In his writings on devotion to Mary he makes a distinction between the adoration due to God and the reverence due to Mary. He also defends depictions of Our Lady in images and icons and consecration to her for which he composed a prayer.[32]

St. Anselm, Benedictine and Archbishop of Canterbury lived from 1033-1109. His writings on Mary are found in sermons, scripture commentaries, prayers and treatises. He treats of her relationship to each person of the Trinity (a relationship upon which St. Louis expounds later in True Devotion), Mary's role in salvation history, her mediation, and her spiritual motherhood. St. Anselm develops also the idea of courtly affection for Mary, calling her "Lady" and of slavery to her. His prayers had a great influence on monastic life in the 12th Century and beyond and he demonstrates a well-balanced Christian piety in regards to devotion to her.[33]

St. Bernard (see above in #27)

St. Bernardine (see above in #27)

St. Thomas Aquinas, a Dominican theologian and another Doctor of the Church lived from 1225-1274. He writes about Mary in his various Summas and commentaries on Scripture. He writes on her role as Mother of God, her freedom from personal sin, her perpetual virginity and the centrality of the Incarnation in salvation history. He speaks of her as a type of mediatrix. He had a very deep personal devotion to Mary.[34]

St. Bonaventure (see above in #8)

John Oecolampadius lived from 1482-1531 and was a German Protestant theologian. He was influential in the Protestantizing of Basle during the Protestant Reformation with the suppression, seizure and pillaging of Catholic churches. He introduced Protestantism into other German cities where he strove for the suppression of all Catholic worship.[35]

St. Louis, referring to various saints and doctors of the Church, makes the observation that chosen souls are entirely devoted to her whereas the condemned have no love for her. Devotion to her is necessary to salvation because without her Jesus would not have been born. We live our lifestyle of true devotion in the company of great saints and doctors of the Church.

> *41. The figures and words of the Old and New Testaments prove this. The sentiments and examples of the saints confirm it. Reason and experience teach and demonstrate it. Even the devil and his crew, constrained by the force of truth, have often been obliged to avow it in spite of themselves. Among all the passages of the holy Fathers and Doctors, of which I have made an ample collection in order to prove this truth, I shall for brevity's sake quote but one: "To be devout to you, O holy Virgin," says St. John Damascene, "is an arm of salvation which God gives to those whom he wishes to save."*

Sacred Scripture, Tradition, reason and experience all lead to the same conclusion and mutually support each other that devotion to Mary cannot but lead to salvation. This devotion does not detract from the saving action of the sacrifice of Jesus upon the cross, but makes that sacrifice a reality by virtue of her motherhood.

> *42. I could bring forward here many anecdotes which prove the same thing, and among others one which is related in the chronicles of St. Francis. This same saint saw in ecstasy a great ladder ascending into Heaven, at the top of which stood the Blessed Virgin and by which it was shown him he must ascend to reach Heaven. There is another related in the chronicles of St. Dominic. There was an unfortunate heretic near Carcassonne, where St. Dominic was preaching the Rosary, who was possessed by a legion of fifteen thousand devils. These evil spirits were compelled, to their confusion, by the command of our Blessed Lady, to avow many great and consoling truths touching devotion to the Blessed Virgin; and they did this with so much force and so much clearness that it is impossible to read this authentic account and the eulogy which the devil made, in spite of himself, of devotion to the most holy Virgin Mary, without shedding tears of joy, however lukewarm we may be in our devotion to her.*

Who's Who?

St. Francis of Assisi (Giovanni Bernadone) lived from 1181/1182 to 1226 in Italy. He was the founder of the Franciscan Friars Minor and was a stagmatist and mystic. This story is supposedly related in the Little Flowers of St. Francis.

St. Dominic (Dominic Guzman) born in Spain, is the founder of the Order of Preachers. He lived from 1170 to 1221. This same story is related in de Montfort's Secret of the Rosary #101-104. Of particular interest to this paragraph is the following confessions of the evil spirits who say that Mary "uncovers [their] hidden plots, breaks [their] snares and makes [their] temptations useless and ineffective."[36] De Montfort will develop these themes later in True Devotion.

St. Louis provides this example of the evil spirits who must avow the power of devotion to Our Lady. Hence, he cites the saints on the one hand and the demons on the other to make a universal case that devotion to Our Lady leads to Jesus and to salvation. This proof should encourage those devoted to her to persevere in this time-honored and proved tradition of the Church.

§2 Still more necessary to those called to a special perfection

> *43. If devotion to the most holy Virgin Mary is necessary to all men simply for working out their salvation, it is still more so for those who are called to any special perfection; and I do not think anyone can acquire an intimate union with Our Lord and a perfect fidelity to the Holy Spirit without a very great union with the most holy Virgin, and a great dependence on her assistance.*

Priests are called to a particular perfection. St. Louis emphasizes that true devotion to Jesus through Mary leads to priestly sanctity and apostolic fruitfulness. The Charismatic Renewal and individual charisms work well when the lifestyle of true devotion to Jesus through Mary and the life in the Spirit are in union. It is Mary's role to lead the soul through the three stages of the spiritual life to reach its goal which is divine union. Those three stages are the purgative, illuminative, and unitive ways. Growth in the charismatic gifts attains a new depth and intensity in the lifestyle of true devotion.

> *44. It is Mary alone who has found grace before God (Lk. 1:30) without the aid of any other mere creature; it is only through her that all those who have since found grace before God have found it at all; and it is only through her that all those who shall come afterward shall find it. She was full of grace when she was greeted by the Archangel Gabriel (Lk. 1:28), and she was superabundantly filled with grace by the Holy Spirit when He covered her with His unspeakable shadow (Lk. 1:35); and she has so augmented this double plenitude from day to day and from moment to moment that she has reached a point of grace immense and inconceivable—in such wise that the most High has made her the sole treasurer of His treasures and the sole dispenser of His graces to ennoble, to exalt and to enrich whom she wishes; to give*

entry to whom she wills into the narrow way of Heaven; to bring whom she wills, and in spite of all obstacles, through the narrow gate of life; and to give the throne, the scepter and the crown of king to whom she wills. Jesus is everywhere and always the Fruit and the Son of Mary; and Mary is everywhere the veritable tree who bears the Fruit of life, and the true Mother who produces it.

Scriptures

St. Louis alludes to three sections from the scene of the Annunciation in the Gospel of Luke. The first is in 1:30 NAB: "Then the angel said to her, 'Do not be afraid, Mary, for you have found favor with God.'" Then he alludes to Luke 1:28: "And coming to her [Gabriel] said, 'Hail, favored one! The Lord is with you.'" And finally, Luke 1:35: "And the angel said to her in reply, 'The Holy Spirit will come upon you, and the power of the Most High will overshadow you. Therefore the child to be born will be called holy, the Son of God.'"

The overshadowing of the Holy Spirit upon Mary (already full of grace) leads to an "immense and inconceivable" portion of grace which she, in turn, dispenses to her children. St. Louis demonstrates an "unveiling" or "revealing" of this grace as it progresses from being known to God alone; to the angelic revelation of this grace, and finally to the operation of the Holy Spirit who overshadows her with so much "more" grace that she conceives in her womb new life, the Son of God. This grace in relation to Mary's spiritual motherhood with her children:

*Ennobles them—with a new dignity and nobility as children of God;

*Exalts them—it lifts them up when they have fallen into sin;

*Enriches them—with the treasures of graces from Heaven;

*Gives entry into the narrow way of heaven—with the spirit of renunciation and the taking up of one's cross;

*Brings them through the narrow gate of life—by bringing them without obstacles to Jesus who is the gate for the sheep and the Way, the Truth and the Life;

*Gives them the throne, scepter, and crown of a king—Mary keeps us rooted in our baptismal graces as priest, prophet and king. Mary is the tree who produces the fruit of her womb, Jesus.

As we live true devotion we enter into the deep waters of our baptismal graces and receive graces from her hands for which we would not even have thought to ask.

The handing over of everything to Mary obtains for us innumerable graces. We should never tire of asking for graces from her hands.

45. It is Mary alone to whom God has given the keys of the cellars (Cant. 1:3) of divine love and the power to enter into the most sublime and secret ways of perfection, and the power likewise to make others enter in there also. It is Mary alone who has given to the miserable children of Eve, the faithless, entry into the terrestrial paradise; that they may walk there agreeably with God, hide there securely against their enemies, feed themselves there deliciously, without further fear of death, on the fruit of the trees of life and of the knowledge of good and evil, and drink in long draughts the heavenly waters of that fair fountain which gushes forth there with abundance; or rather, since she is herself that terrestrial paradise, that virgin and blessed earth from which Adam and Eve, the sinners, have been driven, she gives no entry there except to those whom it is her pleasure to make saints.

Scriptures

Canticles 1:3 Douay: "Draw me: we will run after thee to the odour of thy ointments. The king hath brought me into his storerooms: we will be glad and rejoice in thee, remembering thy breasts more than wine: the righteous love thee."

Song of Songs 1:4 NAB: "Draw me!—We will follow you eagerly! Bring me O king, to your chambers. With you we rejoice and exult, we extol your love; it is beyond wine: how rightly you are loved."

St. Louis, quoting from Song of Songs, intimates that Mary alone has been given the authority to guard the Father's treasure of graces and to lead into the mystery of the Godhead those whom she pleases. She has received the "key" to His heart. Mary not only has the key, but is the key, the means by which we arrive at spiritual perfection. God has given Mary the power to lead souls to perfection.

St. Louis identifies Mary as the new paradise on earth. Mary draws souls to herself in order that they may walk with God and become saints. In Mary her saints hide from their enemies. (These enemies are the "powers and principalities" of which St. Paul speaks in his letter to the Ephesians 6:12.) In her they feed themselves on the fruit of the tree of life which is Jesus, the Eucharist without fear of eternal death. In her they drink heavenly waters—the Holy Spirit who is the fountain of living water. All are called to sanctity in conformity with God's holy will. Mary brings us through the "secret ways of perfection." That is, she knows our souls and teaches us individually and personally how to be holy. How much we need to entrust our soul to her in love, confidence and trust and believe that she knows what she is doing with our lives!

46. All the rich among the people, to make use of an expression of the Holy Spirit (Ps 44:13) according to the explanation of St. Bernard—all the rich among the people shall supplicate her face from age to age and particularly at the end of the world; that is to say, the greatest saints, the souls richest in graces and virtues, shall be the most assiduous in praying to our Blessed Lady, and in having her always present as their perfect model for imitation and their powerful aid for help.

Psalm 44:13 CCD: "And the city of Tyre is here with gifts; the rich among the people seek your favor."

Psalm 45:11-12a NAB:"Listen, my daughter and understand; pay me careful heed. Forget your people and your father's house, that the king might desire your beauty."

Alluding to Psalm 45, St. Louis states that the "rich" (those to whom much has been given) will recognize her power and position with God the Father. They will seek her out for more graces and treasures. Mary desires to make us all rich in the gifts of the Kingdom of Heaven, of which she is the treasurer and the key. She is the special help and intercessor for the great saints of the last days. To become a great saint, then, it would seem that one would have a great love and devotion to Mary. These saints imitate her virtues, and become virtuous themselves, but also receive her powerful protection against the Evil One.

§3 Especially necessary to the great saints of the latter times.

47. I have said that this would come to pass, particularly at the end of the world and indeed presently because the Most High with His holy Mother has to form for Himself great saints who shall surpass most of the other saints in sanctity as much as the cedars of Lebanon outgrow the little shrubs, as has been revealed to a holy soul whose life has been written by M. De Renty.

Who's Who?

Marie des Vallées is the "holy soul" mentioned above. She was a French mystic who lived from 1590-1656. She was a demoniac who suffered the pains of hell. St. Jean Eudes exorcised her and became her spiritual director. He subsequently collected four volumes of her sayings[37].

Gaston Jean Baptiste de Renty (1611-1649) was born in Normandy, France. Educated by Jesuits as a child he wrote treatises on mathematics. Undergoing a powerful conversion after reading The Imitation of Christ he desired to become a Carthusian monk. His parents refused him permission and he dedicated himself to the poor and sick and gave catechetical instructions to lodgers. Nine years after his death his body still remained intact and was placed in a marble tomb. He was widely known in his lifetime for his sanctity.[38]

St. Louis anticipates an era of greater sanctity than ever seen before. This greater sanctity is the fruit of God working in the souls of those devoted to the Blessed Mother.

48. These great souls, full of grace and zeal, shall be chosen to match themselves against the enemies of God, who shall range on all sides; and they shall be singularly devout to our Blessed Lady, illuminated by her light, strengthened with her nourishment, led by her spirit, supported by her arm and sheltered under her protection, so that they shall fight with one hand and build with the other. With the one hand they shall fight, overthrow and crush the heretics with their heresies, the schismatics with their schisms, the idolaters with their idolatries and the sinners with their impieties. With the other hand they shall build (Esd 4:7) the temple of the true Solomon and the mystical city of God, that is to say, the most holy Virgin, called by the Fathers the "Temple of Solomon" and the "City of God." By their words and their examples they shall draw the whole world to true devotion to Mary. This shall bring upon them many enemies, but shall also bring many victories and much glory for God alone. This is what God revealed to St. Vincent Ferrer, the great apostle of his age, as he has sufficiently noted in one of his works. This is what the Holy Spirit seems to have prophesied in the fifty-eighth Psalm: "And they shall know that God will rule Jacob and all the ends of the earth; they shall return at evening and shall suffer hunger like dogs and shall go round about the city." (Ps. 58: 14-15). This city which men shall find at the end of the world to convert themselves in, and to satisfy the hunger they have for justice is the most holy Virgin, who is called by the Holy Spirit the "City of God." (Ps. 86:3).

Scriptures

Although St. Louis alludes to Esdras 4:7 the text is actually found in the Challoner-Douay in 2 Esdras 4:17/Nehemiah 4:17 which states: "Of them that built on the wall and that carried burdens, and that laded: with one of his hands he did the work, and with the other he held a sword."

In the NAB this is found in Nehemiah 4:11 which states: "...as they rebuilt the wall. The load carriers, too, were armed; each did his work with one hand and held a weapon with the other."

Psalm 58:14-15 CCD: "Consume them in wrath; consume, till they are no more; that men may know that God is the ruler of Jacob, yes, to the ends of the earth. Each evening they return, they snarl like dogs and prowl about the city;..."

Psalm 59:14-15 NAB: "Then people will know God rules over Jacob, yes, even to the ends of the earth. Each evening they return, growling like dogs, prowling the city."

Ps 86:3 Douay: "Glorious things are said of you, O city of God!"

Ps 87:3 NAB: " Glorious things are said of you, O city of God!"

St. Louis speaks powerfully in this paragraph about building up the true devotion to Jesus through Mary in the world. He employs the imagery of Nehemiah in citing the rebuilding of the Temple in Jerusalem which depicts the crushing of one's enemies on the one side and the building up of the love of God on the other hand. These enemies of God will recognize His omnipotence as they are converted. They will be converted in the new "city" who is the Virgin Mary. Just as Zion is the city for her children, the mother of the Jews, so will Mary be the mother of all who dwell in this new city of God, those whom she has claimed and brought into life with God.

Who's Who?

St. Vincent Ferrer was a Spanish Dominican who lived from 1350 to 1419. He joined the Dominican order in 1367. Around 1398, St. Vincent became deathly ill and had an apparition of Jesus, St. Dominic and St. Francis. Upon his miraculous recovery, he began a twenty-year apostolate of missionary preaching on the importance of penance and preparation for the coming judgment. He performed miracles everywhere he went and thousands converted to Catholicism. One of those who heard his preaching was Bernardine of Siena (mentioned earlier). The reference St. Louis mentions in this paragraph occurs in St. Vincent's writing, "On the Spiritual Life."[39]

The charism of these great saints will be an apostolate of apologetics to refute heresy. At the same time they will build Marian devotion. These saints are "chosen" by God for this vocation. St. Louis presents an epoch of persecution against the Church. The saints by their preaching and lifestyle will inspire many souls to true devotion. In fact, St. Louis states they shall draw the "whole world." The devil will resist their efforts and these saints will encounter much resistance and suffering.

The great saints of the latter days, those who live in the new city of God, in Mary will both defend the city from its enemies and build it up into virtue and holiness in imitation of Mary's virtues. They will:

One hand	Other hand
Defend church teaching	Build true devotion

Mary is the "city of God" in which conversion occurs and in which justice is decided for those who persevere in righteousness. Those who practice this lifestyle of true devotion will be chosen by Mary herself according to God's will who will ultimately give glory to God. This lifestyle in order to be effective, must be deeply rooted in humility so that one does not take upon himself the victory. The "battle" terminology is consistent with the spiritual warfare already mentioned concerning the "powers and principalities". The image of building and defending belongs to those men and women consecrated to their Queen.

Application of the Lifestyle of True Devotion

1. What does it mean that Mary has a right to my mind and my body? How do I grant her that right and what is my duty in relation to her rights as Queen-mother?

2. How do I recognize Mary as the Queen of my heart?
3. How is my relationship with Mary different than with other saints?
4. Where do I see Mary's influence in the lives of the great saints?
5. How has my life been ennobled and enriched by the lifestyle of true devotion? What do I need to do to be more faithful to its practice?
6. How has Mary called me over the years to have a greater love for her, the terrestrial paradise of God?
7. How has Mary illuminated my life, strengthened me in grace, led me to Jesus, sheltered me from the Evil One and protected me from temptation?

Article Three

Providential Function of Mary in the Latter Times

49. It was through Mary that the salvation of the world was begun, and it is through Mary that it must be consummated. Mary hardly appeared at all in the first coming of Jesus Christ, in order that men, as yet but little instructed and enlightened on the Person of her Son, should not remove themselves from Him in attaching themselves too strongly and too grossly to her. This would have apparently taken place if she had been known, because of the admirable charms which the Most High had bestowed even upon her exterior. This is so true that St. Denis the Areopagite tells us in his writings that when he saw our Blessed Lady he would have taken her for a divinity, because of her secret charms and incomparable beauty, had not the faith in which he was well established taught him the contrary. But in the second coming of Jesus Christ, Mary has to be made known and revealed by the Holy Spirit in order that, through her, Jesus Christ may be known, loved and served. The reasons which moved the Holy Spirit to hide His spouse during her life, and to reveal her but very little since the preaching of the Gospel, subsist no longer.

Who's Who?

St. Denis the Areopagite was the first bishop of Athens and died a martyr's death around the year 95 during the persecution of the Roman Emperor Domitian. He appears in the Acts of the Apostles as one of St. Paul's converts (Acts 17).[40]

St. Louis places in opposition the two comings of Christ. In the first advent, Mary remains hidden so as not to detract attention from her Son that men and women would be drawn directly to Him. In the second advent, Mary has to be made known and revealed by the Holy Spirit so that Jesus may be known, loved and served better. It is God's will that Mary should lead the way and be instrumental in the second coming. The French is more strongly translated "Mary must be known" (Marie doit être connue).

The action of the Holy Spirit is reversed in these two advents. In the first, He hides His spouse; in the second, He reveals her. In our practice of the true devotion, we co-operate with the Holy Spirit who continues to reveal Mary to us. We never reach the satisfaction of saying we know all about her, but in humility we deepen our relationship with her.

I. Existence of This Function and Reasons for It.

50. God, then, wishes to reveal and make known Mary, the masterpiece of His hands in these latter times:

1st Because she hid herself in this world and put herself lower than the dust by her profound humility, having obtained from God and from His Apostles and Evangelists that she should not be made manifest.

2nd Because, as she is the masterpiece of the hands of God, as well here below by grace as in Heaven by glory, He wishes to be glorified and praised in her by those who are living upon the earth.

3rd As she is the dawn which precedes and reveals the Sun of Justice, who is Jesus Christ, she must be seen and recognized in order that Jesus Christ may also be.

4th Being the way by which Jesus came to us the first time, she will also be the way by which He will come the second time, though not in the same manner.

5th Being the sure means and the straight and immaculate way to go to Jesus Christ and to find Him perfectly, it is by her that the souls who are to shine forth especially in sanctity have to find Our Lord. He who shall find Mary shall find life (Prov. 8:35), that is, Jesus Christ, who is the Way, the Truth and the Life. (John 14:6). But no one can find Mary who does not seek her; and no one can seek her who does not know her; for we cannot seek or desire an unknown object. It is necessary, then, for the greater knowledge and glory of the Most Holy Trinity, that Mary should be more than ever known.

6th Mary must shine forth more than ever in mercy, in might and in grace, in these latter times; in mercy, to bring back and lovingly receive the poor strayed sinners who shall be converted and shall return to the Catholic Church; in might, against the enemies of God, idolaters, schismatics, Mahometans, Jews and souls hardened in impiety, who shall rise in terrible revolt against God to seduce all those who shall oppose them and to make them fall by promises and threats; and finally, she must shine forth in grace, in order to animate and sustain the valiant soldiers and faithful servants of Jesus Christ, who shall battle for His interests.

7ᵗʰ And lastly, Mary must be terrible to the devil and his crew, as an army ranged in battle, principally in these latter times, because the devil, knowing that he has but little time, and now less than ever, to destroy souls, will every day redouble his efforts and his combats. He will presently raise up cruel persecutions and will put terrible snares before the faithful servants and true children of Mary, whom it gives him more trouble to conquer than it does to conquer others.

Scriptures

St. Louis cites from Proverbs 8:35 Douay: "He that shall find me, shall find life, and shall have salvation from the Lord"

Proverbs 8:35 NAB: "For he who finds me finds life, and wins favor from the Lord."

John 14:6 Douay/NAB state: "Jesus said to [Thomas], "I am the way and the truth and the life. No one comes to the Father except through me.""

St. Louis quotes here two Scriptures both of which he applies to finding life through Mary (who leads us to Jesus). Mary always leads her children away from death to life; away from sin to grace. She always leads us to Jesus and salvation.

St. Louis presents here seven reasons why God wishes to reveal Mary in preparation for the second coming of Christ. 1) She fulfilled her vocation to hiddenness during her lifetime. 2) He wants to reveal His masterpiece of creation. 3) Intrinsically linked to Jesus as His mother, she precedes His revelation. 4) It is she who brings Him into the world. 5) She is the direct route to Jesus. She is necessary for those called to sanctity to go directly to Him. To know Mary is to seek her all the more. Knowledge of Mary glorifies the Trinity and leads one into the life of the Trinity. 6) Three of Mary's attributes are expressed: "mercy, might and grace." She manifests mercy in the conversion of sinners. She displays might in defeating various enemies of God and His kingdom; and she dispenses grace for her faithful children by breathing life into their souls. She leads them to Jesus in the sacraments and strengthens them in the weariness of the spiritual warfare of good and evil. 7) Lastly, in this spiritual warfare against Satan and his demons, Mary's servants pose him the greatest threat because of the strength of their Queen and the ultimate victory of her Son.

In our consecration to Mary we receive her protection as well as assurance that we cannot go astray from Jesus. This is especially important for those people who sincerely strive to be holy. Mary protects us from the Evil One while keeping us focused on Jesus, the Church and salvation in Heaven.

I. Exercise of this Function

§1 In the Struggle against Satan.

51. It is principally of these last and cruel persecutions of the devil, which shall go on increasing daily till the reign of Antichrist, that we ought to understand that first and celebrated prediction and curse of God pronounced in the terrestrial paradise against the serpent. It is to our purpose to explain this here for the glory of the most holy Virgin, for the salvation of her children and for the confusion of the devil: "I will put enmities between thee and the woman and thy seed and her seed; she shall crush thy head, and thou shalt lie in wait for her heel" (Gen. 3:15).

Scriptures

Genesis 3:15 Douay: "I will put enmity between you and the woman, between your seed and her seed; He shall crush your head, and you shall lie in wait for his heel."

Genesis 3:15 NAB: "I will put enmity between you and the woman, and between your offspring and hers; He will strike at your head, while you strike at his heel."

St. Louis develops in this paragraph from Genesis 3 the curse God placed between the woman (fulfilled in Mary), her seed (Jesus) and the head of the serpent (Satan). This curse which is the punishment due to original sin continues to manifest itself in the struggle between the children of Mary and the children of the Evil One. The victory is accomplished in the death and resurrection of Jesus Christ, yet the battles of the spiritual warfare continue.

Mary exercises this role as the one who crushes the head of the serpent in two ways: in struggles against Satan and in the formation of apostles. St. Louis states that Satan's influence in the world is increasing. We can see the effects of his influence in the world and the popularization of demonic themes in our own century. Those who practice true devotion engage in this spiritual warfare as Mary's soldiers, relying on Gods' strength—not their own. These temptations and persecutions present no obstacle to those children devoted to Mary, as she protects them and teaches them to discern his snares and traps. She will illuminate our minds as to the persons, places and things that serve to take us away from the love of God.

52. God has never made and formed but one enmity; but it is an irreconcilable one, which shall endure and grow even to the end. It is between Mary, His worthy Mother, and the devil—between the children and servants of the Blessed Virgin, and the children and tools of Lucifer. The most terrible of all the enemies which God has set up against the devil is His holy Mother Mary. He has inspired her, even since the days of the earthly paradise—though she existed then only in His idea—with so much hatred against that cursed enemy of God, with so much ingenuity in unveiling the malice of that ancient serpent, with so much power to conquer, to overthrow and to crush that proud, impious rebel, that he fears her not only more than all angels and men, but in a sense more than God Himself. Not that the anger, the hatred and the power of God are not infinitely greater than those of the Blessed Virgin, for the perfections of Mary are limited; but first, because Satan, being proud, suffers infinitely more from being beaten and punished by a little and humble handmaid of God, and her humility humbles him more than the divine power; and secondly, because God has given Mary such great power against the devils that—as they have often been obliged to confess, in spite of themselves, by the mouths of the possessed—they fear one of her sighs for a soul more than the prayers of all the saints, and one of her threats against them more than all other torments.

God Himself formed the enmity between Satan and Mary, between her who is the Mother of the Living and him who is a "murderer from the beginning" (John 8:44). God has given Mary the grace to find nothing attractive in him, i.e., to hate him; to unveil his evilness; to conquer, overthrow and crush him. Her humility is power. Her humility becomes our humility through the lifestyle of true devotion and consequently her power becomes our power through the same means. She teaches us the strategy of how to unveil and overpower his temptations and tricks by recognizing that which is deceptive, that which is illusory, that which leads to death, and that which leads to pride.

53. What Lucifer has lost by pride, Mary has gained by humility. What Eve has damned and lost by disobedience, Mary has saved by obedience. Eve, in obeying the serpent, has destroyed all her children together with herself, and has delivered them to him; Mary, in being perfectly faithful to God, has saved all her children and servants together with herself, and has consecrated them to His Majesty.

Eve	Mary
Disobedient	Obedient
Destroyed her children	Saves her children
Gave them to Satan	Consecrates them to God

54. God has not only set an enmity, but enmities, not simply between Mary and the devil, but between the race of the holy Virgin and the race of the devil; that is to say, God has set enmities, antipathies and secret hatreds between the true children and servants of Mary and the children and slaves of the devil. They have no love for each other. They have no sympathy for each other. The children of Belial, the slaves of Satan, the friends of the world (for it is the same thing) have always up to this time persecuted those who belong to our Blessed Lady, and will in the future persecute them more than ever; just as Cain, of old, persecuted his brother Abel, and Esau his brother Jacob, who are the figures of the reprobate and the predestinate. But the humble Mary will always have the victory over that proud spirit, and so great a victory that she will go so far as to crush his head, where his pride dwells. She will always discover the malice of the serpent. She will always lay bare his infernal plots and dissipate his diabolical counsels[41], and even to the end of time will guard her faithful servants from his cruel claw.

But the power of Mary over all the devils will especially shine forth in the latter times, when Satan will lay his snares against her heel; that is to say, her humble slaves and her poor children, whom she will raise up to make war against him. They shall be little and poor in the world's esteem, and abased before all like the heel, trodden underfoot and persecuted as the heel is by the other members of the body. But in return for this they shall be rich in the grace of God, which Mary shall distribute to them abundantly. They shall be great and exalted before God in sanctity. Superior to all other creatures by their lively zeal, and so well sustained with God's assistance that, with the humility of their heel, in union with Mary, they shall crush the head of the devil and cause Jesus Christ to triumph.

The enmity continues to the generations of servants of Mary and servants of Satan. St. Louis foresees greater persecution coming from the world and the devil against the Marian devotees.

In spiritual warfare and demonic oppression, Mary will always be victorious because of her humility over Satanic pride. Mary's guidance in spiritual warfare and discernment of spirits is to:

-- "discern the malice of the serpent." Mary will help her children recognize through the gifts of the Holy Spirit, her Spouse, when the Evil One is present and how he is afflicting the soul, e.g., by the imagination, memory, etc. Like picking up a rock from the ground and finding a snake underneath, Mary will give her devotees the grace to recognize his presence and remove the rock of hiding.

--"lay bare his infernal plots." She will remove the illusions of the angel of light—Lucifer—so that that which appears to be good may make its evil defects clear and apparent.

--"dissipate his diabolical counsels." Mary provides her servants with the grace to recognize the operation of many evil spirits and their various aspects, attributes and characteristics as they work to torment her children. She will help her devotees not only to recognize them, but to prevent their communications and interactions.

--"guard her faithful servants." Above all, Mary uses her Queenship to protect her children from the many unseen dangers they daily encounter and she obtains for them numerous graces and assistance from the angels.

Mary's own army of devotees will be humble as she is. They will not be recognized for any worldly accomplishments, which will make them more docile in receiving graces from her. They will be strong in spiritual warfare because of their zeal and humility, and the Lord will raise them to great holiness to be victorious in the defeat of the Evil One.

The power to overcome the Evil One will be the deep union they experience with Mary through the lifestyle of true devotion. Her heel becomes their heel and together they crush the head of the serpent in fulfillment of God's promise.

§2 In the formation of the apostles of the Latter Times

55. In a word, God wishes that His holy Mother should be at present more known, more loved, more honored than she has ever been. This, no doubt, will take place if the predestinate enter, with the grace and light of the Holy Spirit, into the interior and perfect practice which I will disclose to them shortly. Then they will see clearly, as far as faith allows, that beautiful Star of the Sea. They will arrive happily in harbor, following its guidance, in spite of the tempests and the pirates. They will know the grandeurs of that Queen, and will consecrate themselves entirely to her service as subjects and slaves of love. They will experience her sweetness and maternal goodness, and they will love her tenderly like well-beloved children. They will know the mercies of which she is full, and the need they have of her help; and they will have recourse to her in all things, as to their dear advocate and Mediatrix with Jesus Christ. They will know what is the surest, the easiest, the shortest and the most perfect means of going to Jesus Christ; and they will give themselves to Mary, body and soul, without reserve, that they may belong entirely to Jesus Christ

In order for God's will to transpire that Mary should be more known, loved, and honored, there needs to be chosen souls dedicated to the lifestyle of true devotion. Those who follow the lifestyle of true devotion will experience:

--a greater awareness of Mary's presence
--a greater strength during temptations
--a deeper appreciation of her dignity and Queenship
--a deeper desire to serve her
--a sensible awareness of her motherhood
--a more ardent love for her as their mother

--a greater recognition of how much they need her help
--a more fervent zeal to seek her intercession in all that they do
--a greater focus on Jesus
--a sacrificial self-donation to the Mother, who will give them to the Son.

> *56. But who shall those servants, slaves and children of Mary be? They shall be ministers of the Lord who, like a burning fire, shall kindle the fire of divine love everywhere. They shall be "like sharp arrows in the hand of the powerful" Mary to pierce her enemies (Ps 126:4). They shall be the sons of Levi, well purified by the fire of great tribulation, and closely adhering to God (1 Cor. 6:17), who shall carry the gold of love in their heart, the incense of prayer in their spirit, and the myrrh of mortification in their body. They shall be everywhere the good odor of Jesus Christ to the poor and to the little, while at the same time, they shall be an odor of death to the great, to the rich and to the proud worldlings.*

Scriptures

Psalm 126:4-5 Douay which says: "Like arrows in the hand of a warrior are the sons of one's youth. Happy the man whose quiver is filled with them; they shall not be put to shame when they contend with enemies at the gate."

Psalm 127:4-5 NAB: "Like arrows in the hand of a warrior are the children born in one's youth. Blessed are they whose quivers are full. They will never be shamed contending with foes at the gate."

1 Cor 6:17 Douay: "But he who cleaves to the Lord is one spirit with him."

1 Cor 6:17 NAB: "But whoever is joined to the Lord becomes one spirit with him."

St. Louis describes that these apostles of Mary in the last times will be like arrows directed by Mary's arm and going in the direction and purpose for which she aims them. They will be purified of disordered attachments so that they are in union with the Lord and seek only to do His will. The purification involves the pain of separation and dying to one's self-will. The pain of dying to one's strong will is not to be underestimated or avoided, it must be endured for the sake of future glory.

These chosen souls will especially be priests. Love, prayer and mortification are necessary for priests. These virtues are precious treasures to be presented to Jesus, and they are prepared especially by Mary within the soul of each priest. They are just as precious as the gifts of gold, frankincense and myrrh the Wisemen presented to Him at His birth. The relationship of the priest and Mary is a unique relationship. The priest, because of the sacrament of Holy Orders, acts in the "person of Christ" (in persona Christi). Mary forms him differently due to his very specific priestly tasks and mission and his unique conformity to Jesus.

57. They shall be clouds thundering and flying through the air at the least breath of the Holy Spirit; who, detaching themselves from everything and troubling themselves about nothing, shall shower forth the rain of the Word of God and of life eternal. They shall thunder against sin; they shall storm against the world; they shall strike the devil and his crew; and they shall pierce through and through, for life or for death, with their two-edged sword of the Word of God (Eph. 6:17), all those to whom they shall be sent on the part of the Most High.

Scriptures

Ephesians 6:17 CCD: "And take unto you the helmet of salvation and the sword of the spirit, that is, the word of God."

Ephesians 6:17 NAB: "And take the helmet of salvation and the sword of the Spirit, which is the word of God."

St. Louis refers to St. Paul's letter to the Ephesians in which St. Paul equips his apostles to fight in their battle against evil. St. Louis arms his apostles of the latter times especially with this armor of the Word of God—their preaching.

St. Louis alludes to the "rain of the Word of God," an expression which occurs in the Prophet Isaiah: "For just as from the heavens the rain and snow come down and do not return there till they have watered the earth, making it fertile and fruitful, giving seed to him who sows and bread to him who eats, so shall my word be that goes forth from my mouth. It shall not return to me void, but shall do my will, achieving the end for which I sent it" (Isaiah 55:10). This ministry of preaching will be directed against sin, against worldliness. It will overthrow demonic activity and fill its preachers with missionary zeal. Priests who live the true devotion will receive Mary's assistance in this renewed ministry of preaching. She obtains special graces for their word to affect souls. By means of a priest's consecration to Mary, he preaches with a new tongue; that is, Mary inspires his words as she gives herself completely to her consecrated priest-son. She unveils for him the Word of God and the Word-made-Flesh.

58 They shall be the true apostles of the latter times, to whom the Lord of Hosts shall give the word and the might to work marvels and to carry off with glory the spoils of His enemies. They shall sleep without gold or silver, and, what is more, without care, in the midst of the other priests, ecclesiastics, and clerics (Ps. 67:14); and yet they shall have the silvered wings of the dove to go, with the pure intention of the glory of God and the salvation of souls, wheresoever the Holy Spirit shall call them. Nor shall they leave behind them, in

the place where they have preached, anything but the gold of char-
ity, which is the fulfillment of the whole law. (Rom 13:10).

Scriptures

Psalm 67:14 Douay: "Though you rested among the sheepfolds, the wings of the dove shone with silver, and her pinions with a golden hue."

Psalm 68:14 NAB: "Every household will share the booty, perhaps a dove sheathed with silver, its wings covered with yellow gold."

Romans 13:10 CCD: "Love does no evil to a neighbor. Love therefore is the fulfillment of the Law."

Romans 13:10 NAB: "Love does no evil to the neighbor; hence, love is the fulfillment of the law."

In these two Scripture references, St. Louis alludes to the battle that these apostles will wage. They will be victorious in their ministry because the victory will be the Lord's, even though the apostles will reap the benefits of their labors. In every place where they shall labor for the building of the "city of God" (true devotion) they will leave in their wake charity. These priests will be true apostles empowered with the charisms of preaching and miracles. They will be devoted to poverty without peer pressure from their brother priests. The priest who consecrates himself to Mary experiences a new power in his priestly work as the Holy Spirit operates through him more dynamically. This is because the Holy Spirit comes to the priest-soul consecrated to Mary because He recognizes her special presence in him. The priest, imbued with a new humility, is also the recipient of new charisms or augmented charisms through Mary's hands that are necessary to his priestly ministry. The priest's soul having already gone through the ontological change at ordination in order to be "in persona Christi" now receives additional graces through his consecration to Jesus through Mary such that Mary protects his priestly identity as much as she protected the life of Jesus in His infancy.

> *59. In a word, we know that they shall be true disciples of Jesus Christ, walking in the footsteps of His poverty, humility, contempt of the world, charity; teaching the narrow way of God in pure truth, according to the holy Gospel, and not according to the maxims of the world; troubling themselves about nothing; not accepting persons; sparing, fearing and listening to no mortal, however influential he may be. They shall have in their mouths the two-edged sword of the Word of God. They shall carry on their shoulders the blood standard of the Cross, the Crucifix in their right hand and the Rosary in their left, the sacred Names of Jesus and Mary in their hearts, and the modesty and mortification of Jesus Christ in their own behavior. These are the great men who are to come; but Mary is the one who, by order of the Most High,*

shall fashion them for the purpose of extending His empire over that of the impious, the idolaters and the Mahometans. But when and how shall this be? God alone knows. And for us, we have but to hold our tongues, to pray, to sigh and to wait: "With expectation I have waited." (Ps. 39:2)

Scriptures

Psalm 39:2 Douay: "I have waited, waited for the Lord, and he stooped toward me and heard my cry."

Psalm 40:2 NAB: "I waited, waited for the Lord; who bent down and heard my cry…"

While St. Louis zealously describes the formation of these apostles of the last times, he speaks about the importance of waiting for God's time of fulfillment to be made manifest. God alone knows when and how this will all happen.

The marks of these true priest apostles will be: poverty, humility, contempt for the world, charity, orthodoxy, trust, and indifference to popularity. St. Louis alludes to Matthew 22:16: "They sent their disciples to him, with the Herodians, saying, 'Teacher, we know that you are a truthful man and that you teach the way of God in accordance with the truth. And you are not concerned with anyone's opinion, for you do not regard a person's status."

They shall be known for their preaching and their mortified conformity to Christ crucified with the Crucifix (the Wisdom of the Cross) in one hand and the Rosary (true devotion) in the other hand. It is Mary who shall fashion them. The French verb "faire" can also be rendered make, rather than fashion, so that the translation is: "It is Mary who will make them." These priest-apostles shall live in their own person the way of the cross without ostentation or self-importance. This vision for the priest apostles finds fruition and realization in the consecration and the lifestyle of true devotion. St. Louis' hopes are not for a distant future, but are for today for those generous souls who consecrate themselves to Jesus through Mary.

Application of the Lifestyle of True Devotion

1. How am I truly seeking to know Mary?
2. How is the Evil One exercising his influence in the world and how does the lifestyle of true devotion combat it?
3. How am I experiencing temptations and how do I respond to them in light of my consecration?
4. How does Mary help me uncover Satan's temptations in my life?
5. What have Mary and I gained by humility?
6. What "price" have I had to pay for not conforming to the sins of the world?
7. How am I making Mary more known, more loved and more honored?

8. If I am a priest, is my love for Mary typified by an increase of love, prayer and mortification? Have I preached against sin? Have I "stormed" against the world? Have I defeated the works of Satan to establish his kingdom and all his empty promises? Have I lived a life of poverty and humility, charity, and orthodoxy?

Chapter II

Fundamental Truths of Devotion to the Blessed Virgin

60. Having spoken thus far of the necessity of devotion to the most holy Virgin, I must now show in what this devotion consists. This I will do, with God's help, after I shall have first laid down some fundamental truths which shall throw light on that grand and solid devotion which I desire to disclose.

Having completed so far a chapter on the necessity of the Blessed Virgin Mary and devotion to her, St. Louis continues in Chapter Two by expounding on five truths related to devotion to her. These five truths are foundational truths that will lead him to speak specifically about the "true devotion" to Mary.

First Truth

<u>Jesus Christ is the Last End of Devotion to Mary</u>

61. Jesus Christ our Savior, true God and true Man, ought to be the last end of all our other devotions, else they are false and delusive. Jesus Christ is the Alpha and the Omega, the beginning and the end, of all things. We labor not, as the Apostle says, except to render every man perfect in Jesus Christ; because it is in Him alone that the whole plenitude of the Divinity dwells together with all the other plenitudes of graces, virtues and perfections. It is in Him alone that we have been blessed with all spiritual benediction; and He is our only Master, who has to teach us; our only Lord on whom we ought to depend; our only Head to whom we must be united; our only Model to whom we should conform ourselves; our only Physician who can heal us; our only Shepherd who can feed us; our only Way who can lead us; our only Truth whom we must believe; our only Life who can animate us; and our only All in all things who can satisfy us. There has been no other name given under Heaven, except the name of Jesus, by which we can be saved. God has laid no other foundation of our salvation, our perfection or our glory, than Jesus Christ. Every building which is not built on that firm rock is founded upon the moving sand, and sooner or later infallibly will fall. Every one of the faithful who is not united to Him, as a branch to the stock of the vine, shall fall, shall wither, and shall be fit only to be cast into the fire. Outside of Him there exists nothing but error, falsehood, iniquity, futility, death and damnation. But if we are in Jesus Christ and Jesus Christ is in us, we have no condemnation to fear. Neither the angels of Heaven nor the men of earth nor the devils of Hell nor any other creature can injure us; because they cannot separate us from the love of God, which is in Jesus Christ. By Jesus Christ, with Jesus Christ, in Jesus Christ, we can do all things; we can render all honor and glory to the Father in the unity of the Holy Spirit; we can become perfect ourselves, and be to our neighbor a good odor of eternal life (2 Cor 2:15-16).

Scriptures

2 Corinthians 2:15-16 CCD: "For we are the fragrance of Christ for God, alike as regards those who are saved and those who are lost; to these an odor that leads to death, but to those an odor that leads to life. And for such offices, who is sufficient?"

2 Corinthians 2:15-16 NAB: "For we are the aroma of Christ for God among those who are being saved and among those who are perishing, to the latter an odor of death that leads to death, to the former an odor of life that leads to life. Who is qualified for this?"

St. Louis employs these words from St. Paul's letter to the Corinthians to emphasize the end goal of the true devotion which is conformity and divine union with Jesus. As we lead people to Jesus we are the sweet aroma of those being saved and an odor of death to those who are perishing. People will have to choose either for Jesus or against Jesus.

St. Louis is stressing that anything that prevents us from going to Jesus is a false devotion. The goal of true devotion is to lead us deeply into the heart of Jesus by means of His mother. Those who follow Mary by means of this true devotion become a sweet odor to the saved and an unpleasant reminder to those who are rejecting God. One of the realities of the lifestyle of true devotion is that not everyone will understand it. In fact, there will be those opposed to it, but the true devotee must persevere in all charity in truth despite personal persecution.

62. If, then, we establish solid devotion to our Blessed Lady, it is only to establish more perfectly devotion to Jesus Christ, and to provide an easy and secure means for finding Jesus Christ. If devotion to Our Lady removed us from Jesus Christ, we should have to reject it as an illusion of the devil; but so far from this being the case, devotion to Our Lady is, on the contrary, necessary for us—as I have already shown, and will show still further hereafter—as a means of finding Jesus Christ perfectly, of loving Him tenderly, of serving Him faithfully.

If Mary ever leads us away from Jesus it is evidence of a false devotion. On the contrary, Mary helps us to find Him, love Him, and serve Him. One facet in the discernment of spirits for the devotee is that the devil tries to separate us from Jesus. If any part of this lifestyle leads us away from Jesus, the Church, the sacraments, etc. it must be carefully re-examined and called under ecclesiastical authority or the authority of one's spiritual director, pastor or bishop.

> *63. I here turn for one moment to Thee, O sweet Jesus, to complain lovingly to Thy Divine Majesty that the greater part of Christians, even the most learned, do not know the necessary union there is between Thee and Thy holy Mother. Thou, Lord, art always with Mary, and Mary is always with Thee, and she cannot be without Thee, else she would cease to be what she is. She is so transformed into Thee by grace that she lives no more, she is as though she were not. It is Thou only, my Jesus, who lives and reigns in her more perfectly than in all the angels and the blessed. Ah! If we knew the glory and the love which Thou receivest in this admirable creature, we should have very different thoughts both of Thee and her from what we have now. She is so intimately united with Thee that it were easier to separate the light from the sun, the heat from the fire; nay, it were easier to separate from Thee all the angels and the saints than the divine Mary, because she loves Thee more ardently and glorifies Thee more perfectly than all the other creatures put together.*

St. Louis digresses in his treatment of the fundamental truths concerning true devotion in order to pray. In this prayer he complains to the Lord Jesus that so many Christians do not know the union between Him and His mother; between the Sacred Heart and the Immaculate Heart. Mary glorifies and loves her Son with a power that surpasses natural laws. One hears echoes of Romans 8:13: "What can separate us from the love of Christ? "Can a mother forget her infant, be without tenderness for the child of her womb?" (Isaiah 49:15). Nothing can separate the love of Mary from Jesus, and she can never be without tenderness or love for the fruit of her womb.

> *64. After that, my sweet Master, is it not an astonishingly pitiable thing to see the ignorance and the darkness of all men here below in regard to Thy holy Mother? I speak not so much of idolaters and pagans, who, knowing Thee not, care not to know her. I speak not even of heretics and schismatics, who care not to be devout to thy holy Mother, being separated as they are from Thee and Thy holy Church; but I speak of Catholic Christians, and even of doctors among Catholics, who make profession of teaching truths*

to others, and yet know not Thee nor Thy holy Mother, except in a speculative, dry, barren and indifferent manner. These gentlemen speak but rarely of Thy holy Mother and of the devotion we ought to have to her, because they fear, so they say, lest we should abuse it, and do some injury to Thee in honoring Thy holy Mother too much. If they hear or see anyone devout to our Blessed Lady, speaking often of his devotion to that good Mother in a tender, strong and persuasive way, and as a secure means without delusion, as a short road without danger, as an immaculate way without imperfection, and as a wonderful secret for finding and loving Thee perfectly, they cry out against him, and give him a thousand false reasons by way of proving to him that he ought not to talk so much of our Blessed Lady; that there are great abuses in that devotion; and that we must direct our energies to destroy these abuses, and to speak of Thee, rather than to incline the people to devotion to our Blessed Lady, whom they already love sufficiently. We hear them sometimes speak of devotion to our Blessed Lady, not for the purpose of establishing it and persuading men to embrace it, but to destroy the abuses which are made of it; and all the while these teachers are without piety or tender devotion toward Thyself, simply because they have none for Mary. They regard the Rosary and the Scapular as devotions proper for weak and ignorant minds, without which men can save themselves; and if there falls into their hands any poor client of Our Lady who says his Rosary, or has any other practice of devotion toward her, they soon change his spirit and his heart. Instead of the Rosary, they counsel him the seven Penitential Psalms. Instead of devotion to the holy Virgin, they counsel him devotion to Jesus Christ. O my sweet Jesus, do these people have Thy spirit? Do they please Thee in acting thus? Does it please Thee when, for fear of displeasing Thee, we neglect doing our utmost to please Thy Mother? Does devotion to thy holy Mother hinder devotion to Thyself? Does she attribute to herself the honor we pay her? Does she head a faction of her own? Is she a stranger who has no connection with Thee? Does it displease Thee that we should try to please her? Do we separate or alienate ourselves from Thy love by giving ourselves to her and honoring her?

St. Louis speaks directly to Jesus, again in a stylistic digression, posing nine questions to Him asking how devotion to His mother could ever lead one away from Him. Each rhetorical question receives a negative response.

The adversaries and opponents of true devotion in St. Louis' time and in our own time will protest that there are abuses in this devotion by emphasizing Mary too much. They will claim that these abuses must be destroyed and that one should speak of Mary less and Jesus more. St. Louis repeatedly states through the <u>True Devotion</u> that because Mary reserves nothing to herself, all the "attention" she receives is handed over to Jesus.

St. Louis devotes considerable text to the opposition he has received from theologians who dispute his treatment of true devotion. He describes the approach of these theologians vis-à-vis Mary as speculative, dry, barren and indifferent. Their fear, he contends, is that by honoring Mary too much, one might bring dishonor to Jesus. On the contrary true devotion to Jesus through Mary leads to:

--a secure means to arriving at union with Jesus without delusions;
--a short road without danger;
--an immaculate way without imperfection;
--a wonderful secret for finding and living in Jesus.

> 65. Yet, my sweet Master, the greater part of the learned could not discourage devotion to Thy holy Mother more, and could not show more indifference to it, even if all that I have just said were true. Thus have they been punished for their pride! Keep me, Lord, keep me from their sentiments and their practices, and give me some share of the sentiments of gratitude, esteem, respect and love which Thou hast in regard to Thy holy Mother, so that the more I imitate and follow her, the more I may love and glorify Thee.

Jesus relates to Mary with gratitude, esteem, respect and love. St. Louis maintains that the more we imitate and follow Mary, the more we glorify the Lord. In our lifestyle of true devotion, Mary simply leads us to the greater glory of God; never to her herself.

> 66. So, as if up to this point I had still said nothing in honor of Thy holy Mother, "give me now the graces to praise Thee worthily," in spite of all her enemies, who are Thine as well; and grant me to say loudly with the saints, "let not that man presume to look for the mercy of God who offends His holy Mother."

Enemies of Mary are also enemies of Jesus Christ. If we dishonor Jesus' mother, we dishonor Him. True devotion shows us how to honor them both; the one as the perfect act of God's creation and the other as God Himself.

> 67. Make me love Thee ardently, so that I may obtain of Thy mercy a true devotion to Thy holy Mother, and inspire the whole earth with it; and for that end, receive the burning prayer which I offer to Thee with St. Augustine and Thy other true friends: "Thou art Christ, my holy Father, my tender God, my great King, my

good Shepherd, my one Master, my best Helper, my most Beautiful and my Beloved, my living Bread; my Priest forever, my Leader to my country, my true Light, my holy Sweetness, my straight Way, my excellent Wisdom, my pure Simplicity, my pacific Harmony, my whole Guard, my good Portion, my everlasting Salvation. Christ Jesus, my sweet Lord, why have I ever loved, why in my whole life have I ever desired anything except Thee, Jesus my God? Where was I when I was not in Thy mind with Thee? Now, from this time forth, do ye, all my desires, grow hot, and flow out upon the Lord Jesus; run, ye have been tardy thus far; hasten whither ye are going; seek whom ye are seeking. O Jesus, may he who loves Thee not, be anathema; may he who loves Thee not, be filled with bitterness! O sweet Jesus, may every good feeling that is fitted for Thy praise, love Thee, delight in Thee, admire Thee. God of my heart and my Portion, Christ Jesus, may my heart faint away in spirit and mayest Thou be my life within me! May the live coal of Thy love grow hot within my spirit, and break forth into a perfect fire; may it burn incessantly on the altar of my heart; may it glow in my innermost being; may it blaze in hidden recesses of my soul; and in the day of my consummation, may I be found consummated with Thee. Amen."

St. Louis prays to Jesus for the personal gift of true devotion to His Mother with the apostolic and missionary aim of making this devotion known to the whole world. His prayer, truly inspired by the Holy Spirit, sets our hearts on fire with the same zeal to spread this devotion "to the whole world."

Application of the Lifestyle of True Devotion

1. Is the greater love for Jesus the reason for my consecration and living the true devotion? What prevents me or competes with my attention for loving Jesus wholeheartedly?
2. Has my devotion to Mary ever led me away from Jesus?
3. Does my consecration and lifestyle of true devotion give a good example to other people on how to love Jesus?
4. When were the times in my life when I scoffed devotion to Mary as being idolatrous or as taking away devotion to Jesus? Do I suffer from those thoughts? Lord Jesus, have I ever been an enemy of your mother in my attempt to love you?
5. Do I pray every day for the gift of true devotion recognizing that the gift comes from God and not from myself?

Second Truth

<u>We Belong to Jesus And Mary As Their Slaves</u>

68. We must conclude from what Jesus Christ is with regard to us that, as the Apostle says (1 Cor. 6:19-20), we do not belong to ourselves but are entirely His, as His members and His slaves, whom He has bought at an infinitely dear price, the price of all His Blood. Before Baptism we belonged to the devil, as his slaves; but Baptism has made us true slaves of Jesus Christ, who have no right to live, to work or to die, except to bring forth fruit for that God-man (Rom. 7;4); to glorify Him in our bodies and to let Him reign in our souls, because we are His conquest, His acquired people and His inheritance. It is for the same reason that the Holy Spirit compares us: (1) to trees planted along the waters of grace, in the field of the Church, who ought to bring forth their fruit in their season; (2) to the branches of a vine of which Jesus Christ is the stock, and which must yield good grapes; (3) to a flock of which Jesus Christ is the Shepherd, and which is to multiply and give milk; (4) to a good land of which God is the Husbandman, in which the seed multiplies itself and brings forth thirtyfold, sixtyfold and a hundredfold. (Ps. 1:3; John 15:2; 10:11; Matthew 13:8). Jesus Christ cursed the unfruitful fig tree (Mt. 21:19), and pronounced sentence against the useless servant who had not made any profit on his talent. (Mt. 25:24-30). All this proves to us that Jesus Christ wishes to receive some fruit from our wretched selves, namely our good works, because those works belong to Him alone: "Created in good works, in Christ Jesus " (Eph. 2:10)—which words of the Holy Spirit show that Jesus Christ is the sole beginning, and ought to be the sole end, of all our good works, and also that we ought to serve Him, not as servants for wages, but as slaves of love. I will explain what I mean.

<u>Scriptures</u>

1 Cor. 6:19-20 NAB: "Do you not know that your body is a temple of the Holy Spirit within you, whom you have from God, and that you are not your own? For you have been purchased at a price. Therefore glorify God in your body."

Romans 7:4 NAB: "In the same way, my brothers, you also were put to death to the law through the body of Christ, so that you might belong to another, to the one who was raised from the dead in order that we might bear fruit for God."

Ps. 1:3 Douay: "He is like a tree planted near running water, that yields its fruit in due season, and whose leaves never fade, [whatever he does, prospers]."

Psalm 1:3 NAB: "They are like a tree planted near streams of water, that yields its fruit in season; its leaves never wither; whatever they do prospers."

John 15:2, 10:11 NAB: "He takes away every branch in me that does not bear fruit, and everyone that does he prunes so that it bears more fruit." "I am the good Shepherd. A good shepherd lays down his life for the sheep."

Matthew 13:8 NAB: "But some seed fell on rich soil, and produced fruit, a hundred or sixty or thirtyfold."

Matthew 21:19 NAB: "Seeing a fig tree by the road, he went over to it, but found nothing on it except leaves. And he said to it, 'May no fruit ever come from you again.' And immediately the fig tree withered."

Matthew 25:24-30 NAB: "Then the one who had received the one talent came forward and said, 'Master, I knew you were a demanding person, harvesting where you did not plant and gathering where you did not scatter; so out of fear I went off and buried your talent in the ground. Here it is back. His master said to him in reply, 'You wicked, lazy servant! So you knew that I harvest where I did not plant and gather where I did not scatter? Should you not then have put my money in the bank so that I could have got it back with interest on my return? Now then! Take the talent from him and give it to the one with ten. For to everyone who has, more will be given and he will grow rich; but from the one who has not even what he has will be taken away. And throw this useless servant into the darkness outside, where there will be wailing and grinding of teeth.'"

Ephesians 2:10 NAB: "For we are his handiwork, created in Christ Jesus for the good works that God has prepared in advance, that we should live in them."

In these many Scripture references that St. Louis cites in this paragraph, he is making the point: We belong to Jesus Christ in virtue of His saving us from eternal damnation through the victory of His death and resurrection. As a result, in gratitude for this salvation we are to bear fruit for God, by means of our cooperation with His graces and by leading a virtuous life. We are designed to be fruitful and St. Louis compares us to the tree which bears fruit, to the branch that needs constant pruning by the vinedresser in order to bear good fruit, and that we are to be like rich soil to produce an abundant harvest. Jesus expects us to be faithful servants in bearing good fruit which has been God's design for us since the beginning. We serve Jesus consequently as slaves of love, as St. Louis demonstrates below.

> *69. Here on earth there are two ways of belonging to another and of depending on his authority: namely, simple service and slavery, whence we derive the words "servant" and "slave." By common service among Christians a man engages himself to serve another during a certain time, at a certain rate of wages or of recompense. By slavery a man is entirely dependent on another during his whole life, and must serve his master without claiming any wages or reward, just as one of his beasts, over which he has the right of life and death.*

St. Louis begins his introduction to the slavery of love by establishing a preliminary distinction between slaves and servants.

Slave	Servant
-Entire dependence on the master	-Limited and engaged work
-Expects no reward or recompense	-Expects to be compensated.
-Has no rights for his work.	-Has rights

> 70. *There are three sorts of slavery: a slavery of nature, a slavery of constraint and a slavery of will. All creatures are slaves of God in the first sense: "The earth is the Lord's and the fullness thereof" (Ps. 23:1); the demons and the damned are slaves in the second sense; the just and the saints in the third. Because by slavery of the will we make choice of God and His service above all things, even though nature did not oblige us to do so, slavery of the will is the most perfect and most glorious to God, who beholds the heart (1 Kings 16:7), claims the heart (Proverbs 23:26), and calls Himself the God of the heart (Psalm 72:26), that is, of the loving will.*

<u>Scriptures</u>

Psalm 23:1 Douay: "The Lord's are the earth and its fullness; the world and those who dwell in it."

Psalm 24: 1 NAB: "The earth is the Lord's and all it holds, the world and those who live there."

*1 Kings 16:7=1 Samuel 16:7 Douay: "And the Lord said to Samuel: Look not on his countenance, nor on the height of his stature: because I have rejected him, nor do I judge according to the look of man: for man seeth those things that appear, but the Lord beholdeth the heart."

1 Samuel 16:7 NAB: "But the Lord said to Samuel: 'Do not judge from his appearance or from his lofty stature, because I have rejected him. Not as man sees does God see, because man sees the appearance but the Lord looks into the heart.'"

Proverbs 23:26 Douay: "My son, give me thy heart: and let thy eyes keep my ways."

Proverbs 23:26 NAB: "My son, give me your heart, and let your eyes keep to my ways."

Psalm 72:26 Douay: "Though my flesh and my heart waste away, God is the rock of my heart and my portion forever."

Psalm 73:26 NAB: "Though my flesh and my heart fail, God is the rock of my heart, my portion forever."

St. Louis uses these Scriptures to develop his teaching on slavery. All of creation belongs to God, God alone probes the mystery of man's heart and has rights to that heart in which the soul resides. Man through faith should recognize that it is God to whom his whole heart ought rightfully to belong. In our lifestyle of true devotion we give our hearts and wills over to Jesus through Mary. This is not done easily and at once, and there may be many false starts and retreats to selfishness, but continuously and with repeated mortification and growth in the spiritual life, we see the necessity of entering into the divine will and trusting in divine providence at every moment of our lives. We begin to recognize the paradox that "he who loses his life will find it." (Matthew 10:39)

> *71. There is an entire difference between a servant and a slave: (1ˢᵗ) A servant does not give all he is, all he has and all he can acquire, by himself or by another, to his master; but the slave gives himself whole and entire to his master, all he has and all he can acquire, without any exception. (2ⁿᵈ) The servant demands wages for the services which he performs for his master; but the slave can demand nothing whatever assiduity, whatever industry, whatever energy he may have at his work. (3ʳᵈ) The servant can leave his master when he pleases, or at least when the time of his service expires; but the slave has no right to quit his master at will. (4ᵗʰ) The master of the servant has no right of life and death over him, so that if he should kill him like one of his beasts of burden, he would commit an unjust homicide; but the master of the slave has by law a right of life and death over him, so that he may sell him to anybody he likes, or kill him as if he stood on the same level as one of his horses. (5ᵗʰ) Lastly, the servant is only for a time in his master's service; the slave, always.*

St. Louis makes further distinctions between slaves and servants. While these distinctions may no longer exist in modern culture, his point is well taken.

Slave	Servant
--gives everything	--holds back
--demands nothing	--demands payment
---has no right to anything	--has the right to leave
--his/her life belongs to the master	--his/her life is his own
--relationship endures until death	--temporary service

Vocabulary

Assiduity- constant application or diligence.

> *72. There is nothing among men which makes us belong to another more than slavery. There is nothing among Christians*

which makes us more absolutely belong to Jesus Christ and His holy Mother than the slavery of the will according to the example of Jesus Christ Himself, who took on Himself the form of a slave for love of us (Phil. 2:7); and also according to the example of the holy Virgin, who called herself the servant and slave of the Lord (Luke 1:38). The Apostle calls himself, as by a title of honor, "the slave of Christ." Christians are often so called in the Holy Scriptures; and the word for the designation, "servus," as a great man has truly remarked, signified in olden times a slave in the completest sense, because there were no servants then like those of the present day. Masters were served only by slaves or freedmen. This is what the Catechism of the holy Council of Trent, in order to leave no doubt about our being slaves of Jesus Christ, expresses by an unequivocal term, in calling us mancipia Christi, "slaves of Jesus Christ."

Scriptures

Phil. 2:7 NAB: "Rather, [Jesus] emptied himself, taking the form of a slave, coming in human likeness; and found human in appearance, he humbled himself, becoming obedient to death, even death on a cross."

Luke 1:38 NAB: "Mary said, 'Behold, I am the handmaid of the Lord. May it be done to me according to your word.' Then the angel departed from her."

Romans 1:1 NAB: " Paul, a slave of Christ Jesus, called to be an apostle and set apart for the gospel of God…"

St. Louis identifies Jesus and Mary from the Scriptures as those who made themselves slaves of love for God. Jesus through the divine condescension of becoming man and Mary who proclaims for the record of human history that she is the handmaid of the Lord both extol this whole-hearted renunciation to God.

We belong to Jesus and Mary by slavery of the will out of love, not out of constraint. By becoming a slave of Christ we become a slave of love because "God is love" (John 4:8). As we live and practice the true devotion we become slaves of love to Jesus through Mary. We make our own whole-hearted renunciation of all that we are and all that we have: past, present and future and place everything into the hands of Mary.

73. Now that I have given these explanations, I say that we ought to belong to Jesus Christ, and to serve Him not only as mercenary servants, but as loving slaves who, as a result of their great love, give themselves up to serve Him in the quality of slaves simply for the honor of belonging to Him. Before Baptism we were the slaves of the devil. Baptism has made us the slaves of Jesus

Christ: Christians must needs be either the slaves of the devil or the slaves of Jesus Christ.

St. Louis implies that we cannot serve two masters. As baptized Christians we must belong to Jesus, not as hired men, but with the total renunciation of our lives.

74. What I say absolutely of Jesus Christ, I say relatively of Our Lady. Since Jesus Christ chose her for the inseparable companion of His life, of His death, of His glory and of His power in Heaven and upon earth, He gave her by grace, relatively to His Majesty, all the same rights and privileges which He possesses by nature. "All that is fitting to God by nature is fitting to Mary by grace," say the saints; so that, according to them, Mary and Jesus, having but the same will and the same power, have also the same subjects, servants and slaves.

Jesus gave Mary rights and privileges by grace. Mary then has the same subjects, servants and slaves as He does. We can legitimately make our renunciation through her hands.

75. We may, therefore, following the sentiments of the saints and of many great men, call ourselves and make ourselves the loving slaves of the most holy Virgin, in order to be, by that very means, the more perfectly the slaves of Jesus Christ. Our Blessed Lady is the means Our Lord made use of to come to us. She is also the means which we must make use of to go to Him. For she is not like all other creatures who, if we should attach ourselves to them, might rather draw us away from God than draw us near Him. The strongest inclination of Mary is to unite us to Jesus Christ, her Son; and the strongest inclination of the Son is that we should come to Him through His holy Mother. It is to honor and to please Him, just as it would be to do honor and pleasure to a king to become more perfectly his subject and his slave by making ourselves the slaves of the queen. It is on this account that the holy Fathers, and St. Bonaventure after them, say that Our Lady is the way to go to Our Lord: "The way of coming to Christ is to draw near to her."

We become slaves of Mary in order to become perfect slaves of Jesus according to St. Augustine. Mary is different from all other creatures because attachment to her leads us to Jesus, unlike attachment to earthly creatures which only ends in leading us to them. St. Bonaventure states that it honors and pleases Jesus that we go to Him through His holy Mother. As we live the true devotion we honor Jesus and please Him by surrendering all things into His mother's hands. This is an "easy" way to please His Sacred Heart without painful or burdensome self-imposed penances.

> *76. Moreover, if, as I have said, the holy Virgin is the Queen and Sovereign of Heaven and earth, has she not then as many subjects and slaves as there are creatures? St. Anselm, St. Bernard, St. Bernardine, St. Bonaventure say: "All things, the Virgin included, are subject to the empire of God: Behold, all things and God included, are subject to the empire of the Virgin." Is it not reasonable that among so many slaves of constraint there should be some of love, who of their own good will, in the quality of slaves, should choose Mary for their Mistress? What! Are men and devils to have their voluntary slaves, and Mary to have none? What! Shall a king hold it to be for his honor that the queen, his companion, should have slaves over whom she has the right of life and death, because the honor and power of the one is the honor and power of the other; and yet are we to think that Our Lord, who as the best of all sons has divided His entire power with His holy Mother, shall take it ill that she too has her slaves? Has He less respect and love for His Mother than Ahasuerus had for Esther, or than Solomon had for Bathsheba? Who shall dare say so, or even think so?*

Scriptures

Consult the Book of Esther for the relationship between Queen Esther and King Ahasuerus.

Consult 1 Kings 1-2 for the relationship between the Queen-Mother Bathsheba and her son King Solomon.

All the earth is subject to Mary as Queen Mother. She exercises queenship over all the slaves of nature, constraint and love. St. Louis makes the point that just as there are men who give their lives over to evil, so ought there be those who freely give their lives over to Mary. In the comparison of these Old Testament Kings, the point is that Jesus, being God, has more respect for His Mother (the Mother of God) than did Solomon. Jesus is honored by those who make themselves slaves of love to His Mother upon whom He has conferred royal dignity.

> *77. But whither is my pen hurrying me? Why am I stopping here to prove a thing so plain? If we do not wish to call ourselves slaves of the Blessed Virgin, what matter? Let us make ourselves, and call ourselves, slaves of Jesus Christ; for that is being the slave of the holy Virgin, inasmuch as Jesus is the fruit and the glory of Mary; and it is this very thing which we do perfectly by the devotion of which we are hereafter to speak.*

St. Louis continues to clarify to anyone who would oppose him that slavery to Mary is synonymous with slavery to Jesus.

<u>Application of the Lifestyle of True Devotion</u>

1. Is Jesus the sole beginning and the sole end of all my good works? How much of my good works are contaminated by self-consciousness and pride?
2. Have I acted more as a servant or as a slave in my relationship to Jesus?
3. How does my attachment to Mary lead me to Jesus? How does my attachment to other creatures lead me away from Jesus?

Third Truth

<u>We Need Mary In Order To Die to Ourselves</u>

78. Our best actions are ordinarily stained and corrupted by our corrupt nature. When we put clean, clear water into a vessel which has a foul and evil smell, or wine into a cask the inside of which has been tainted by another wine which has been in it, the clear water and the good wine are spoilt, and readily take on the bad odor. In like manner, when God puts into the vessel of our soul, spoilt by original and actual sin, His graces and heavenly dews, or the delicious wine of His love, His gifts are ordinarily spoilt and corrupted by the bad leaven and the evil which sin has left within us. Our actions, even the most sublime and virtuous, feel the effects of it. It is therefore of great importance in the ac-quiring of perfection –which, it must be remembered, is only ac-quired by union with Jesus Christ—to rid ourselves of everything that is bad within us; otherwise Our Lord, who is infinitely pure and hates infinitely the least stain upon our souls, will not unite Himself to us, and will cast us out from His presence

The spiritual gifts can be corrupted due to the effects of original sin in us. There are root tendencies or sins called the seven capital sins which include: pride, envy, anger, gluttony, lust, sloth and avarice. Renunciation of these root sins is the key to perfection. The beginning stage of the purgative way, or the way of begin-ners, consists in purifying oneself of these tendencies towards sin. Mary, who is without sin, leads us to the imitation of her virtues by obtaining for us the grace of self-knowledge that we may recognize these tendencies operative in ourselves and the way the devil tempts us to sin in each of these areas. St. Louis moves his treatment of the truths of devotion to Mary to a demonstration of how she leads us to self-knowledge by helping us rid ourselves of that which in our nature tends toward sin.

> *79. To rid ourselves of self we must: (1ˢᵗ) Thoroughly recognize, by the light of the Holy Spirit, our inward corruption, our incapacity for every good thing useful for salvation, our weakness in all things, our inconstancy at all times, our unworthiness of every grace, and our iniquity in every position. The sin of our first father has spoilt us all, soured us, puffed us up and corrupted us, as the leaven sours, puffs up and corrupts the dough into which it is put. The actual sins which we have committed, whether mortal or venial, pardoned though they may be, have nevertheless increased our concupiscence, our weakness, our inconstancy and our corruption, and have left evil remains in our souls. Our bodies are so corrupted that they are called by the Holy Spirit bodies of sin (Romans 6:6), conceived in sin (Ps. 50:7), nourished in sin, and capable of all sin—bodies subject to thousands of maladies, which go on corrupting from day to day, and which engender nothing but disease, vermin and corruption. Our soul, united to our body, has become so carnal that it is called flesh: "All flesh having corrupted its way" (Gen. 6:12). We have nothing for our portion but pride and blindness of spirit, hardness of heart, weakness and inconstancy of soul, concupiscence, revolted passions, and sicknesses in the body. We are naturally prouder than peacocks, more groveling than toads, more vile than unclean animals, more envious than serpents, more gluttonous than hogs, more furious than tigers, lazier than tortoises, weaker than reeds, and more capricious than weathercocks. We have within ourselves nothing but nothingness and sin, and we deserve nothing but the anger of God and everlasting Hell.*

Scriptures

Romans 6:6 Douay: "For we know that our old self has been crucified with him, in order that the body of sin may be destroyed, that we may no longer be slaves to sin"

Romans 6:6 NAB: "We know that our old self was crucified with him, so that our sinful body might be done away with, that we might no longer be in slavery to sin."

Psalm 50:7 Douay: "Indeed, in guilt was I born, and in sin my mother conceived me:"

Psalm 51:7 NAB: "True, I was born guilty, a sinner, even as my mother conceived me."

70

Genesis 6:12 Douay: "God saw that the earth was corrupt; for all men lived corruptly on the earth."

Genesis 6:12 NAB: "When God saw how corrupt the earth had become, since all mortals led depraved lives on earth…"

St. Louis refers to these Scriptures to illustrate the original sin which we inherited from Adam and Eve which has rendered the body subject to disease, aging and death. He also alludes to the fact that the nobility of the soul has been influenced by the disordered pleasures of the body and no longer seeks to serve and please God, but rather seeks its own desires. St. Louis presents the first stage of dying to oneself as a period of self-knowledge. Mortal and venial sins have damaged our souls and have increased our concupiscence. We need the grace of insight to illuminate our conscience so that we can recognize in ourselves:

--our inward corruption;

--our incapacity for good things for salvation;

--our inconstancy;

--our unworthiness;

--our iniquity.

The Catechism of the Catholic Church teaches in regards to concupiscence: "Yet certain temporal consequences of sin remain in the baptized, such as suffering, illness, death and such frailties inherent in life as weakness of character, and so on, as well as an inclination to sin that Tradition calls concupiscence. ..[it] 'is left for us to wrestle with, it cannot harm those who do not consent but manfully resist it by the grace of Jesus Christ.'" [1]

This moral corruption includes: pride, obduracy, inconstancy, concupiscence, revolted passions, and bodily ills. More specifically St. Louis identifies: pride, groveling, vile behavior, envy, gluttony, fury, laziness, weakness, and capriciousness. Because of this corruption he maintains that our sins deserve Hell were it not for grace. Without the help of grace we are lost in our own nothingness.

Our lifestyle of true devotion begins with the knowledge of how much we need God. Having consecrated ourselves to Mary, one of her first actions is to show us how much we need a Savior—how much we need her Son.

> *80. After this, ought we to be astonished if Our Lord has said that whoever wishes to follow Him must renounce himself and hate his own life, and that whosoever shall love his own life shall lose it and whosoever shall hate it, shall save it? (Jn. 12:25). He who is infinite Wisdom does not give commandments without reason, and He has commanded us to hate ourselves only because we so richly deserve to be hated. Nothing is worthier of love than God, and nothing is worthier of hatred than ourselves.*

Scriptures

John 12:25 NAB: "Whoever loves his life loses it, and whoever hates his life in this world will preserve it for eternal life."

In this reference to the Gospel of John, St. Louis identifies the Jewish notion that to hate one's life means really to love it less. The idea is, that to hate one's own life means that one loves life in Christ all the more and thereby gains salvation for choosing Jesus rather than self. Our Lady teaches us to choose Jesus daily and to renounce daily our self-love.

> *81. (2nd) In order to rid ourselves of self, we must die to ourselves daily. That is to say, we must renounce the operations of the powers of our soul and of the sense of our body. We must see as if we saw not, understand as if we understood not, and make use of the things of this world as if we made no use of them at all. (1 Cor. 7:29-31). This is what St. Paul calls dying daily. (1 Cor. 15:31). "Unless the grain of wheat falling into the ground die, itself remains alone," and brings forth no good fruit. (Jn. 12:24-25). If we do not die to ourselves and if our holiest devotions do not incline us to this necessary and useful death, we shall bring forth no fruit worth anything, and our devotions will become useless. All our good works will be stained by self-love and our own will; and this will cause God to hold in abomination the greatest sacrifices we can make and the best actions we can do; so that at our death we shall find our hands empty of virtues and of merits and we shall not have one spark of pure love, which is only communicated to souls dead to themselves, souls whose life is hidden with Jesus Christ in God (Col. 3:3).*

Scriptures

1 Cor. 7:29-31 NAB: "I tell you, brothers, the time is running out. From now on, let those having wives act as not having them, those weeping as not weeping, those rejoicing as not rejoicing, those buying as not owning, those using the world as not using it fully. For the world in its present form is passing away."

1 Cor. 15:31 NAB: "Every day I face death; I swear it by the pride in you [brothers] that I have in Christ Jesus our Lord."

John 12:24-25 NAB: "Amen, amen, I say to you, unless a grain of wheat falls to the ground and dies, it remains just a grain of wheat; but if it dies, it produces much fruit. Whoever loves his life loses it, and whoever hates his life in this world will preserve it for eternal life."

Colossians 3:3 NAB: "For you have died, and your life is hidden with Christ in God."

In these Scriptures, St. Louis gives examples of how to die to self. He emphasizes detachment from the things of this world, including being detached from one's own ideas, plans, and projects. Once we have died in this sense, and live in Christ Jesus, then we are able to bear fruit, because it is the power of Christ working through us. Even our good intentions can be stained with pride and self-love and the desire to have things done "my way." The lifestyle of true devotion requires us to put all our good actions into Mary's hands whose purity perfects our impure motives. The more we hide with her in Jesus Christ, the more we will receive the pure love of Jesus Christ.

The next step St. Louis presents in ridding ourselves of self is the stage of renunciation and mortification. This mortification must occur daily.

> *82. (3rd) We must choose, therefore, among all the devotions to the Blessed Virgin, the one which draws us most toward this death to ourselves, inasmuch as it will be the best and the most sanctifying. For we must not think that all that shines is gold, that all that tastes sweet is honey, or that all that is easy to do and is done by the greatest number is the most sanctifying. As there are secrets of nature by which natural operations are performed more easily, in a short time and at little cost, so also are there secrets in the order of grace by which supernatural operations, such as ridding ourselves of self, filling ourselves with God, and becoming perfect, are performed more easily. The practice which I am about to disclose is one of these secrets of grace, unknown to the greater number of Christians, known even to few of the devout, and practiced and relished by a lesser number still. But by way of beginning the explanation of this practice, let us consider a fourth truth which is a consequence of the third.*

We must choose the best Marian devotion which enhances mortification and renunciation as it will be the most fruitful. This lifestyle is the best way to empty ourselves of self-love in order to be filled with the pure love of Christ. It does "mortify" or "put to death" our strong desires and appetites in order that we may be free from our own desire to control and be bossy with the Lord. True devotion is a secret of grace which leads us directly and quickly into the mysteries of the Kingdom of God by making us humble and dependent like little children. It is like a spiritual shortcut to sanctity which allows one to:

--die to self;
--be filled with God;
--become perfect.

Application of the Lifestyle of True Devotion

1. How does Mary help me to see and to renounce my tendencies towards selfishness?
2. How does Mary help me to recognize my own incapacity to do anything good without God's grace?
3. How does Mary remind me that my dignity as a baptized son or daughter is much greater than the animals that act by natural instincts?

4. How does Mary teach me that "nothing is worthier of love than God"?
5. How does my practice of the true devotion enable me to die to self and make sacrifices?
6. How does Mary show me how to live a life "hidden with Jesus Christ in God"?
7. How do I manifest my desire to die to self in my devotion to Mary?

Fourth Truth

We Need Mary as Our Mediatrix With our Mediator, Jesus Christ

83. It is more perfect, because it is more humble, not to approach God of ourselves without taking a mediator. Our nature, as I have just shown, is so corrupted that if we rely on our own works, efforts and preparations in order to reach God and please Him, it is certain that our good works will be defiled or be of little weight before God in inducing Him to unite Himself to us and to hear us. It is not without reason that God has given us mediators with His majesty. He has seen our unworthiness and our incapacity; He has had pity on us; and in order to give us access to His mercies, he has provided us with powerful intercessors with His Grandeur, so that to neglect these mediators, and to draw near to His Holiness directly, and without any recommendation, is to fail in humility. It is to fail in respect toward God, so high and so holy. It is to make less account of that King of Kings than we should make of a king or prince of this earth, whom we would not willingly approach without some friend to speak for us.

To employ the mediation of Mary is an act of profound humility. God finds this act of humility pleasing because it is the same way by which His Son chose to come into the world. Going to the Father by means of a mediator parallels going to a president by means of his ambassador or secretary.

84. Our Lord is our advocate and Mediator of redemption with God the Father. It is through Him that we ought to pray, in union with the whole Church, Triumphant and Militant. It is through Him that we have access to the Majesty of the Father, before whom we ought never to appear except sustained and clothed with the merits of His Son, just as the young Jacob came before his father Isaac in the skins of the kids to receive his blessing.

Jesus Christ is the one true mediator between God and man. The Church teaches this clearly as most recently expressed in Pope John Paul II's encyclical letter Redemptoris Mater: "The Church knows and teaches with St. Paul that there is only one mediator: 'For there is one God, and there is one mediator between God and men, the man Christ Jesus, who gave himself as a ransom for all' (1 Tim. 2:5-6)" 'the maternal role of Mary towards people in no way obscures or diminishes the unique mediation of Christ, but rather shows its power': it is mediation in Christ."[2]

Our lifestyle of true devotion doesn't displace Jesus in favor of His Mother. It sees Mary's role "in Christ." Hers is a role in salvation history that nobody else shares.

> *85. But have we not need of a mediator with the Mediator Himself? Is our purity great enough to unite us directly to Him, and by ourselves? Is He not God, in all things equal to His Father, and consequently the Holy of Holies, as worthy of respect as His Father? If through His infinite charity He has made Himself our bail and our Mediator with God His Father, in order to appease Him and to pay Him what we owed Him, are we, on that account, to have less respect and less fear for His majesty and His Sanctity? Let us say boldly with St. Bernard that we have need of a mediator with the Mediator Himself, and that it is the divine Mary who is the most capable of filling that charitable office. It was through her that Jesus Christ came to us, and it is through her that we must go to Him. If we fear to go directly to Jesus Christ, our God, whether because of His infinite greatness or because of our vileness or because of our sins, let us boldly implore the aid and intercession of Mary, our Mother. She is good, she is tender, she has nothing in her austere and forbidding, nothing too sublime and too brilliant. In seeing her, we see our pure nature. She is not the sun, which by the brightness of its rays blinds us because of our weakness; but she is fair and gentle as the moon (Cant. 6:9), which receives the light of the sun, and tempers it to make it more suitable to our capacity. She is so charitable that she repels none of those who ask her intercession, no matter how great sinners they have been; for, as the saints say, never has it been heard since the world was the world that anyone has confidently and perseveringly had recourse to our Blessed Lady and yet has been repelled. She is so powerful that none of her petitions has ever been refused. She has but to show herself before her Son to pray to Him, and straightaway He grants her desires, straightaway He receives her prayers. He is always lovingly vanquished by the prayers of His dearest Mother, who bore Him and nourished Him.*

Scriptures

Canticles 6:9 Douay: "Who is that that cometh forth as the morning rising, fair as the moon, bright as the sun, terrible as an army set in array?"

Song of Songs 6:10 NAB: "Who is this that comes forth like the dawn, as beautiful as the moon, as resplendent as the sun, as awe-inspiring as bannered troops?"

St. Louis develops the idea from Song of Songs that Mary receives her strength and power and loveliness from God, just as the moon receives its light from the sun. She is not the source of salvation or holiness, but reflects it from the Father to her children.

St. Louis introduces this paragraph by posing four rhetorical questions concerning Mary's role as a "mediator of intercession." The concept of mediator in intercession is key to understanding Mary's role in relationship to her Son. Her mediation is an act of love which does not diminish to any degree Jesus' role as the one Mediator with God the Father.

Pope John Paul II treats of Mary's mediation when he states: "At Cana in Galilee there is shown only one concrete aspect of human need, apparently a small one of little importance ("They have no wine"). But it has a symbolic value: this coming to the aid of human needs means, at the same time, bringing those needs within the radius of Christ's messianic mission and salvific power. Thus there is a mediation: Mary places herself between her Son and mankind in the reality of their wants, needs and sufferings. She puts herself 'in the middle,' that is to say she acts as a mediatrix not as an outsider, but in her position as mother. She knows that as such she can point out to her Son the needs of mankind, and in fact, she 'has the right' to do so. Her mediation is thus in the nature of intercession: Mary 'intercedes' for mankind."[3]

> *86. All this is taken from St. Bernard and St. Bonaventure, so that according to them, we have three steps to mount to go to God: the first, which is nearest to us and the most suited to our capacity is Mary; the second is Jesus Christ; and the third is God the Father. To go to Jesus, we must go to Mary; she is our mediatrix of intercession. To go to God the Father, we must go to Jesus; for He is our mediator of redemption. Now the devotion that I am about to bring forward observes this order perfectly.*

St. Louis identifies three steps to God the Father:

1st) Mary, the mediator of intercession (which requires on our part an act of humility to approach her)

2nd) →Jesus, Mediator of Redemption (which requires faith. Through the lifestyle of true devotion this faith has been purified of selfishness and embellished with grace due to Mary's intercession for us with Jesus)

3rd) →God the Father.

Application of the Lifestyle of True Devotion

1. How has choosing Mary to be my mediator of intercession with God the Father increased my humility? How has it affected my understanding of His grandeur?
2. How have I prayed better "through, with and in Jesus" as a result of my lifestyle of true devotion to Jesus through Mary?
3. How do I see my pure nature when seeing Mary? How does my prayer change with Mary when I am in a state of sin and when I am in a state of grace? What have I learned about Mary being the nearest and easiest step to God?

Fifth Truth

<u>We Need Mary In Order to Preserve the Graces and Treasures We have Received From God</u>

> *87. It is very difficult, considering our weakness and frailty, to preserve in ourselves the graces and treasures which we have received from God: (1ˢᵗ) Because we have this treasure, which is worth more than Heaven and earth put together, in frail vessels, i.e., in a corruptible body and in a weak and inconstant soul, which a mere nothing disturbs and dejects: "We have this treasure in earthen vessels" (2 Cor. 4:7).*

<u>Scriptures</u>

2 Cor. 4:7 NAB: "But we hold this treasure in earthen vessels, that the surpassing power may be of God and not from us."

In this Scripture, St. Louis points out that it is difficult to preserve the graces we have received due to an inconstant soul and corruptible body. We are being transformed into glory according to St. Paul, and St. Louis would have us be transformed and molded into Jesus Christ by a perfect mold, Mary, who, neither corrupt nor inconstant, is the perfect vessel for containing our treasure chest of grace.

In this and the following two paragraphs St. Louis treats of the temptations that come from outside of us--from the world, the flesh and the devil. Here St. Louis has described the temptation that comes from the flesh due to its tendency towards pleasure. Mary is the remedy for the temptations of the flesh.

> *88. (2ⁿᵈ) Because the devils, who are skillful thieves, wish to surprise us unawares, and to strip us. They watch day and night for the favorable moment. For that end they go round about us*

incessantly to devour us and to snatch from us in one moment, by a sin, all the graces and merits we have gained for many years. Their malice, their experience, their stratagems and their number ought to make us fear this misfortune immensely, especially when we see how many persons fuller of grace than we are, richer in virtues, better founded in experience and far higher exalted in sanctity, have been surprised, robbed and unhappily pillaged. Ah! How many cedars of Lebanon, how many stars of the firmament, have we not seen fall miserably, and in the twinkling of an eye lose all their height and their brightness! Whence comes that sad and curious change? It was not for want of grace, which is wanting to no man; but it was for want of humility. They thought themselves capable of guarding their own treasures. They trusted in themselves, relied upon themselves. They thought their house secure enough, and their coffers strong enough, to keep the precious treasure of grace. It is because of that scarcely perceptible reliance upon themselves, though all the while it seemed to them that they were relying only on the grace of God, that the most just Lord permitted them to be robbed by leaving them to themselves. Alas! If they had but known the admirable devotion which I will unfold presently, they would have confided their treasure to a Virgin powerful and faithful, who would have kept it for them, as if it had been her own possession; nay, who would have even taken it as an obligation of justice on herself to preserve it for them.

In this second paragraph St. Louis is teaching about the temptations that come from the Devil and the evil spirits. This is a very important paragraph on the nature of the evil spirits who tempt us. They tempt us relentlessly to sever and damage the relationship we have with God. There are distinct patterns to their temptations, and these include some of the following:

One of their first objectives is to disrupt our prayer lives. If they succeed in preventing us from praying (by suggesting to us a multitude of reasons why not to pray) then they have already gained a significant advantage over our soul.

A second area is in our dependence upon material things. The evil spirits will try to lead us to a disordered attachment to material things, especially the accumulation or the earning of money. This disordered attachment will cause division within the family or the soul even at the expense of attending Mass and making time to pray. The hunger (temptation) for earning more money increases as we satisfy that temptation. Jesus reminds us in Matthew 6:24: "Man cannot serve both God and mammon for he will love the one and hate the other." The love of money above the love of God is a diabolical goal.

The evil spirits also operate on our psyche by trying to tempt us with anxieties and worries so that we will lose trust in God. This excessive worry can lead to obsessive fear and preoccupation which deprives us of the peace which Jesus came to give to the world. Satan is the master of exaggeration and these exaggerated worries about a future which does not yet exist can create for those souls striving for holiness great distress and temptation to doubt in God's Divine Providence.

Another aspect of temptation in our daily lives from the evil spirits is to complain and curse God for when "bad" things happen to us, rather than seeing in them an occasion of grace and trust that all things work out for the good of those who love Him. Once we turn on God we can begin to see Him as the enemy of our souls, and not Satan and his minions. Another aspect of the devil's tactics is to create divisions, misunderstandings and lack of respect. This division is clearly seen in families, religious communities, between spouses, parents and their children, etc. The more Satan can divide, the more he can conquer an individual soul, family, community or nation.

The evil spirits are extremely successful in temptations to lust, immorality and immodesty. Not only does this appeal to our sexual nature, but the temptations can many times be satisfied in our technological age in solitude through access to the Internet, chat rooms, videos, etc. Satan is not opposed to using modern technology and whatever means available to cause our ruin and to incite our pride to rebel against "old fashioned" mores.

The list of temptations is not limited to these alone, but also includes lies, gossip, foul language, inordinate curiosity, deceit, injustice, vanity, etc.[4] The Virgin Mary, however, and the lifestyle of true devotion is a counter to these temptations because she has enmity against him. Through the lifestyle of true devotion St. Louis shows how devotion to Mary and imitation of her virtues allow the soul to overcome, or at least through Mary's intercession, to grow in the discernment of spirits and to recognize the snares of the evil one.

The decisive fault by which we succumb to temptation is our lacking in humility. Those who rely upon their own strength (and not upon the Virgin Mother) will fall. The Lord permits these falls into sin—not that He desires or causes them. But that by them we ought to grow in humility and in a recognition of a greater dependence upon Mary.

> 89. (3rd) It is difficult to persevere in justice because of the strange corruption of the world. The world is now so corrupt it seems inevitable that religious hearts should be soiled, if not by its mud, at least by its dust; so that it has become a kind of miracle for anyone to remain in the midst of that impetuous torrent without being drawn in by it, in the midst of that stormy sea without being drowned in it or stripped by the pirates or the corsairs, in the midst of that pestilent sea without being infected by it. It is the Virgin, alone faithful, in whom the serpent has never had part, who works this miracle for those who serve her in that sweet way which I have shortly to unfold.

In this third paragraph, St. Louis treats of the temptations arising from the world.

Due to the culture of death in which we live, it is difficult for religious people to persevere in holiness. One is surrounded and bombarded by corruption in faith and morals. It is nearly impossible not to be affected by it in one way or another; that is, by "mud" or "dust." It is Mary alone who can protect us from the culture of death and godlessness since she has never been contaminated by the world, the flesh or the devil. Our lifestyle of true devotion really protects us from the evil which comes from the world because we are consecrated to the new Mother of the living.

Application of the Lifestyle of True Devotion

1. How does living true devotion help preserve in my soul the graces God has given me?
2. How has my lack of humility caused me to commit sin? What are my greatest occasions for sin? What time of day or night am I most susceptible to temptations?
3. How has conferring my graces to Mary's care affected my response to temptation, sin and remaining in a state of grace?
4. How does the world daily affect my religious and devotional life?
5. What have I gained in self-knowledge about my vulnerability to temptations coming from the world, the flesh and the devil? What has Mary taught me about myself and my inclinations to sin?

CHAPTER III

CHOICE OF TRUE DEVOTION TO THE BLESSED VIRGIN

90. Having laid down these five truths let us continue. Today, more than ever, we must take pains in choosing true devotion to our Blessed Lady, because, more than ever before, there are false devotions to our Blessed Lady which are easily mistaken for true ones. The devil, like a false coiner and a subtle and experienced sharper, has already deceived and destroyed so many souls by a false devotion to the Blessed Virgin that he makes a daily use of his diabolical experience to plunge many others by this same way into everlasting perdition; amusing them, lulling them to sleep in sin, under the pretext of some prayers badly said or of some outward practices which he inspires. As a false coiner does not ordinarily counterfeit anything but gold or silver, and very rarely other metals, because they are not worth the trouble, so the evil spirit does not for the most part counterfeit other devotions, but only those to Jesus and Mary—devotion to Holy Communion and to our Blessed Lady—because they are among other devotions what gold and silver are among other metals.

St. Louis moves to a presentation now of the true devotion by illustrating first certain aspects of false devotions that separate them from what he will present as the best of all devotions to Mary.

The devil himself inspires us to false devotions to Mary preventing us from entering into the true devotion as described by St. Louis. It is to his diabolical advantage to counterfeit something so valuable and he doesn't bother with false devotions in the case of other saints. The flaws in the "counterfeited" devotion, however, can be recognized by its effect on the interior life. These counterfeit devotions are described in the following paragraphs.

91. It is then very important to recognize, first of all, false devotions to our Blessed Lady, in order to avoid them, and true devotion, in order to embrace it; secondly, which of the many practices of true devotion to our Blessed Lady is the most perfect, the most agreeable to her, the most glorious to God, and the most sanctifying for ourselves, so that we may adopt that one.

St. Louis sets out to demonstrate seven types of false devotions to help the reader identify and avoid them. Then, in Article Two, after presenting the true devotion, he wants to show us which is the most perfect practice of the many practices he will describe for our sanctification. In our lifestyle of true devotion we may humbly recognize aspects of ourselves in these false devotees. That humble recognition is a valuable moment for conversion and deepening of our consecration and lifestyle.

Application of the Lifestyle of True Devotion

1. How does the devil try to prevent me from living the true devotion to Jesus through Mary?
2. How do I evaluate a true devotion to Mary from a counterfeit one? What does the counterfeiter (that is, the devil) gain from deceiving me?

Article One

False Devotions to the Blessed Virgin and False Devotees

92. I find seven kinds of false devotees and false devotions to Our Lady, namely: 1. The critical devotees; 2. The scrupulous devotees; 3. The external devotees; 4. The presumptuous devotees; 5. The inconstant devotees; 6. The hypocritical devotees; 7. The interested devotees.

1. Critical devotees

93. The critical devotees are, for the most part, proud scholars, rash and self-sufficient spirits, who have at heart some devotion to the holy Virgin, but who criticize nearly all the practices of devotion which simple people pay simply and holily to their good Mother, because these practices do not fall in with their own humor and fancy. They call in doubt all the miracles and pious stories recorded by authors worthy of faith, or drawn from the chronicles of religious orders: narratives which testify to us the mercies and the power of the most holy Virgin. They cannot see, without uneasiness, simple and humble people on their knees before an altar or an image of Our Lady, sometimes at the corner of a street, in order to pray to God there; and they even accuse them of idolatry, as if they adored the wood or the stone. They say that, for their part, they are not fond of these external devotions, and that they are not so credulous as to believe so many tales and stories that are told about Our Lady. When they are told how admirably the Fathers of the Church praised the Blessed Virgin, they either reply that the Fathers spoke as professional orators, with exaggeration; or they misinterpret their words. These kinds of false devotees and of proud and worldly people are greatly to be feared. They do an infinite wrong to devotion to Our Lady; and they are but too successful in alienating people from it, under the pretext of destroying its abuses.

There is predominantly a lack of love in all of the false devotions which St. Louis presents. True devotion disposes us to love by leading us into the Immaculate Heart of Mary. The critical devotees suffer from intellectual pride. This is the attitude of proud scholars and intellectuals who scoff at the pious practices and devotions to Our Lady practiced by the faithful. In their pride they have done even further damage by leading many simple souls away from Our Lady telling them that such devotion to her is idolatry. There is worldliness and pride in the critical devotees who reject even the Tradition of the Church. In paragraph #104, St. Louis says of them that "they believe nothing and criticize everything."

2. Scrupulous Devotees

94. The scrupulous devotees are those who fear to dishonor the Son by honoring the Mother, to abase the one in elevating the other. They cannot bear that we should attribute to Our Lady the most just praise which the holy Fathers have given her. It is all they can do to endure that there should be more people before the altar of the Blessed Virgin than before the Blessed Sacrament—as if the one were contrary to the other, as if those who prayed to our Blessed Lady did not pray to Jesus Christ through her. They are unwilling that we should speak so often of Our Lady and address her so frequently. Here are some of their favorite sayings; "Why so many Rosaries, so many confraternities and so many external devotions to the Blessed Virgin? There is much ignorance in all this. It makes a mummery of our religion. Speak to us of those who are devout to Jesus Christ." (Yet they often name Him without raising their hats—I say this by way of parenthesis.) "We must have recourse to Jesus Christ; He is our only Mediator. We must preach Jesus Christ; this is the solid devotion." What they say is in a certain sense true, but in the application they make of it, namely, to hinder devotion to our Blessed Lady, very dangerous; and it is, under pretext of a greater good, a subtle snare of the evil one. For the more we honor the Blessed Virgin, the more we honor Jesus Christ, because we honor Mary only that we may the more perfectly honor Jesus, since we go to her only as the way by which we are to find the end we are seeking, which is Jesus.

Scrupulous devotees are motivated by fear. They are afraid that honoring Mary too much can dishonor her Son. They neglect to realize that praying to Mary means praying to Jesus. All prayers go to Him through her and she retains nothing for herself. The deception in this false devotion is to cause confusion and doubt that one is denying Jesus the adoration due Him; when in fact, honoring His mother (whom He gave to us on Calvary) renders Him great praise.

> 95. *The Church, with the Holy Spirit, blesses Our Lady first, and Our Lord second: "Blessed art thou among women, and blessed is the fruit of thy womb, Jesus." It is not that Mary is more than Jesus or even equal to Him—that would be intolerable heresy; but it is that, in order to bless Jesus more perfectly, we must begin by blessing Mary. Let us then say, with all the true clients of Our Lady, in opposition to these false scrupulous devotees, "O Mary, thou art blessed among all women, and blessed is the fruit of thy womb, Jesus."*

St. Louis uses the structure of the Hail Mary (Luke 1:41) to emphasize that blessing Mary first leads to blessing Jesus more perfectly. He reiterates that Mary is not equal to or greater than Jesus. See also #104 where St. Louis states that scrupulous devotees are "afraid of being too devout out of respect to Jesus Christ."

3. External Devotees

> 96. *External devotees are persons who make all devotion to our Blessed Lady consist in outward practices. They have no taste except for the exterior of this devotion, because they have no interior spirit of their own. They will say quantities of Rosaries with the greatest precipitation; they will hear many Masses distractedly; they will go, without devotion, to processions; they will enroll themselves in all her confraternities—without amending their lives, without doing any violence to their passions, or without imitating the virtues of that most holy Virgin. They have no love but for the sensible part of devotion, without having any relish for its solidity. If they have not sensible sweetness in their practices, they think they are doing nothing; they get all out of joint, throw everything up, or do everything at random. The world is full of these exterior devotees, and there are no people who are more critical than they of men of prayer, who foster an interior spirit as the essential thing, without, however, disregarding that outward modesty which always accompanies true devotion.*

External devotion, devoid of interiority, leads to superficiality. A lack of interiority is characterized by: rushed prayers, distractions, failure to enter into a deeper conversion to the message of the Gospel, avoidance of mortification, insipidity, and lack of growth in the virtues. It is characterized by those who seek emotional gratification in their prayers. A fruit of the lifestyle of true devotion is humility which distinguishes the true devotee from the false. St. Louis states in #104 concerning the external devotees that for them: "all devotion consists in the outward practices." The external devotee is also one who preoccupies himself with busyness with the idea that he has to be "doing" something for God all the time.

4. Presumptuous Devotees

97. Presumptuous devotees are sinners abandoned to their passions, or lovers of the world, who under the fair name of Christians and clients of our Blessed Lady conceal pride, avarice, impurity, drunkenness, anger, swearing, detraction, injustice or some other sin. They sleep in peace in the midst of their bad habits, without doing any violence to themselves to correct their faults, under the pretext that they are devout to the Blessed Virgin. They promise themselves that God will pardon them; that they will not be allowed to die without confession; and that they will not be lost eternally because they say the Rosary, because they fast on Saturdays, because they belong to the Confraternity of the Holy Rosary, or wear the Scapular, or are enrolled in other congregations, or they wear the little habit or little chain of Our Lady. They will not believe us when we tell them that their devotion is only an illusion of the devil and a pernicious presumption likely to destroy their souls. They say that God is good and merciful; that He has not made us to condemn us everlastingly; that no man is without sin; that they shall not die without confession; that one good act of contrition at the hour of death is enough; that they are devout to Our Lady, wear the Scapular, say daily, without fail and without vanity, seven Our Fathers and seven Hail Marys in her honor; and that they sometimes say the Rosary and the Office of Our Lady, besides fasting and other things. To give authority to all this, and to blind themselves still further, they quote certain stories which they have heard or read—it does not matter to them whether they be true or false—relating how people have died in mortal sin without confession, and then, because in their lifetime they sometimes said some prayers or went through some practices of devotion to Our Lady, how they have been raised to life again in order to go to confession or their soul has been miraculously retained in their bodies till confession; or through the clemency of the Blessed Virgin they have obtained from God, at the moment of death, contrition and pardon of their sins and so have been saved; and that they themselves expect similar favors.

98. Nothing in Christianity is more detestable than this diabolical presumption. For how can we truly say that we love and honor our Blessed Lady when by our sins we are pitilessly piercing, wounding, crucifying and outraging Jesus Christ, her Son? If Mary laid down a law to herself, to save by her mercy this sort of people, she would be authorizing crime and helping crucify and outrage her Son. Who would ever dare think of such a thing?

Presumptuous devotees hide their sins under the pretext of being "Marian." Presumption is a defect of pride in which one thinks he is capable of doing something beyond his ability. These false devotees aspire to greatness and high degrees of prayer without passing through the lower degrees. They have no desire to build the interior life on humility, renunciation or faithfulness to the present moment.[5] In the context in which St. Louis is speaking these are the devotees who claim salvation without having recourse to conversion or penance because they use Mary's name to get them into Heaven. St. Louis forcefully states that to commit sin under Mary's aegis is a type of false devotion proceeding from a diabolical illusion. One cannot freely oppose Jesus and hurt others while claiming to love Jesus' mother Mary at the same time. St. Louis asks the question who would dare to set enmity between the Mother and the Son? Mary does not authorize or encourage the crucifying of her Son through her children's sins.

99. I say that thus to abuse devotion to Our Lady, which, after devotion to Our Lord in the Blessed Sacrament, is the holiest and solidest of all devotions, is to be guilty of a horrible sacrilege, which, after the sacrilege of an unworthy Communion, is the greatest and least pardonable of all sacrileges. I confess that, in order to be truly devout to our Blessed Lady, it is not absolutely necessary to be so holy as to avoid every sin, though this were desirable; but this much at least is necessary, and I beg you to lay it well to heart: (1) to have a sincere resolution to avoid at least all mortal sin, which outrages the Mother as well as the Son; (2) to do violence to ourselves to avoid sin; (3) to enroll ourselves in confraternities, to say the Rosary or other prayers, to fast on Saturdays and the like.

St. Louis describes two types of sacrilege: (1) making an unworthy Communion and (2) sinning while presuming Mary will save one. The Church teaches that a sacrilege "consists in profaning or treating unworthily the sacraments and other liturgical actions, as well as persons, things or places consecrated to God. Sacrilege is a grave sin especially when committed against the Eucharist, for in this sacrament the true Body of Christ is made substantially present for us."[6] An unworthy Communion occurs when one receives the Eucharist in a state of mortal sin. Pope John Paul II emphasizes the importance of Confession before receiving the Eucharist when he states: "Along these same lines, The <u>Catechism of the Catholic Church</u> rightly stipulates that 'anyone conscious of a grave sin must receive the sacrament of Reconciliation before coming to Communion.' I therefore desire to reaffirm that in the Church there remains in force, now and in the future, the rule by which the Council of Trent gave concrete expression to the Apostle Paul's stern warning when it affirmed that, in order to receive the Eucharist in a worthy manner, 'one must first confess one's sins, when one is aware of mortal sin.'"[7] The lifestyle of true devotion always leads to personal and ongoing conversion. This is a necessary and key aspect of knowing if one is actually practicing this devotion.

The lifestyle involves the basic Christian duty to:

--avoid mortal sin;
--practice mortification;
--pray and fast.

> *100. These good works are likewise wonderfully useful for the conversion of a sinner, however hardened he may be. If my reader be such a one, even though he have one foot in the abyss, I would advise him to practice them, but only on condition that he do so with the intention of obtaining from God, through the intercession of the Blessed Virgin, the grace of contrition and pardon of sins and the grace to conquer his evil habits, and not to remain quietly in the state of sin, contrary to his remorse of conscience, the example of Jesus Christ and the saints and the maxims of the holy Gospel.*

The lifestyle of true devotion aids a person in conquering bad habits by the return to the Sacrament of Reconciliation, by a greater self-knowledge, by strengthening the will and by helping to make a firm amendment not to sin and to avoid all the near occasions of sin. These would be some of the fundamental points of the Act of Contrition; a necessary prayer for the ongoing conversion involved in this lifestyle and in achieving union with God. Concerning presumptuous devotees, St. Louis says in #104 that they are the ones who "wallow in sin."

5. Inconstant Devotees

> *101. The inconstant devotees are those who are devout to our Blessed Lady by fits and starts. Sometimes they are fervent and sometimes lukewarm. Sometimes they seem ready to do anything for her, and then a little afterward, they are not like the same people. They begin by taking up all the devotions to her, and enrolling themselves in the confraternities; and then they do not practice the*

rules with fidelity. They change like the moon, and Mary puts them under her feet with the crescent, because they are changeable and unworthy to be reckoned among the servants of that faithful Virgin who have for their special graces fidelity and constancy. It were better for such persons not to burden themselves with so many prayers and practices but to choose a few and fulfill them with faithfulness and love, in spite of the world, the devil and the flesh.

Inconstancy in the spiritual life afflicts beginners who begin to make progress in holiness. When the graces which are experienced in a less sensible manner recede, the soul grows weary and begins to relax its efforts. We begin to shorten or avoid prayer, we relax or quit our penances and begin to shop around for a more exciting spiritual life that satisfies our curiosity, vanity or sensuality. Inconstant devotees lack temperance and prudence. They are easily stimulated to exuberance but are unable to persevere in a commitment. They pick and choose devotions with superficiality. St. Louis states that true devotees are identified by their fidelity and constancy. The cure for such inconstant souls is to practice one devotion well, with a renewed resolve of the will and with frequent recourse to spiritual direction and the making of a good examination of conscience.[8] These types of devotees who fail to make true devotion a lifestyle "give up devotion under the least temptation." (Cf. #104) The lifestyle of true devotion should be practiced with patience, fidelity and a recognition of how much one can undertake from the many recommendations suggested.

6. Hypocritical Devotees

> *102. We have still to mention the false devotees to our Blessed Lady who are hypocritical devotees, who cloak their sins and sinful habits with her mantle, in order to be taken by men for what they are not.*

Hypocrisy is another defect of pride and vainglory. It hides its vices under the appearance of virtue.[9] Hypocritical devotees are those who fake it. They want to appear to be children of Mary when in fact they are children of sin. St. Louis states that these false devotees "do true devotion in order to pass for good people" (#104).

7. Interested Devotees

> *103. There are also the interested devotees, who have recourse to Our Lady only to gain some lawsuit, or to avoid some danger, or to be cured of some illness, or for some other similar necessity, without which they would forget her altogether. All these are false devotees, pleasing neither to God nor to His holy Mother.*

This type of false devotee uses Mary for self-interested gain. St. Louis states that they use her to get out of trouble or to obtain for themselves some advantage. Otherwise they would have no devotion to her. Each of these false devotions serves as a warning for us (the true devotees) not to slip into them.

> *104. Let us then take great care not to be of the number of the critical devotees, who believe nothing and criticize everything; nor of the scrupulous devotees, who are afraid of being too devout to Our Lady, out of respect to Our Lord; nor of the exterior devotees, who make all their devotion consist in outward practices; nor of the presumptuous devotees, who, under the pretext of their false devotion to the Blessed Virgin, wallow in their sins; nor of the inconstant devotees, who from levity change their practices of devotion, or give them up altogether, at the least temptation; or of the hypocritical devotees, who join confraternities and wear the liveries of the Blessed Virgin in order to pass for good people; nor, finally, of the interested devotees, who have recourse to Our Lady only to be delivered from bodily evils, or to obtain temporal goods."*

Here St. Louis summarizes this section on false devotees with a warning for us not to follow them. We, however, as true children of Mary are to follow the true way he is about to describe.

Application of the Lifestyle of True Devotion

1   How have I in my mistaken pride led people away from Mary? How have I been led away from Mary by intellectuals or academic scholars who have misrepresented her?

2.   Do I feel competition between my devotion to Mary and my worship of Jesus? Do I worry that I may be offending Jesus by time spent with Mary?

3.   Do I focus too much on the exterior aspects of the true devotion? Have I failed to cultivate an interior spirit of quiet, recollection and self-surrender to Our Lady?

4.   Have I used my consecration to Mary as an excuse to commit sin and not to strive for perfection—knowing that she will get me off the hook at the hour of my death?

5.   Do I strive to avoid sin? Practice mortification and self-control?

6.   Do I jump from one Marian devotion to another depending upon the latest book I've read or the latest Marian apparition?

7.   Do I pretend to be holy in my public life, while my private life is in shambles?

8.   Do I practice the true devotion in hope that Mary will obtain things for me?

Article Two

True Devotion to the Blessed Virgin

I. Characteristics

105. After having laid bare and condemned the false devotions to the most holy Virgin, we must, in a few words, give the characteristics of true devotion. It must be: 1. Interior, 2. Tender, 3. Holy, 4. Constant, and 5. Disinterested.

(1ˢᵗ) Interior

106. True devotion to Our Lady is interior; that is, it comes from the mind and the heart. It flows from the esteem we have for her, the high idea we have formed of her greatness, and the love which we have for her.

In this first of five characteristics of the lifestyle of true devotion, St. Louis states that it must proceed from the mind and the heart.

The Mind→esteems Mary; holds her greatness in high regard with an understanding of her dignity.

The Heart→loves her with the heart of a child.

The interiority of this devotion focusing on the esteem and greatness of Mary opposes the exploitation which occurs in the disinterested false devotee just seen. Our lifestyle of true devotion is interior, balanced between the intellect and the will or the mind and the heart. It is also essentially a personal devotion in that it is a relationship between two persons (Mary and the soul) created in the image and likeness of God who are capable of knowing and loving each other and giving glory to God for their relationship.

(2ⁿᵈ) Tender

107. It is tender; that is, full of confidence in her, like a child's confidence in his loving mother. This confidence makes the soul have recourse to her in all its bodily and mental necessities, with much simplicity, trust and tenderness. It implores the aid of its good Mother at all times, in all places and above all things; in its doubts, that it may be enlightened; in its wanderings, that it may be brought into the right path; in its temptations, that it may be supported; in its weaknesses, that it may be strengthened; in its falls, that it may be lifted up; in its discouragements, that it may be cheered; in its scruples, that they may be taken away; in the crosses, toils and disappointments of life, that it may be consoled under them. In a word, in all the evils of body and mind, the soul ordinarily has recourse to Mary, without fear of annoying her or displeasing Jesus Christ.

Another characteristic of true devotion is that it is tender. One has recourse to Mary with simplicity, trust and the tenderness that flows from love. It is opposed to the interested devotees who have recourse to Mary in order to be delivered from their bodily ills or who are looking out for themselves only. The lifestyle of true devotion seeks Mary's intercession at all times. It is not inconstant, but rather one is in a continuous relationship with her. It has some of the following effects:
--an illumination and clarification when in doubt;
--a return to the Lord when distracted by the world, the flesh and the devil;
--a support during temptations;
--a strengthening due to moral weakness;
--a lifting up after having sinned and being brought to Jesus in the Sacraments;
--a cheer and consolation during periods of discouragement;
--the removal of scruples;
--a consolation in bodily, mental and spiritual sufferings.

When we enter into this deeper relationship with Mary by virtue of our consecration, we begin to experience the effects of this devotion. The tenderness of which St. Louis speaks is not a saccharine piety, but is a response to love.

(3ʳᵈ) Holy

108. True devotion to Our Lady is holy; that is to say, it leads the soul to avoid sin and to imitate the virtues of the Blessed Virgin, particularly her profound humility, her lively faith, her blind obedience, her continual prayer, her universal mortification, her divine purity, her ardent charity, her heroic patience, her angelic sweetness, and her divine wisdom. These are the ten principal virtues of the most holy Virgin.

The actual lifestyle of true devotion involves imitating Mary's virtues. These virtues lead one to holiness. The Second Vatican Council teaches that: "...the followers of Christ still strive to increase in holiness by conquering sin. And so they raise their eyes to Mary who shines forth to the whole community of the elect as a model of the virtues. Devotedly meditating on her and contemplating her in the light of the Word made man, the Church with reverence enters more intimately into the supreme mystery of the Incarnation and becomes ever increasingly like her Spouse."[10]

The ten virtues that St Louis lists should not be glossed over lightly, but should be reviewed carefully. Nine of the virtues are presented below as a means of deepening our understanding of their value in our own spiritual lives.

(1) <u>Humility</u> is a supernatural virtue, which, through the self-knowledge it imparts, inclines us to reckon ourselves at our true worth and to seek self-efface-ment and contempt. Humility is based both in truth and justice. Truth causes us to know ourselves just as we are and justice inclines us to act upon that knowledge. To attain this self-knowledge we must see what in us belongs to God, and what belongs to ourselves. Spiritual writers have listed varying degrees of humility. Among them is St. Benedict's twelve degrees. The first seven concern interior acts of humility and there are four that concern exterior acts of humility. They include the following:

1. The fear of God which induces us to keep the commandments.
2. Obedience to God's will.
3. Obedience to one's superiors out of love for God
4. Patient obedience in difficult circumstances without complaining.
5. The admission of secret faults to one's superior.
6. The acceptance of privations and menial task which one feels is below one's station.
7. To consider oneself as inferior to others.
8. To avoid drawing attention to oneself.
9. To be silent when there is no good reason to speak.
10. Moderation of laughter which is uncouth, sneering or boisterous.
11. Reserve in speech, choosing to be quiet and humble.
12. Modesty of behavior; modesty of the eyes, posture.[11]

While these degrees of humility are written for Benedictine monks they can be applied to those who live in the world. Mary practiced these aspects of humility to perfection and obtains for us that same grace when we practice the lifestyle of true devotion. For the growth of this virtue, one can grow in humility by practicing one of these aspects of humility each month, and thus have a yearlong training in humility in the school of Mary. These virtues are not to be studied, but exercised.

(2) <u>Faith</u> is a theological virtue that inclines the mind, under the influence of the will and of grace, to yield a firm assent to revealed truths, because of the au-thority of God. This virtue enables us to believe truths from God and the Church with our whole being. Faith must be the foundation of the spiritual life uniting us to God. Pope John Paul II speaking of Mary's faith states:

"As the Council teaches, 'The obedience of faith' (Rom. 16:26) must be given to God who reveals, an obedience by which man entrusts his whole self freely to God." This description of faith found perfect realization in Mary. The 'decisive' moment was the Annunciation, and the very words of Elizabeth: 'And blessed is she who believed' refer primarily to that very moment. Indeed, at the Annunciation Mary entrusted herself to God completely, with the 'full submission of intellect and will,' manifesting 'the obedience of faith' to him who spoke to her through his messenger. She responded, therefore, with all her human feminine 'I,' and this response of faith included both perfect cooperation with 'the grace of God that precedes and assists' and perfect openness to the action of the Holy Spirit, who 'constantly brings faith to completion by his gifts.'"[12]

We practice faith in the lifestyle of true devotion by firm assent to revealed truth from God and the Church's interpretations of these truths. Mary helps us to grow in faith by the illumination in our minds of God's truths. If there are areas of Church teaching we don't understand, Mary obtains for us the grace of insight when we have recourse to her.

(3) Obedience is a supernatural, moral virtue which inclines us to submit our will to that of our lawful superiors, in so far as they are the representatives of God. This virtue relates to the absolute submission we owe to God and to His lawful representatives. As with humility, there are also degrees of obedience. The 1st degree is to observe the Commandments and the teachings of the Church. It also means that one conforms to the orders of lawful superiors. The 2nd degree is the submission of one's will to the Father, without complaint, even, and especially in the midst of hardships. The 3rd degree is the submission of one's judgment without consideration of the reasons for a particular command. For the obedience to be perfect it has to be supernatural (we are to see Jesus present in our superiors), universal (we comply with every command of a superior, not just the ones we like) and entire: it is prompt—motivated by love one obeys with readiness. Without reservation—one obeys in all things, not just selectively. Persevering—not to quit no matter the length or difficulty of the obedience. Even cheerful—obedience can be cheerful when one keeps in mind the person of Jesus present in the superior.[13] Mary's obedience to God is perfect obedience and she fulfills every one of these requirements. When we consecrate ourselves to her, she obtains for us the grace to imitate her practice of these same virtues. When we struggle with authority and disobedience Our Lady helps us purify our hearts of a disordered self-will or of deep traumas that prevent our wholehearted surrender to God's will. She helps with the healing we all need in order to grow in these virtues.

(4) Prayer is defined as an elevation of our soul to God to offer Him our homage and ask His favors, in order to grow in holiness for His glory. It takes a human effort to focus our attention on Him while at the same time not being distracted by the things of the world. This lifting up of the mind and heart to God involves a colloquy in which we wait for God to answer us. There are different forms of prayer which include: adoration, thanksgiving, reparation and petition. Adoration acknowledges God's supreme dominion and our absolute dependence upon Him. Thanksgiving—We owe to God all that we are and all that we have. He has a right to this gratitude since He continuously bestows his mercies upon us. Reparation—the prayer by which we repair the injustices and misuse of God's gifts which have offended Him. Petition—by the prayer of petition we ask God for what we need due to our own poverty before Him. By means of the lifestyle of true devotion we pray by Mary, with Mary, in Mary and for Mary who perfects in us all these aspects of prayer. She shows us how to adore Him, thank Him, make reparation

and ask Him for our daily needs.[14] By means of our consecration the addition or superimposition of Mary's prayer to ours gives it a much greater value and beauty and enables us to pray more purely.

(5) Mortification is the struggle against our evil inclinations in order to subject them to the will and the will to God. It is the practice of overcoming the obstacles that block the soul from making progress in holiness. The goal of all mortification is union with God and the reversal of our vices to virtues. Practices of mortification include the exterior senses: 1) Mortification of the eyes. The avoidance of persons, places or things that incline us to sin against modesty and chastity. It includes particularly gazing at people, magazines, immoral videos, Internet, etc. (2) Mortification of the ear and tongue—We avoid saying anything that could hurt somebody, gossip, obscene words, dirty jokes. We also do not listen to such things. It particularly involves our use of the TV and media and unhealthy conversations at work, home or school. The act of mortification involves not asking questions simply out of curiosity, engaging in gossip and saying things that build people up rather than destroy them. We also mortify the interior senses which would be the memory and imagination. We practice this by not conjuring up past memories that are dangerous and avoiding frequent daydreaming. On the positive side, one should employ the memory and imagination in helpful piety, by devotion to the Scriptures, and the mysteries of the faith.[15] Mary helps us to develop the spirit of mortification and a deep interior silence and hunger for silence. The more we grow in mortification, the more we grow in holiness because we decrease evil tendencies in ourselves and increase the practice of virtue. Little progress can be made in the spiritual life without mortification. Those for whom mortification is difficult will find themselves strengthened by Mary's intercession.

(6) Chastity as a virtue checks whatever is inordinate in voluptuous pleasures. This virtue also consists of degrees. The 1st degree of chastity consists in refraining from consent to any thought, fancy, feeling or action contrary to this virtue. The 2nd degree involves ridding oneself immediately of every thought, image or impression that could tarnish chastity. The 3rd degree consists in mastering the senses and thoughts that give one a certain composure when dealing with sexual matters. The 4th degree is a perfect preservation from all inordinate feelings related to sexuality. Chastity is protected by four other virtues: (1) humility which allows one to recognize his weakness and to flee from the occasion of sin; (2) mortification by which one struggles against the body's love for pleasure; (3) Devotion to one's duties which keeps one occupied with worthwhile endeavors so that one doesn't become idle and restless; and finally, (4) love for God which should fill one's heart, preventing one from giving himself over to dangerous affections and attractions.[16] Mary who is "all pure" covers us with her chastity by means of the lifestyle of true devotion. This particular grace of chastity is truly God's gift to us through His mother for generations of children starving for purity of mind and body.

(7) Charity is a theological virtue that causes us to love God above all things, for His own sake, in the way in which He loves Himself, and to love the neighbor

for God's sake. Charity is directed in two directions: towards God and towards one's neighbor. We love our neighbor because God is in him. One loves God with one's whole heart, mind, soul and strength. Charity is the most sanctifying of all the virtues because it is of the very essence of perfection. It contains all the virtues and it perfects all of them, causing all of the virtues to be directed towards the love of God. Charity unites the mind, the will and the heart to God. It unites all of our energies towards the service of God. The Second Vatican Council teaches concerning Mary's charity that: "In an utterly singular way she cooperated by her obedience, faith, hope, and burning charity in the Savior's work of restoring supernatural life to souls. For this reason she is a mother to us in the order of grace…By her maternal charity, Mary cares for the brethren of her Son who still journey on earth surrounded by dangers and difficulties, until they are led to their happy father-land."[17] The consecration and lifestyle of true devotion is rooted in love of God and neighbor. As we progress in living true devotion, our charity deepens and becomes stronger while we become more detached from the human objects of our charity—not a cold detachment or disinterest, but a detachment from the need to be thanked and appreciated and an attachment to loving for the sake of God's will alone. Mother Mary obtains this increase in charity with perfect timing for people, places and circumstances.

(8) Patience is the virtue that makes us withstand with equanimity of soul, for the love of God, and in union with Jesus Christ, all physical and moral sufferings. The goal of patience is to suffer without complaining, bitterness or rebellion against God's Providence. Our inspiration to be patient derives from desiring to do God's will in all things. There are degrees of patience. For those just beginning the spiritual life patience is accepted as coming from God without resentment or complaints. One accepts it in reparation for sins and to purify one's heart and it is accepted despite one's natural aversion to it. For those more advanced, patience is exercised by an eagerness to embrace suffering in order to make us more like Jesus. One follows Him more closely in carrying one's cross. The most advanced degree of patience is expressed in the desire for and the love of suffering for the sake of God whom one wishes to glorify and for the sake of souls for whose sanctification one wants to labor.[18] The lives of the great saints are distinguished by this virtue of patience. As Mary's rule is to form new and greater saints in the latter days, we who practice this lifestyle grow in patience. Obstacles which previously overwhelmed us are placed in the proper perspective as being merely manifestations of God's Divine Providence. We begin to see all things in relation to Divine Providence and love His Will despite our personal likes or dislikes.

(9) Wisdom is a gift of the Holy Spirit which perfects the virtue of charity. The gift of wisdom contains two elements one of which is light which illumines the mind which enables it to rightly judge the things of God. The second element is a supernatural taste which acts upon the will and enables it to relish the things of God as by a sort of natural attraction. Wisdom is a gift which perfects the virtue of charity by enabling us to discern God and divine things in their ultimate principles and by giving us a relish for them. Wisdom allows charity to increase in the soul.

This is a gift which one must long for and desire. We must acquire the habit of seeing how all things proceed from God and are related back to God.[19] Pope John Paul II states: "Through this gift [of wisdom] the entire life of the individual Christian, with all its events, hopes, plans, and achievements, is caught up in the breath of the Spirit, who permeates it with Light 'from on high' as is attested to by many chosen souls in our day…In all of these souls the 'great things' that the Spirit did in Mary are repeated. May she whom pious tradition venerates as the 'Sedes sapientiae [Seat of Wisdom]' lead each of us to taste interiorly divine things."[20] Mary obtains for us by means of this lifestyle to view all things according to God's will and to get us to see the "big picture" in life beyond our narrow scope of reality. If we practice these virtues in imitation of Mary we will experience the fruits of the Holy Spirit in our souls and a more intimate and loving union with the Lord.

(4ᵗʰ) Constant

> *109. True devotion to Our Lady is constant. It confirms the soul in good, and does not let it easily abandon its spiritual exercises. It makes it courageous in opposing the world in its fashions and maxims, the flesh in its wearinesses and passions, and the devil in his temptations; so that a person truly devout to our Blessed Lady is neither changeable, irritable, scrupulous nor timid. It is not that such a person does not fall, or change sometimes in the sensible feeling of devotion. But when he falls, he rises again by stretching out his hand to his good Mother. When he loses the taste and relish of devotion, he does not become disturbed because of that; for the just and faithful client of Mary lives by the faith (Heb. 10:38) of Jesus and Mary, and not by natural sentiment.*

<u>Scriptures</u>

Hebrews 10:38 NAB: "But my just one shall live by faith, and if he draws back I take no pleasure in him."

This quotation from Hebrews (which is really a quotation from Habakkuk 2:3-4) stresses the belief that when the sweetness of devotion passes, the power and strength of faith in Christ remains. This perseverance requires confidence and patience.

The practice of true devotion leads to constancy of religious practice. Constancy in effort consists in struggling and suffering to the end, without yielding to weariness, discouragement or indolence. Perseverance against weariness and discouragement is a gift from God and we must return courageously to the task at hand.[21] In response to the allurements, weariness and temptations of the world, the flesh and the devil, true devotion makes a soul courageous. The sensible appetites are purified. The relationship of the constant devotee is one of complete dependence—even after sin. Of note also, is that St. Louis states that "when he loses the taste and relish of devotion" and not "if" he loses it, indicating that a certain aridity of soul is necessary for growth in the spiritual life. This aridity leads to a deepening of faith as we see expressed in the writings of St. John of the Cross when he discusses the dark night of the sense and of the soul. Mary conducts the soul through that dryness of sense experience into a stronger faith in which the natural sentiments and attachments must be purified. Our lifestyle of true devotion will necessarily include some very dry moments and feelings of the "absence" of God. These feelings are not to be feared, but to be endured with faith and trust.

(5th) Disinterested

> *110. Lastly, true devotion to Our Lady is disinterested; that is to say, it inspires the soul not to seek itself but only God, and God in His holy Mother. A true client of Mary does not serve that august Queen from a spirit of lucre and interest, nor for his own good, whether temporal or eternal, corporal or spiritual, but exclusively because she deserves to be served, and God alone in her. He does not love Mary because she obtains favors for him, or because he hopes she will, but solely because she is so worthy of love. It is on this account that he loves and serves her as faithfully in his disgusts and drynesses as in his sweetnesses and sensible fervors. He loves her as much on Calvary as at the marriage of Cana. Oh, how agreeable and precious in the eyes of God and of His holy Mother is such a client of our Blessed Lady, who has no self-seeking in his service of her! But in these days how rare is such a sight! It is that it may be less rare that I have taken my pen in hand to put on paper what I have taught with good results, in public and in private, during my missions for many years.*

The practice of true devotion perfects a soul in seeking God and not himself. A child of Mary serves her out of love not for material gain or advantage. Hence the phrase, "slave of love." It is also noteworthy that this true devotion is so complete that one is devoted to Mary both in "good times and in bad"; that is, in times of dryness and sweetness; in suffering and in joy. St. Louis continues the idea from the preceding paragraph of the suffering and joy which require constancy in this devotion. As we make progress in this lifestyle we realize that we consecrate ourselves to Mary, not for what we might get out of it, but in order to love her (and Jesus) better.

> *111. I have now said many things about the most holy Virgin; but I have many more to say, and there are infinitely more which I shall omit, either from ignorance, inability or want of time, in unfolding the plan for forming a true client of Mary and a true disciple of Jesus Christ.*

All the work of this devotion is aimed at the spiritual formation of devotees to Mary and true Christian disciples. St. Louis remarks that such devotion and discipleship is rare even in his own time. How much more in our present century! Our generation requires the new evangelization or the re-evangelization of Christians. Part of that new evangelization is the renewal of authentic Marian devotion—the true devotion to Jesus through Mary.

> *112. Oh, but my labor will have been well expended if this little writing, falling into the hands of a soul of good dispositions—a soul well-born of God and of Mary, and not of blood, nor of the will of the flesh, nor of the will of woman (Jn. 1:13)—should unfold to him, and should by the grace of the Holy Spirit inspire him with the excellence and the value of that true and solid devotion to our Blessed Lady which I am going presently to describe. If I knew that my guilty blood could serve in engraving upon anyone's heart the truths which I am writing in honor of my true Mother and Sovereign Mistress, of whose children and slaves I am the least, I would use my blood instead of ink to form the letters, in the hope of finding some good souls who, by their fidelity to the practice which I teach, should compensate my dear Mother and Mistress for the losses which she has suffered through my ingratitude and infidelities.*

Scriptures

John 1:13 CCD: "Who were born not of blood, nor of the will of the flesh, nor of the will of man, but of God."

John 1:13 NAB: "Who were born not by natural generation nor by human choice nor by a man's decision but of God."

St. Louis' reference to John's Gospel reminds us that Jesus made "children of God" those who accepted His Gospel. In the same way, St. Louis hopes that those who read this book will be born of God and not of the Evil One who rules the kingdom of the world.

The practice and inspiration to live the spiritual lifestyle of true devotion to Jesus through Mary is an act of the Holy Spirit. There is a reparatory value to the lifestyle of true devotion as well in that it repairs the damage done to Our Lady's honor by those who mistreat her. This practice consoles Mary's heart by forming children especially devoted to her whom she can lead into the Sacred Heart of Jesus her Son. Those who live this practice are the answer to his prayer, for they are the "souls of good disposition" in whom the seed of true devotion will be great fruit.

> *113. I feel myself more than ever encouraged to believe and to hope for the fulfillment of all that I have deeply engraven upon my heart and have asked of God these many years, namely, that*

sooner or later the Blessed Virgin shall have more children, servants and slaves of love than ever; and that by this means, Jesus Christ, my dear Master, shall reign in hearts more than ever.

St. Louis' fervent prayer is to raise up children for Mary and disciples of Jesus Christ. He has prayed for some time that this teaching on true devotion would take shape and provide a rule of life for the formation of Mary's children.

> *114. I clearly foresee that raging beasts shall come in fury to tear with their diabolical teeth this little writing and him whom the Holy Spirit has made use of to write it—or at least to smother it in the darkness and silence of a coffer, that it may not appear. They shall even attack and persecute those who shall read it and carry it out in practice. But what matter? On the contrary, so much the better! This very foresight encourages me, and makes me hope for great success, that is to say, for a great squadron of brave and valiant soldiers of Jesus and Mary, of both sexes, to combat the world, the devil and corrupted nature, in those more-than-ever perilous times which are about to come. "He who reads, let him understand." (Mt. 24:15). "He who can receive it, let him receive it." (Mt. 19:12).*

Scriptures

Matthew 24:15 NAB: "When you see the desolating abomination spoken of through Daniel the prophet standing in the holy place (let the reader understand), then those in Judea must flee to the mountains…"

Matthew 19:12 NAB: "Some are incapable of marriage because they were born so; some, because they were made so by others; some, because they have renounced marriage for the sake of the kingdom of heaven. Whoever can accept this ought to accept it."

St. Louis comments from the Gospel of Matthew that this work of true devotion will be presented to the world, but not everybody will be able to receive it or to understand it—only those to whom the mystery has been revealed.

This is one of St. Louis' most important passages. Its prophetic message is doubly important. First, it speaks about the actual burial of the manuscript during the French Revolution. It was found by one of the Montfort Fathers in 1842 safely buried in a chest. Second, he prophesies to our own generation; that is, to those who will attempt to promote, spread and live the spirituality of true devotion to Jesus through Mary. These "raging beasts" will be made manifest in family, friends, colleagues, proud scholars, evil spirits, etc. who will attempt to prevent Mary from having more children.

This prophetic knowledge fills St. Louis with greater zeal to labor for his Queen, resolved that after the period of trial there will be great graces. The time of grace will be marked by the courageous men and women who promote and live the lifestyle of true devotion.

<u>Application of the Lifestyle of True Devotion</u>

1. Do I practice the lifestyle of true devotion with love for Jesus and Mary?
2. Am I confident that Mary will truly provide for my every need in virtue of my consecration to her?
3. Do I try every day to imitate the ten principal virtues of Mary?
4. How do I remain committed to practicing true devotion even when I feel like nothing is happening in my soul?
5. Do I practice this devotion in order to love God all the more without self-interest?
6. Has the practice of this lifestyle allowed Jesus to reign in my heart more and more?

II. Practices

1ˢᵗ Common practices, both interior and exterior

115. There are several interior practices of true devotion to the Blessed Virgin. Here are the principal ones, stated compendiously: (1) to honor her as the worthy Mother of God, with the worship of hyperdulia; that is to say, to esteem her and honor her above all the other saints, as the masterpiece of grace, and the first after Jesus Christ, true God and true man; (2) to meditate on her virtues, her privileges and her actions; (3) to contemplate her grandeurs; (4) to makes acts of love, of praise, of gratitude to her; (5) to invoke her cordially; (6) to offer ourselves to her and unite ourselves with her; (7) to do all our actions with the view of pleasing her; (8) to begin, to continue and to finish all our actions by her, in her, with her and for her, in order that we may do them by Jesus Christ, in Jesus Christ, with Jesus Christ and for Jesus Christ, our Last End. We will presently explain this last practice.

These eight interior practices speak for themselves. Some technical terms include the word "hyperdulia" which is the theological term signifying the veneration due to Mary. It occurs between "dulia" the honor paid to the saints and "latria" the worship due to God alone as has been mentioned earlier in this commentary in paragraph thirty-nine.[22] Mary's virtues have already been listed earlier. Her privileges can be discussed as they occur in the prayer entitled, "Little Crown of Mary." Mary's crown consists of twelve titles originating from the Book of Revelation 12:1 which states: "A great sign appeared in the sky, a woman clothed with the sun, with the moon under her feet, and on her head a crown of twelve stars." Each of these twelve stars is adorned with a privilege of Mary, not limited to, but including the following salutations and honors: 1. Her Divine Maternity; 2. Her ineffable virginity; 3. Her purity without stain; 4. Her innumerable virtues; 5. Her royalty; 6. Her magnificence; 7. Her universal mediation; 8. The strength of her rule; 9. Her mercy towards sinners; 10. Her mercy towards the poor; 11. Her mercy towards the just; and 12. Her mercy towards the dying.[23]

Other privileges can be extracted from the Litany of Loreto. These include:

(1) The Maternal titles: Mother of God, Virgin of Virgins, Mother of Christ, Mother of Divine Grace, Mother Most Pure, Mother Most Chaste, Mother Undefiled, Mother Inviolate, Mother Most Amiable, Mother Most Admirable, Mother of Good Counsel, Mother of Our Creator, Mother of Our Reedemer. Her grandeurs (greatness) come from the same Litany and include:

(2) The Virgin titles: Virgin Most Prudent, Virgin Most Venerable, Virgin Most Renowned, Virgin Most Powerful, Virgin Most Merciful, Virgin Most Faithful.

(3) The Mystic titles include: Mirror of Justice, Seat of Wisdom, Cause of our Joy, Spiritual Vessel, Vessel of Honor, Singular Vessel of Devotion, Mystical Rose, Tower of David, Tower of Ivory, House of Gold, Ark of the Covenant, Gate of Heaven, Morning Star.

(4) The Mercy titles include: Health of the Weak, Refuge of Sinners, Consoler of the Afflicted, Help of Christians.

(5) The Queen titles include: Queen of Angels, Queen of Patriarchs, Queen of Prophets, Queen of Apostles, Queen of Martyrs, Queen of Confessors, Queen of Virgins, Queen of All Saints, Queen Conceived without Sin, Queen of the Rosary, Queen of Peace.[24]

In the lifestyle of true devotion one can meditate upon any of these titles of her greatness or privileges to great advantage. It would be appropriate to do so on any of her feast days, or during the months of October and May, traditionally dedicated to Our Lady.

116. True devotion to Our Lady also has several exterior practices, of which the following are the principal ones: (1) to enroll ourselves in her confraternities and enter her congregations; (2) to join the religious orders instituted in her honor; (3) to proclaim her praises; (4) to give alms, to fast and to undergo outward and inward mortifications in her honor; (5) to wear her liveries, such as the Rosary, the Scapular or the little chain; (6) to recite with attention, devotion and modesty the holy Rosary, composed of fifteen decades of Hail Marys in honor of the fifteen principal mysteries of Jesus Christ; or five decades, which is one third of the Rosary, either in honor of the five Joyful Mysteries, which are the Annunciation, the Visitation, the Nativity of Jesus Christ, the Purification, and the Finding of Our Lord in the temple; or in honor of the five Sorrowful Mysteries, which are the Agony of Our Lord in the Garden of Olives, His Scourging, His Crowning with Thorns, His Carrying of the Cross, and His Crucifixion; or in honor of the five Glorious Mysteries, which are the Resurrection, the Ascension, the Descent of the Holy Spirit at Pentecost, the Assumption of our Blessed Lady, body and soul, into Heaven, and her Coronation by the Three Persons of the Most Holy Trinity. We may also say a chaplet of six or seven decades in honor of the years which we believe Our Lady lived on earth; or the Little Crown of the Blessed Virgin, composed of three Our Fathers and twelve Hail Marys, in honor of her crown of twelve stars or privileges; or the Office of Our Lady, so universally received and recited in the Church; or the little Psalter of the holy Virgin, which St. Bonaventure composed in her honor, and which is so tender and so devout that one cannot say it without being moved by it; or fourteen Our Fathers and Hail Marys in honor of her fourteen joys; or some other prayers, hymns and canticles of the Church, such as the Salve Regina, the Alma, the Ave Regina Coelorum, or the Regina Coeli, according to the different seasons; or the Ave Maris Stella, the O Gloriosa Domina, the Magnificat, or some other practices of devotion, of which books are full; (7) to sing, or have sung, spiritual canticles in her honor; (8) to make a number of genuflections or reverences, while saying, for example, every morning, sixty or a hundred times, Ave Maria, Virgo Fidelis ("Hail Mary, Faithful Virgin"), to obtain from God through her the grace to be faithful to the graces of God during the day; and then again in the evening, Ave Maria, Mater Misericordiae ("Hail Mary, Mother of Mercy") to ask pardon of God through her for the sins that we have committed during the day; (9) to take care of her confraternities, to adorn her altars, to crown and ornament her images; (10) to carry her images, or to have them carried, in procession, and to carry a picture or an image of her about our own persons, as a mighty arm against the evil spirit; (11) to have copies of her name or picture made and placed in churches, or in houses, or on the gates and entrances into cities, churches and houses; (12) to consecrate ourselves to her in a special and solemn manner.

To this list of exterior practices one would add the luminous mysteries of the Rosary (the Baptism of Jesus, The Wedding Feast at Cana, the Preaching of the Kingdom of God, the Transfiguration, and the Institution of the Eucharist) and first Saturday devotions as well as prayers in reparation for the sins against the Immaculate Heart of Mary as revealed in Fatima. These sins against Mary's Immaculate Heart are: sins against her Immaculate Conception, sins against her Perpetual Virginity, sins against her Divine Maternity, sins of those who try publicly to implant in children's hearts indifference, contempt and hatred against our Immaculate Mother; and the sins of those who directly insult her in her sacred images. These exterior practices in themselves do not require much commentary, but the practice thereof reinforces the lifestyle of true devotion and safeguard the interior dispositions of love.

> *117. There are numerous other practices of true devotion toward the Blessed Virgin which the Holy Spirit has inspired in saintly souls and which are very sanctifying; they can be read at length in the Paradise Opened to Philagius of Father Barry, the Jesuit, in which he has collected a great number of devotions which the saints have practiced in honor of Our Lady—devotions which serve marvelously to sanctify our souls, provided they are performed as they ought to be, that is to say, (1) with a good and pure intention to please God only, to unite ourselves to Jesus Christ as to our Last End, and to edify our neighbor; (2) with attention and without voluntary distraction; (3) with devotion, equally avoiding precipitation and negligence; (4) with modesty, and a respectful and edifying posture of the body.*

Who's Who?

Paul Boursier de Barry, a French Jesuit, was born 1587 and died 1661. Not only was he a member of the Jesuits, he was also rector of three Jesuit colleges and Provincial. He wrote a number of devotional works on Mary, Joseph and the saints. The full title of the text to which St. Louis refers is <u>Paradise Opened to Philagius by One Hundred Devotions to the Mother of God, Easy to Practice on her Feasts and Octaves Which Occur Each Month of the Year</u>. It was first printed in 1636.[25]

St. Louis lists four criteria for the devout practice of these exterior devotions which aid in cultivating the interior devotions. One ought to perform these acts:

1. To please God and to edify others;
2. With attention and recollection;
3. With devotion;
4. With modesty and respect.

The long list of exterior devotions should not be intimidating to the devotee, but he or she should employ those types which are most suitable to his state in life and strive for depth of devotion rather than quantity.

Application of the Lifestyle of True Devotion

1. How am I practicing daily, weekly, monthly, the eight interior practices of this lifestyle that St. Louis describes in paragraph 115?

2. How am I practicing daily, weekly, monthly, the eight exterior practices described in paragraph 116?

2nd Its perfect practice.

118. But after all, I loudly protest that, having read nearly all the books which profess to treat of devotion to Our Lady, and having conversed familiarly with the best and wisest of men of these latter times, I have never known nor heard of any practice of devotion toward her at all equal to the one which I now wish to unfold; demanding from the soul, as it does, more sacrifices for God, ridding the soul more of itself and of its self-love, keeping it more faithfully in grace and grace more faithfully in it, uniting it more perfectly and more easily to Jesus Christ; and finally, being more glorious to God, more sanctifying to the soul and more useful to our neighbor than any other of the devotions to her.

In this paragraph St. Louis describes the perfect practice of devotion to Mary. He begins here his introduction to the most perfect devotion by stating that he has carefully studied all the others. The lifestyle of true devotion excels all others that he has researched in the following ways:

1. It demands more sacrifices to offer to God;
2. It rids the soul more of self-love;
3. It keeps the soul more in the state of grace;
4. It unites it more easily to Jesus Christ;
5. It is more glorious to God;
6. The soul grows more in holiness;
7. It is more useful to one's neighbor.

119. As the essential of this devotion consists in the interior which it ought to form, it will not be equally understood by everybody. Some will stop at what is exterior in it, and will go no further, and these will be the greatest number. Some, in small number, will enter into its inward spirit; but they will only mount one step. Who will mount to the second step? Who will get as far as the third? Lastly, who will so advance as to make this devotion his habitual state? He alone to whom the spirit of Jesus Christ shall have revealed this secret, the faultlessly faithful soul whom He shall conduct there Himself, to advance from virtue to virtue, from grace to grace, from light to light, until he arrives at the transformation of himself into Jesus Christ, and to the plenitude of

His age on earth and of His glory in Heaven.

St. Louis is realistic in his expectation that not everybody will understand what the true devotion to Jesus through Mary is all about. It is essentially an interior disposition and way of life that require constant cultivation. St. Louis speaks about the difficulties along the way. He explains that the greatest number will be attracted to the exterior practices of the devotion because they are the easiest, most obvious and the most active. Such souls will not advance very far unless they penetrate into the interior practices. Others will advance to the interior practices, such as those who make the consecration, but don't faithfully maintain the lifestyle. The key to constancy in this devotion will be the habitual exercise of doing all things by-with-in-for Mary in order to do them by-with-in-for Jesus, as will be explained further.

Those faithful souls who advance from "light to light" must also pass through periods of darkness as is necessary for any kind of advancement in the spiritual life. These passive purifications are necessary in order for one to die to self and to grow spiritually. During this time of trial one experiences a sensible darkness and has to live by the light of faith. Faith is purified during these trials and virtue is ultimately strengthened. Pope John Paul II speaks about this darkness of faith when he states: "Like St. John of the Cross, St. Louis Marie insists above all on the purity of faith and on its essential (and often painful) darkness (cf. Secret of Mary, 51-52). It is a contemplative faith which, renouncing sensible and extraordinary things, penetrates the mysterious depths of Christ. So, in his prayer, St. Louis Marie addresses the Mother of the Lord, saying: "I do not ask for visions or revelations, for sensible devotion or even spiritual pleasures... As for my portion here on earth, I wish only to have a share in yours, that is to have simple faith without seeing or tasting" (ibid., 69). The Cross is the culminating point of Mary's faith, as I wrote in the Encyclical Redemptoris Mater: 'Through this faith Mary is perfectly united with Christ in his self-emptying...This is perhaps the deepest kenosis of faith in human history.' (no. 18)"[26]

St. Louis returns in this paragraph to the idea of "secret." He states that those who fully enter into the interior lifestyle of the true devotion are those who have received this secret from Jesus. This secret consists in the possession of wisdom and the love of the Cross which God gives as a gift which is beyond all human understanding. It is a mystery and is not accessible for everybody—especially for those who are blinded by their own pride[27]

Application of the Lifestyle of True Devotion

1. Am I making progress in practicing true devotion? That is, am I progressing from the exterior practices, to the interior, to the habitual practice?

Part Two

Perfect Devotion to the Blessed Virgin Mary

Chapter 1

Nature of Perfect Devotion to the Blessed Virgin or Perfect Consecration to Jesus Christ

120. *All our perfection consists in being conformed, united and consecrated to Jesus Christ; and therefore the most perfect of all devotions is, without any doubt, that which the most perfectly conforms, unites and consecrates us to Jesus Christ. Now, Mary being the most conformed of all creatures to Jesus Christ, it follows that, of all devotions, that which most consecrates and conforms the soul to Our Lord is devotion to His holy Mother, and that the more a soul is consecrated to Mary, the more it is consecrated to Jesus. Hence it comes to pass that the most perfect consecration to Jesus Christ is nothing else but a perfect and entire consecration of ourselves to the Blessed Virgin, and this is the devotion which I teach; or, in other words, a perfect renewal of the vows and promises of holy Baptism.*

St. Louis reaffirms that the lifestyle of true devotion is directed towards perfect consecration of the soul to Jesus. Mary is not the end, but the means to this consecration. Because Mary is the most conformed to Jesus, then devotion to her leads a soul to Jesus. " The more a soul is consecrated to Mary, the more it is consecrated to Jesus." Mary leads one then into the heart of that perfect Christian consecration which is Baptism. The renewal of the Baptismal promises ratifies our consecration to Christ. In Baptism, we reject Satan and all his empty promises and we choose the Kingdom of God. Mary helps us reject Satan, by pointing out his snares and temptations, and leads us into a personal relationship with the Trinity in the Kingdom of God.

Article One

A Perfect and Entire Consecration of Oneself to the Blessed Virgin

121. *This devotion consists, then in giving ourselves entirely to Our Lady, in order to belong entirely to Jesus through her. We must give her (1) our body, with all its senses and members; (2) our soul, with all it powers; (3) our exterior goods of fortune, whether present or to come; (4) our interior and spiritual goods, which are our merits and our virtues, and our good works, past,*

present and future. In a word, we must give her all we have in the order of nature and in the order of grace, and all that may become ours in the future, in the orders of nature, grace and glory; and this we must do without the reserve of so much as one cent, one hair, or one least good action; and we must do it also for all eternity; and we must do it, further, without pretending to, or hoping for, any other recompense for our offering and service except the honor of belonging to Jesus Christ through Mary and in Mary—as though that sweet Mistress were not (as she always is) the most generous and the most grateful of creatures.

What constitutes the lifestyle of true devotion to Jesus through Mary? It is one's entire self-donation to Our Lady without exception. This entire gift of one's self includes the following:

1. Each sense: our sight, touch, hearing, tasting, smell. Every cell, muscle, fiber, organ and bone, etc.
2. Our soul with its memory, intellect, imagination and will.
3. All our money, property, possessions, income, bills, debts, clothes, toys, etc.
4. All the merits of our prayers and sacrifices as well as our spiritual and corporal works of mercy.
5. Everything from our past, present and future. We include even our sins, vices, temptations, imperfections, etc.

This self-donation is so complete that we do not hope for any reward from her because of this offering except to belong completely to her Son, Jesus. This "reward" includes any spiritual consolations, gifts or material advantages.

Notice that this paragraph contains the heart of the Prayer of Consecration.

122. Here we must note that there are two things in the good works we perform, namely, satisfaction and merit; in other words, their satisfactory or impetratory value, and their meritorious value. The satisfactory or impetratory value of a good action is that action inasmuch as it satisfies for the pain due to sin, or obtains some new grace; the meritorious value, or the merit, is the good action inasmuch as it merits grace now and eternal glory hereafter. Now, in this consecration of ourselves to Our Lady, we give her all the satisfactory, impetratory and meritorious value of our actions; in other words, the satisfactions and the merits of all our good works. We give her all our merits, graces and virtues—not to communicate them to others, for our merits, graces and virtues are, properly speaking, incommunicable, and it is only Jesus Christ, who, in making Himself our surety with His Father, is able to communicate His merits—but we give her them to keep them, augment them and embellish them for us, as we shall explain by

*and by. Our satisfactions, however, we give her to communicate
to whom she likes, and for the greatest glory of God.*

Here it is helpful to define some theological terms so as not to get lost in the
beautiful and sublime offering St. Louis is presenting to those who will follow the
lifestyle of true devotion. First some definitions:

A <u>meritorious</u> act has for its main object the increase of grace for the individual soul and an increase of eternal glory. The value of merit is personal and cannot
be transferred to somebody else.

A <u>satisfactory</u> act has for its object the removal of the temporal punishment
still due to sin. Satisfactory value may be transferred from the person performing
the good work and applied to another. This is because the temporal punishment
due to sin is in the nature of a debt which can be "paid off," The "paying off" of
a debt can be transferred to somebody else's "account." The satisfactory value of
good works can also be applied to souls in purgatory so that these souls may benefit. The person who is doing the praying may renounce and sacrifice all of the
fruits of his good works to be applied to these very souls.

<u>Impretratory</u> value means the efficacy of prayer for the living or the dead. This
good work of prayer appeals to the goodness, love and liberality of God. Fervent
and unceasing prayer gains a hearing with God simply by virtue of the work of
prayer and as such is efficacious.[1]

All that having been said, what St. Louis is saying is that by this consecration
to Our Lady, all of the meritorious value that could be applied to our souls (and
cannot be transferred to another) is entrusted to Mary who will embellish it, augment it and guard it. The satisfactory value of our good works (which can be transferred) is entrusted to her likewise, but we don't specify to which person, living or
dead, we want the value of those actions to go. The impetratory value of our good
works, which means our prayers for others, is likewise entrusted to Mary to be applied at her discretion—which is always perfectly in conformity with God's will:
for His glory and the salvation of souls. St. Louis will state below in #123 that not
even religious orders make such consecrations of the fruits of their good works.
In this regard, he emphasizes the totality and absoluteness of this consecration of
handing over all things of nature—and of grace—to Mary.

123. It follows from this that:

> *1ˢᵗ. By this devotion we give to Jesus Christ in the most perfect
> manner, inasmuch as it is by Mary's hands, all we can give Him,
> and far more than by any other devotions in which we give Him
> either a part of our time, or a part of our good works, or a part of
> our satisfactions and mortifications; because here everything is
> given and consecrated to Him, even the right of disposing of our
> interior goods and the satisfactions which we gain by our good
> works day after day. This is more than we do even in a religious*

order. In religious orders we give God the goods of fortune by the vow of poverty, the good of the body by the vow of chastity, our own will by the vow of obedience, and sometimes the liberty of the body by the vow of cloister. But we do not by these vows give Him the liberty or the right to dispose of the value of our good works; and we do not strip ourselves, as far as a Christian man can do so, of that which is dearest and most precious, namely, our merits and our satisfactions.

Thus, this self-donation in all its totality is given to Jesus by means of Mary. The self-donation is so total and perfect that is surpasses the other consecrated religious vows of poverty, chastity, obedience (and sometimes stability) taken in religious orders. By this perfect consecration we create a type of "fourth vow" by which we give to Jesus and consecrate to Him the right to dispose of all the value of our merits and satisfactions. This fourth vow is taken by all who consecrate themselves to Jesus through Mary: laity, clergy and religious.

124. 2ⁿᵈ. A person who is thus voluntarily consecrated and sacrificed to Jesus Christ through Mary can no longer dispose of the value of any of his good actions. All he suffers, all he thinks, all the good he says or does, belongs to Mary, in order that she may dispose of it according to the will of her Son and His greatest glory—without, however, that dependence interfering in any way with the obligations of the state we may be in at present or may be placed in for the future; for example, without interfering with the obligations of a priest who, by his office or otherwise, ought to apply the satisfactory and impetratory value of the Holy Mass to some private person. For we make the offering of this devotion only according to the order of God and the duties of our state.

The "totus tuus" ("all yours") is truly all-encompassing; both the good and the bad of the person; body, mind and soul; and his life belongs to Mary that she may present it to Jesus. This consecration, however, does not interfere with the duties of one's state in life. In other words, it does not contradict the duties and obligations of married life; the single life; or the priestly/clerical life. If anything, it perfects these states of life and makes them more fruitful because Mary gives herself entirely to the soul consecrated to her.

125. 3ʳᵈ. We consecrate ourselves at one and the same time to the most holy Virgin and to Jesus Christ; to the most holy Virgin as to the perfect means which Jesus Christ has chosen whereby to unite Himself to us, and us to Him; and to Our Lord as to our Last End, to whom, as our Redeemer and our God, we owe all we are.

St. Louis here reiterates that Mary is the means to arrive at Jesus. Jesus is the "Last End" and the one to whom we owe all that we are offering to Him. We are really doing nothing more than we ought to do in the first place.

Application of the Lifestyle of True Devotion

1. Do I give everything to Mary through this consecration without hoping for any recompense? What areas of my life do I still have difficulty surrendering to her?
2. When I pray for myself and for others and offer things up for them, do I offer them all by means of Mary to Jesus?
3. How do I consciously give to Mary the value of all my good works? How do I monitor myself from taking the credit for prayer requests being answered? When people ask me to pray for them do I refer all prayer requests to Our Lady at least in my heart? Do I evangelize about the efficacy of the true devotion?
4. How do I give all that I suffer to Mary?

Article Two

A Perfect Renewal of the Vows of Holy Baptism

126. I have said that this devotion may rightly be called a perfect renewal of the vows or promises of holy Baptism. For every Christian, before his Baptism, was the slave of the devil, seeing that he belonged to him. He has in his Baptism, by his own mouth or by his sponsor's solemnly renounced Satan, his pomps and his works; and he has taken Jesus Christ for his Master and Sovereign Lord, to depend upon Him in the quality of a slave of love. That is what we do by the present devotion. We renounce, as is expressed in the formula of consecration, the devil, the world, sin and self; and we give ourselves entirely to Jesus Christ by the hands of Mary. Nay, we even do something more; for in Baptism, we ordinarily speak by the mouth of another, our godfather or godmother, and so we give ourselves to Jesus Christ not by ourselves but through another. But in this devotion we do it by ourselves, voluntarily, knowing what we are doing. Moreover, in holy Baptism we do not give ourselves to Jesus by the hands of Mary, at least not in an explicit manner; and we do not give Him the value of our good actions. We remain entirely free after Baptism, either to apply them to whom we please or to keep them for ourselves. But by this devotion we give ourselves to Our Lord explicitly by the hands of Mary, and we consecrate to Him the value of all our actions.

True devotion and the renewal of the Baptismal vows strive to accomplish the same thing.

True Devotion
1. We renounce, devil, world, sin, self.
2. We give ourselves to Jesus by Mary.
3. We give ourselves by our own free will.
4. We give to Jesus the value of all our good actions.

Baptism
1. We renounce Satan, his works and all his empty promises.
2. We proclaim that Jesus Christ is Lord.
3. We become slaves of Love to Jesus.
4. We are given to Jesus by parents and godparents who make an act of faith for us.

127. Men, says St. Thomas, make a vow at their Baptism to renounce the devil and all his pomps. This vow, says St. Augustine, is the greatest and most indispensable of all vows. It is thus also that canonists speak: "The principal vow is the one we make at Baptism." Yet who has kept this great vow! Who is it that faithfully performs the promises of holy Baptism? Have not almost all Christians swerved from the loyalty which they promised Jesus in their Baptism? Whence can come this universal disobedience, except from our forgetfulness of the promises and obligations of holy Baptism, and from the fact that hardly anyone ratifies, of himself, the contract he made with God by those who stood sponsors for him?

St. Louis states that we have not kept our Baptismal promises very well because we have compromised with the Devil and have failed in practicing our faith. And, for the most part, people do not think about or renew their Baptismal promises—with the exception of the annual renewal of Baptismal promises at the Easter Vigil Mass and on Easter Day.

128. This is so true that the Council of Sens, convoked by order of Louis the Debonair to remedy the disorders of Christians, which were then so great, judged that the principal cause of that corruption of morals arose from the oblivion and the ignorance in which men lived of the obligations of holy Baptism; and it could think of no better means for remedying so great an evil than to persuade Christians to renew the vows and promises of Baptism.

Who's Who?

Louis the Debonair is also known as Louis the Pious or Louis I. He was the third son of Charlemagne and ruled as Holy Roman Emperor and King of the Franks from 814 to 840.[2] The Council of Sens, also known as the 6th Council of Paris, was convened in 829.

De Montfort begins to look at the history of the Church and demonstrates its attempt to overcome evil by the renewal of Baptismal promises in the life of the faithful.

> *129. The Catechism of the Council of Trent, the faithful inter-preter of that holy Council, exhorts the parish priests to do the same thing, and to induce the people to remind themselves, and to believe, that they are bound and consecrated as slaves to Our Lord Jesus Christ, their Redeemer and their Lord. These are its words: "The parish priest shall exhort the faithful people so that they may know that it is most just…that we should devote and consecrate ourselves forever to our Redeemer and Lord as His very slaves."*

This quotation from the Council of Trent occurs in the Article of Faith concerning "And in Jesus Christ, His Only Son, Our Lord." It specifically refers to the "Duties owed to Christ our Lord." The key phrase in the original Latin is: "non secus ac mancipia." "Mancipius" is the word for slave. St. Louis uses this text as a reference to induce the reader to become a slave of love to Jesus through Mary in that he has already become a "slave," that is, he owes everything to Jesus, by virtue of his baptism. Hence, the renewal of the baptismal promises and the slavery of love through true devotion complement each other.

> *130. Now, if the Councils, the Fathers and even experience, show us that the best means of remedying the irregularities of Christians is by making them call to mind the obligations of their Baptism, and persuading them to renew now the vows they made then, is it not only right that we should do it in a perfect manner, by this devotion and consecration of ourselves to Our Lord through his holy Mother? I say "in a perfect manner," because in thus consecrating ourselves to Him, we make use of the most perfect of all means, namely, the Blessed Virgin.*

St. Louis concludes that the best way of helping Christians persevere in their faith is by the renewal of their Baptismal promises. Since this is indisputable, then the means to achieve this renewal of vows perfectly is by the devotion and consecration of ourselves to Jesus through Mary. She is the most perfect means. Any other way of renewing our vows would be less perfect than through the hands of our Mother.

131. No one can object to this devotion as being either a new or an indifferent one. It is not new, because the Councils, the Fathers and many authors both ancient and modern speak of this consecration to Our Lord, or renewal of the vows and promises of Baptism, as of a thing anciently practiced, and which they counsel to all Christians. Neither is it a matter of indifference, because the principal source of all disorders and consequently of the eternal perdition of Christians, comes from their forgetfulness and indifference about this practice.

St. Louis asserts here that the neglect of calling to mind our Christian dignity—by the renewal of the Baptismal promises—leads us to compromise with sin. This consequently brings about a cascade of problems in our lives and relationships with others, not to mention putting in jeopardy our eternal salvation.

132. But some may object that this devotion, in making us give to Our Lord, by Our Lady's hands, the value of all our good works, prayers, mortifications and alms, puts us in a state of incapacity for assisting the souls of our parents, friends and benefactors. I answer them as follows:

1ˢᵗ) That it is not credible that our parents, friends and benefactors should suffer from the fact of our being devoted and consecrated without exception to the service of Our Lord and His holy Mother. To think this would be to think unworthily of the goodness and power of Jesus and Mary, who know well how to assist our parents, friends and benefactors, out of our own little spiritual revenue or by other ways.

2ⁿᵈ) This practice does not hinder us from praying for others, whether dead or living, although the application of our good works depends on the will of our Blessed Lady. On the contrary, it is this very thing which will lead us to pray with more confidence; just as a rich person who has given all his wealth to his prince in order to honor him the more, would beg the prince all the more confidently to give an alms to one of his friends who should ask for it. It would even be a source of pleasure to the prince to be given an occasion of proving his gratitude toward a person who had stripped himself to clothe him, and impoverished himself to honor him. We must say the same of our Blessed Lord and of Our Lady. They will never let themselves be outdone in gratitude.

The first objection concerns the possibility of losing the value of our good works when praying for others. St. Louis states that one might object that by placing in Mary's hands our prayer intentions it may deprive those for whom we are praying of some direct benefit of the value of our good works for them. However, our friends and family cannot be deprived of the benefits of our prayers as though they were more powerful than the prayers of Mary to Jesus. To the contrary, it is because of passing all things through Mary's hands that we pray with greater confidence. Our act of trust and surrender to her by means of this lifestyle of true devotion obtains in itself many more graces.

> *133. Some may perhaps say, "If I give to our Blessed Lady all the value of my actions to apply to whom she wills, I may have to suffer a long time in Purgatory." This objection which comes from self-love and ignorance of the generosity of God and His holy Mother, refutes itself. A fervent and generous soul who gives God all he has, without reserve, so that he can do nothing more; who lives only for the glory and reign of Jesus Christ, through His holy mother, and who makes an entire sacrifice of himself to bring it about—will this generous and liberal soul, I say, be more punished in the other world because it has been more liberal and more disinterested than others? Far, indeed, will that be from the truth! Rather, it is toward that soul, as we shall see by what follows, that Our Lord and His holy Mother are the most liberal in this world and in the other in the orders of nature, grace and glory.*

The second objection has to do with fear of losing graces for oneself. This second objection proceeds from the fear of "giving away" any merits for oneself, thereby increasing (or at least not reducing) one's time in purgatory. These graces could have been "spent" on oneself.

St. Louis counters this objection with the reasoning that a soul so well disposed as to do all things by-with-in-for Mary and Jesus cannot expect greater punishment due to his sins than one who is not so consecrated. Especially as one considers that this lifestyle of true devotion involves the constant conversion from sin and growth in the virtues concomitant with those progressing toward Heaven, one ought not see this lifestyle as a detriment towards getting into Heaven any "later."

> *134. But we must now, as briefly as we can, run over the motives which ought to recommend this devotion to us, the marvelous effects it produces in the souls of the faithful, and its practices.*

At this point, St. Louis makes the transition to his presentation of the motives, effects and practices of the lifestyle of true devotion to Jesus through Mary.

Application of the Lifestyle of True Devotion

1. How do I live every day with Jesus as my Master and Lord? Has my Baptism truly changed my life?
2. How have I violated my baptismal promises? How has Mary led me back to a greater fidelity to these same promises?
3. If I am a priest, have I encouraged my parishioners to renew their baptismal promises outside of Easter?
4. How does Mary help me renew my baptismal promises in a "perfect manner"?
5. How does the practice of true devotion make more effective my prayers for my relatives living and deceased? How will my consecration to Mary aid me after death?

Chapter II

Motives of This Perfect Consecration

First Motive: <u>It Devotes Us Entirely to the Service of God</u>

St. Louis begins this longest chapter of his book with the explanation of eight motives or reasons why one should make the perfect consecration to Jesus through Mary. This chapter concludes with an examination of the Jacob/Esau relationship to their mother Rebecca. St. Louis employs this mother-son story as a metaphor for the predestined/saved and reprobate/condemned and their relationship with Mary.

> *135. The first motive, which shows us the excellence of this consecration of ourselves to Jesus Christ by the hands of Mary.*
>
> *If we can conceive on earth no employment more lofty than the service of God—if the least servant of God is richer, more powerful and more noble than all the kings and emperors of this earth, unless they also are the servants of God—what must be the riches, the power and the dignity of the faithful and perfect servant of God, who is devoted to His service entirely and without reserve, to the utmost extent possible? Such is the faithful and loving slave of Jesus in Mary who has given himself up entirely to the service of that King of Kings, by the hands of His holy Mother, and has reserved nothing for himself. Not all the gold of earth nor all the beauties of the heavens can repay him.*

As loving slaves of Jesus in Mary we have chosen the most noble "profession" on earth. In this profession we receive the riches, power and dignity of the Lord. It is a service entirely and wholeheartedly devoted to the Lord without retaining anything for oneself. In this lifestyle we have truly found our vocation in life which is the loving service of God in Jesus Christ through the hands of Mary.

> *136. The other congregations, associations and confraternities erected in honor of Our Lord and His holy Mother, which do such immense good in Christendom, do not make us give everything without reserve. They prescribe to their members only certain practices and actions to satisfy their obligations. They leave them free for all other actions and moments and occupations. But this devotion makes us give to Jesus and Mary, without reserve, all our thoughts, words, actions and sufferings, every moment of our life, in such wise that whether we wake or sleep, whether we eat or drink, whether we do great actions or very little ones, it is always true to say that whatever we do, even without thinking of it,*

is, by virtue of our offering—at least if it has not been intentionally retracted—done for Jesus and Mary. What a consolation this is!

This lifestyle of true devotion requires the donation of every thought, word, action, and suffering. It requires all of our temporal reality—each minute and second is consecrated even when we are asleep. This is not required by any other pious practice. This is a very important point to remember, especially in moments of great temptation, frustration or insult. We can consecrate those moments of pain to Our Blessed Mother who will wrap them in her sweetness and present them as an offering to her Son, who will speedily bless them and bring good out of evil. We consecrate even our sleep, dreams, and nightmares to her to be purified as well.

137. Moreover, as I have already said, there is no other practice equal to this for enabling us to rid ourselves easily of a certain proprietorship, which imperceptibly creeps into our best actions. Our good Jesus gives us this great grace in recompense for the heroic and disinterested action of giving over to Him, by the hands of His holy Mother, all the value of our good works. If He gives a hundredfold even in this world to those who, for His love, quit outward and temporal and perishable goods (MT. 19:29), what will that hundredfold be which He will give to the man who sacrifices for Him even his inward and spiritual goods!

Scriptures

Matthew 19:29 NAB: "And everyone who has given up houses or brothers or sisters or father or mother or children or lands for the sake of my name will receive a hundred times more, and will inherit eternal life."

St. Louis cites this passage from Matthew's gospel of the story of the rich young man to emphasize the overabundant generosity of the Lord who repays a hundred times over what we have sacrificed to Him. St. Louis extends the meaning to include the spiritual sacrifices as well as the material, personal and property mentioned in the gospel. And, of course, how much sweeter will those sacrifices be to the Lord when they are made through the hands of His mother!

This self-donation through consecration purifies us of all selfishness. The Lord receives this divine exchange of self-surrender and gives us His peace. St. Louis reiterates the supreme value of the interior surrender involved in this consecration.

138. Jesus, our great Friend, has given Himself to us without reserve, body and soul, virtues, graces and merits. "He has bought the whole of me with the whole of Himself," says St. Bernard. Is it not then a simple matter of justice and of gratitude that we should give Him all that we can give Him? He has been the first to be liberal toward us; let us, at least, be the second; and then, in life and death and throughout all eternity, we shall find Him still more liberal. "With the liberal He will be liberal."

St. Louis indicates the propriety of giving everything to Jesus, since He has given everything to us. Since in our Christian duty we imitate the Lord, the first thing we do in imitation of Him is to give ourselves away entirely to Him.

<u>Application of the Lifestyle of True Devotion</u>

1. How does being a servant of God enhance my baptismal dignity even further?
2. How is even my sleeping an act of total surrender to Jesus through Mary? Why is that an offering?
3. What does it mean that Jesus will give me a hundredfold in terms of the spiritual goods I give Him?

Second Motive

<u>It Makes Us Imitate the Example of Jesus Christ and the Holy Trinity and Practice Humility</u>

139. The second motive, which shows us how just it is in itself, and how advantageous to Christians, to consecrate themselves entirely to the Blessed Virgin by this practice, in order to belong more perfectly to Jesus Christ.

This good Master did not disdain to shut Himself up in the womb of the Blessed Virgin, as a captive and as a loving slave, and later to be subject and obedient to her for thirty years. It is here, I repeat, that the human mind loses itself, when it seriously reflects on the conduct of the Incarnate Wisdom who willed to give Himself to men—not directly, though He might have done so, but through the Blessed Virgin. He did not will to come into the world at the age of a perfect man, independent of others, but like a poor little babe, dependent on the care and support of this holy Mother. He is that Infinite Wisdom who had a boundless desire to glorify God His Father and to save men; and yet He found no more perfect means, no shorter way to do it, than to submit Himself in all things to the Blessed Virgin, not only during the first eight, ten or fifteen years of His life, like other children, but for thirty years! He gave more glory to God His Father during all that time of submission to and dependence on our Blessed Lady than He would have given Him if He had employed those thirty years in working miracles, in preaching to the whole world and in converting all men—all of which He would have done could He have thereby contributed more to God's glory. Oh, how highly we glorify God when, after the example of Jesus, we submit ourselves to Mary!

Having, then, before our eyes an example so plain and so well known to the whole world, are we so senseless as to imagine that we can find a more perfect or a shorter means of glorifying God than that of submitting ourselves to Mary, after the example of her Son?

St. Louis here presents Jesus' very own life (nine months in the womb and thirty years at home) as the model of care, support and obedience living with Mary. While St. Louis states that Jesus could have glorified God His Father at an earlier age by performing miracles, great works, forming the Apostles, etc., He chose to spend those thirty years in loving submission to His mother which gave more glory to the Father. This loving submission to Mary glorified the Father more, (because of the humility and love it demonstrated for mankind) than any great works He had the "power" to perform instead.

Since Jesus gave us this example of how to glorify God (by obedience to His mother), it would be illogical for us to think we can find a better way to glorify the Father than the way presented by the Son. This devotion is deeply rooted in the humility Jesus demonstrates in His own lifetime to His mother Mary and to the glory of the Father. True devotion glorifies the Father by the direct imitation of the Son.

> 140. *Let us recall here, as a proof of the dependence we ought to have on our Blessed Lady, what I have said above in bringing forward the example which the Father, the Son and the Holy Spirit give of this dependence. The Father has not given, and does not give, His Son, except by her; He has no children but by her, and communicates no graces but through her. The Son has not been formed for the whole world in general, except by her; and He is not daily formed and engendered except by her, in union with the Holy Spirit; neither does He communicate His merits and His virtues except through her. The Holy Spirit has not formed Jesus Christ except by her; neither does He form the members of Our Lord's Mystical Body, except by her; and through her alone does He dispense His favors and His gifts. After so many and such pressing examples of the Most Holy Trinity, can we without extreme blindness dispense with Mary, can we fail to consecrate ourselves to her and depend on her for the purpose of going to God and sacrificing ourselves to God?*

St. Louis makes a Trinitarian summary of God's dependence on Mary. He also poses the question of how it could be possible to bypass the operation of the Trinity who does all things by means of Mary. If this is the method the Trinity has chosen, then it is the best method for us, also.

<pre>
                          Father
                            ↓
Gives us the Son at the Annunciation and Incarnation
Forms us as His children
Communicates graces
                                    ↓

Son   →   BY MARY   ← Holy Spirit
Received human nature   Formed Jesus at Annunciation/Inc.
Formed in souls   Forms members of the Church
Communicates His merits   Dispenses charismatic gifts
and virtues   and graces
</pre>

By means of true devotion we continue the plan which God formed in the beginning of salvation history. Mary and her fiat are key to the Trinity's operation among men in the world.

141. *Here are some passages of the Fathers which I have chosen to prove what has just been said:*

"Mary has two sons, a God-Man and a pure man; she is Mother of the first corporally, of the second spiritually." [Origen and St. Bonaventure]

"This is the will of God, who wished us to have all things through Mary; if, therefore, there is in us any hope, any grace, any salutary gift, we know it comes to us through her." [St. Bernard]

"All the gifts, virtues and graces of the Holy Spirit are distributed by Mary, to whom she wishes, when she wishes, the way she wishes and as much as she wishes." [St. Bernadine of Siena]

"Since you were unworthy to receive the divine graces, they were given to Mary, so that whatever you would have, you would receive through her." [St. Bernard]

142. *God, says St. Bernard, seeing that we are unworthy to receive His graces immediately from His own hand, gives them to Mary, in order that we may have through her whatever He wills to give us; and He also finds His glory in receiving, through the*

hands of Mary, the gratitude, respect and love which we owe Him for His benefits. It is most just, then, that we imitate this conduct of God, in order, as the same St. Bernard says, that grace return to its Author by the same channel through which it came: "That grace should return to the giver by the same channel through which it came." That is precisely what our devotion does. We offer and consecrate all we are and all we have to the Blessed Virgin in order that Our Lord may receive through her mediation the glory and the gratitude which we owe Him. We acknowledge ourselves unworthy and unfit to approach His Infinite Majesty by ourselves; and it is on this account that we avail ourselves of the intercession of the most holy Virgin.

Our unworthiness proceeds from the fact that we are sinners. We say in the Mass just before the reception of Holy Communion, "Lord, I am not worthy to receive you but only say the word and I shall be healed." Mary, having no sin, is more worthy to be the intermediary for receiving graces in order to distribute them to us. Mary also receives from us our prayers and purifies the sinful inclinations and selfishness which mingles with them. St. Louis, quoting from St. Bernard, states that she is the channel of grace designed by God. Mary is the purification filter of our prayers. She is "tota pulchra"—all beautiful.

Jesus is not diminished by this, as has been previously pointed out. He chose this same route of Mary to come into the world and by being lovingly obedient to her.

Mary is once again the mediator of intercession and by this lifestyle of true devotion we pass everything through her immaculate hands to the Father.

> 143. *Moreover, this devotion is a practice of great humility, which God loves above all the other virtues. A soul which exalts itself abases God; a soul which abases itself exalts God. God resists the proud and gives His grace to the humble. If you abase yourself, thinking yourself unworthy to appear before Him and to draw nigh to Him, He descends and lowers Himself to come to you, to take pleasure in you and to exalt you in spite of yourself. On the contrary, when you are bold enough to approach God without a mediator, God flies from you and you cannot reach Him. Oh, how He loves humility of heart! It is to this humility that this devotion induces us, because it teaches us never to draw nigh, of ourselves, to Our Lord, however sweet and merciful He may be, but always to avail ourselves of the intercession of our Blessed Lady, whether it be to appear before God, or to speak to Him, or to draw near to Him, or to offer Him anything, or to unite and consecrate ourselves to Him.*

The practice of true devotion requires humility because we must always keep the proper relationship with God.

St. Louis alludes to the Letter of James 4:6 which states: "… 'God resists the proud, but gives grace to the humble.'"

Humility is derived from the Latin word "humus" (earth). It is an action of bowing toward the earth. Humility is an indispensable virtue and is, in fact, the foundation of all the virtues and the spiritual life. Humility is the antidote to pride through which all sins enter the soul. It is the active recognition of our littleness and inferiority before God—and when we are in a state of sin, we recognize our wretchedness having alienated ourselves from God. Humility is equally important in that it leads us to discretion, and to hide from worldly attentions. Humility also helps us to recognize how totally dependent we are upon God's grace and of ourselves we can do nothing.[3]

Approaching God with a mediator such as His Beloved Mother demonstrates an attitude of humility. St. Louis states we must seek Mary's intercession particularly at five times: (1) appearing before God at death, (2) speaking with Him, (3) entering into His holy presence, (4) offering Him anything, and (5) consecrating ourselves to Him.

Application of the Lifestyle of True Devotion

1. How do I imitate Jesus' humility when I give myself completely to Mary, His Mother?
2. How has my consecration to Jesus through Mary improved my relationship with each person of the Blessed Trinity?
3. Do I love to give myself to God the Father through Mary? Am I self-conscious, hesitant, or doubtful?
4. How has the practice of true devotion enabled me to grow in greater humility?

Third Motive

It Obtains for us the Good Offices of the Blessed Virgin

I. Mary gives Herself to Her Slave of Love

144. *The most holy Virgin, who is a Mother of sweetness and mercy, and who never lets herself be outdone in love and liberality, seeing that we give ourselves entirely to her, to honor and to serve her, and for that end strip ourselves of all that is dearest to us, in order to adorn her, meets us in the same spirit. She also gives her whole self, and gives it in an unspeakable manner, to him who gives all to her. She causes him to be engulfed in the abyss of her graces. She adorns him with her merits;*

she supports him with her power; she illuminates him with her light; she inflames him with her love; she communicates to him her virtues; her humility, her faith, her purity and the rest. She makes herself his bail, his supplement, and his dear all toward Jesus. In a word, as that consecrated person is all Mary's, so Mary is all his, after such a fashion that we can say of that perfect servant and child of Mary what St. John the Evangelist said of himself, that he took the holy Virgin for his own: "The disciple took her for his own." (Jn. 19:27).

Scriptures

John 19:27 NAB: "Then [Jesus] said to the disciple, 'Behold, your mother.' And from that hour the disciple took her into his home."

Just as in John's Gospel, the Beloved Disciple receives the Mother of Jesus and takes her into his home at Jesus' command, so too, does the disciple of true devotion take Mary into his or her life with the same divine blessing.

Following from the fact that we give ourselves entirely to Mary, she in turn gives herself entirely to us. The complete renunciation of ourselves, giving to Mary all that we possess, cling to, and hope for—placing them into her hands—adorns her with a "garment of trust and surrender" that she cannot obtain from her children in any other way. The French verb "orner" has a deeper meaning than just to dress. It also means to make prettier, to confer charm, to decorate and to make more attractive[4]. Mary, in an extended sense not only dresses us, but she in-vests us with her Queenly garment. We become "in-vested" with her:

--Insight
--Love
--Virtues: especially humility, love and purity.

The lifestyle of true devotion clothes us in Mary. It is truly a "rags to riches" story: we give the "rags" of all that we are to her; and she, in turn gives us all the "riches" that she is to us. This is an incredible gift!

145. *It is this which produces in the soul, if it is faithful, a great distrust, contempt and hatred of self, and a great confidence in and self-abandonment to the Blessed Virgin, its good Mistress. A man no longer, as before, relies on his own dispositions, intentions, merits, virtues and good works; because, having made an entire sacrifice of them to Jesus Christ by that good Mother, he has but one treasure now, where all his goods are laid up, and that is no longer in himself, for his treasure is Mary.*

This is what makes him approach Our Lord without servile or scrupulous fear, and pray to Him with great confidence. This is what makes him share the sentiments of the devout and learned Abbot Rupert, who, alluding to the victory that Jacob gained over the angel (Gen. 32:24), said to our Blessed Lady these beautiful words: "O Mary, my Princess, Immaculate Mother of the God-Man, Jesus Christ, I desire to wrestle with that man, namely, the Divine Word, not armed with my own merits but with yours."

Oh, how strong and mighty we are with Jesus Christ when we are armed with the merits and intercession of the worthy Mother of God, who, as St. Augustine says, has lovingly vanquished the Most High.

Scriptures

Genesis 32:24-26 Douay: "He [Jacob] took [his two wives, with the two maid-servants and his eleven children] and sent them across the stream, with every-thing that belonged to him; but Jacob himself remained behind, all alone. Someone wrestled with him until the break of dawn. When he saw that he could not over-come Jacob, he touched the socket of Jacob's thigh so that it was dislocated while Jacob wrestled with him."

Gen. 32:24-26 NAB: "After [Jacob] had taken [his two wives, with the two maidservants and his eleven children] across the stream and had brought over all his possessions, Jacob was left there alone. Then some man wrestled with him until the break of dawn. When the man saw that he could not prevail over him, he struck Jacob's hip at its socket, so that the hip socket was wrenched as they wrestled."

Who's Who?

Abbot Rupert of Deutz was a 12th Century Abbot of the Benedictine Monastery of Deutz, Germany. He lived from around 1070-1129. He wrote a wide range of commentaries on the Old Testament and the New Testament and was a well-known Scriptural exegete for his time.[5]

This complete self-renunciation and self-donation to Mary, emptying ourselves of the good and the bad is a major source of consolation. We have entrusted all of our goods in one safe location. That is where our treasure now is—in Mary. She is our safety deposit box, our hope chest, in which all that is precious to us is stored. When we present ourselves to Jesus we come to Him with our treasure—His moth-er. And beholding the treasure, our mother and His, He cannot help but marvel at the beauty of our prayers and needs.

Servile fear is that fear which serves God for fear of going to hell and suffering eternal punishment. This is an imperfect understanding of fear, although essen-tially a true fear because it allows one to avoid sin. Scrupulous fear is that disor-dered fear in a soul who believes that due to his own sins—for which he believes he is never sufficiently sorry—God will punish him. These two types of fear are opposed to the good virtue of filial fear which drives one to serve God and to avoid

124

sin out of love and only for fear of being separated from Him.[6] In true devotion there can be no servile fear or scrupulous fear only confidence because there is no fear in Mary towards her Son.

II. Mary Purifies Our Good Works, Embellishes Them and Makes Them Acceptable to Her Son.

146. *As by this practice we give to Our Lord, by His Mother's hands, all our good works, that good Mother purifies them, embellishes them and makes them acceptable to her Son.*

1ˢᵗ) She purifies them of all the stain of self-love, and of that imperceptible attachment to created things which slips unnoticed into our best actions. As soon as they are in her most pure and fruitful hands, those same hands, which have never been sullied or idle and which purify whatever they touch, take away from the present which we give her all that was spoiled or imperfect about it.

Mary takes our good works and presents them to Jesus, but first purifies, embellishes and makes them acceptable to Him. By purification she is able to remove the self-love and attachment to creatures, removing all the imperfections caused by selfishness in our offerings to Him. In order to become wholly "attached" to Jesus, we have to become "detached" from creatures—people and things, so that we do not put greater importance on the things than on the Lord Himself. We want all our desires and goals to be directed towards God. Attachment to creatures and too much of a dependence on them can prevent one from growing in holiness. Our detachment from creatures increases with growth in charity and union with God.[7] To be thus detached requires purification that Mary helps to bring about in order to bring the soul to divine union with God.

147. *2ⁿᵈ) She embellishes our works, adorning them with her own merits and virtues. It is as if a peasant, wishing to gain the friendship and benevolence of the king, went to the queen and presented her with a fruit which was his whole revenue, in order that she might present it to the king. The queen, having accepted the poor little offering from the peasant, would place the fruit on a large and beautiful dish of gold, and so, on the peasant's behalf, would present it to the king. Then the fruit, however unworthy in itself to be a king's present, would become worthy of his majesty because of the dish of gold on which it rested and the person who presented it.*

Mary embellishes. That is, she makes our works more beautiful by adorning them with her own merits and virtues which surpass our own. Because she is all beautiful, all that she does is clothed in beauty. She extends that beauty to us and to our projects.

> 148. *3ʳᵈ) She presents these good works to Jesus Christ; for she keeps nothing of what is given her for herself, as if she were our last end. She faithfully passes it all on to Jesus. If we give to her, we give necessarily to Jesus. If we praise her or glorify her, she immediately praises and glorifies Jesus. As of old when St Elizabeth praised her, so now when we praise her and bless her, she sings: "My soul doth magnify the Lord" (Lk. 1:46).*

Scriptures

Luke 1:46 CCD: "My soul magnifies the Lord…"
Luke 1:46 NAB: "And Mary said, 'My soul proclaims the greatness of the Lord.'"

St. Louis has recourse to this scene in Luke's Gospel of the visitation of Mary to her cousin Elizabeth to demonstrate that even during her lifetime Mary refers all praise and honor back to the Father.

Mary passes on everything to Jesus. She empties herself totally to her Son. There is no jealousy or rivalry between the Mother and the Son or competition for our prayers and attentions. Mary refers all things to God. Having once embellished our works and prayers, she takes "no credit" for it when presenting them to the Father, but He recognizes the fragrance of her humility and touch.

> 149. *She persuades Jesus to accept these good works, however little and poor the present may be for that Saint of Saints and that King of Kings. When we present anything to Jesus by ourselves, and relying on our own efforts and dispositions, Jesus examines the offering, and often rejects it because of the stains it has contracted through self-love, just as of old He rejected the sacrifices of the Jews when they were full of their own will. But when we present Him anything by the pure and virginal hands of His well-beloved, we take Him by His weak side, if it is allowable to use such a term. He does not consider so much the thing that is given Him as the Mother who presents it. He does not consider so much whence the offering comes, as by whom it comes. Thus Mary, who is never repelled but always well received by her Son, makes everything she presents to Him, great or small, acceptable to His Majesty. Mary has but to represent it for Jesus to accept it and be pleased with it. St. Bernard used to give to those whom he conducted to perfection this great counsel; "When you want to of-*

fer anything to God, take care to offer it by the most agreeable and worthy hands of Mary, unless you wish to have it rejected."

No matter how poor or insignificant our offering to Jesus, through Mary's intercession everything is presented with such love. Jesus respects our going through the mediation of His mother and the humility with which we go to Him. The quotation from St. Bernard occurs in <u>De Aquaeductu</u>.[8]

> 150. *Is not this what nature itself suggests to the little with regard to the great, as we have already seen? Why should not grace lead us to do the same thing with regard to God, who is infinitely exalted above us and before whom we are less than atoms—especially since we have an advocate so powerful that she is never refused; so ingenious that she knows all the secret ways of winning the heart of God; and so good and charitable that she repels no one, however little and wretched he may be. I shall speak further on of the true figure of these truths in the story of Jacob and Rebecca.*

Mary's advocacy before the Father is never refused and she never tires of interceding for her children because her charity knows no end. Pope John Paul II speaking of Mary's maternal mediation for her children states: "After her Son's departure, her motherhood remains in the Church as maternal mediation: interceding for all her children, the Mother cooperates in the saving work of her Son the Redeemer of the world. In fact the Council teaches that the 'motherhood of Mary in the order of grace…will last without interruption until the eternal fulfillment of all the elect.' With the redeeming death of her Son, the maternal mediation of the handmaid of the Lord took on a universal dimension, for the work of redemption embraces the whole of humanity."[9] The lifestyle of true devotion is a gift of infinite value from the Father to His children for those who are able to receive and accept that gift.

<u>Application of the Lifestyle of True Devotion</u>

1. How have I stripped myself of all that is dearest to me? What does it me that Mary gives her whole self to me?
2. How has my self-abandonment to the Blessed Virgin Mary grown with my practice of true devotion?
3. How have my actions been tainted with self-love? How have I been attached to created things including people?
4. What does it mean that Mary is embellishing my good works? Which works is she embellishing?
5. How does Mary's example of giving everything over to Jesus affect my attitude towards possessions, both material and spiritual?
6. What does it mean in paragraph 150 that "[Mary] repels no one, however little and wretched he may be"?

Fourth Motive

It Is An Excellent Means Of Procuring God's Greater Glory

151. This devotion, faithfully practiced, is an excellent means of making sure that the value of all our good works shall be employed for the greater glory of God. Scarcely anyone acts for that noble end, although we are all under an obligation to do so. Either we do not know where the greater glory of God is to be found, or we do not wish to find it. But our Blessed Lady, to whom we cede the value and merit of our good works, knows most perfectly where the greater glory of God is to be found; and inasmuch as she never does anything except for the greater glory of God, a perfect servant of that good Mistress, who is wholly consecrated to her, may say with the hardiest assurance that the value of all his actions, thoughts and words is employed for the greater glory of God, unless he purposely revokes his offering. Is there any consolation equal to this for a soul who loves God with a pure and disinterested love, and who prizes the glory and interest of God far beyond his own?

The lifestyle of true devotion ensures that everything we do is directed to the glory of God. It is not a devotion ultimately about Mary, it is ultimately about the glory of God. St. Paul states in 1 Corinthians 10:31 that all our actions must tend toward the glory of God: "So whether you eat or drink, or whatever you do, do everything for the glory of God." He further states that to give greater value to our offerings to the Father we do them through Jesus thereby adding His merits to ours: "And whatever you do, in word or in deed, do everything in the name of the Lord Jesus, giving thanks to God the Father through him" (Colossians 3:17). Since Mary forms us in Jesus, and knows best where the glory of God is to be found in any situation in our lives, and she is not sidetracked from seeking God's glory as we are, then by consecrating all things to her, she, presenting them to Jesus and the Father, allows us to give Him perfect glory. This is the most perfect practice of religion.

Application of the Lifestyle of True Devotion

1. How do I understand my obligation to do all things for the greater glory of God?
2. How does it help me that Mary knows where the greater glory of God is to be found in every situation of my life?

Fifth Motive

152. This devotion is an easy, short, perfect and secure way of attaining union with Our Lord, in which union the perfection of a Christian consists.

I. *It is an Easy Way*

It is an easy way. It is the way which Jesus Christ Himself trod in coming to us, and in which there is no obstacle in reaching Him. It is true that we can attain divine union by other roads; but it is by many more crosses and strange deaths, and with many more difficulties, which we shall find it hard to overcome. We must pass through obscure nights, through combats, through strange agonies, over craggy mountains, through cruel thorns and over frightful deserts. But by the path of Mary we pass more gently and more tranquilly.

We do find, it is true, great battles to fight, and great hardships to master; but that good Mother makes herself so present and so near to her faithful servants, to enlighten them in their darkness and their doubts, to strengthen them in their fears, and to sustain them in their struggles and their difficulties, that in truth this virginal path to find Jesus Christ is a path of roses and honey compared with the other paths. There have been some saints, but they have been in small numbers, who have walked upon this sweet path to go to Jesus, because the Holy Spirit, faithful Spouse of Mary, by a singular grace disclosed it to them. Such were St. Ephrem, St. John Damascene, St. Bernard, St. Bernardine, St. Bonaventure, St. Francis de Sales, and others. But the rest of the saints, who are the greater number, although they have all had devotion to our Blessed Lady, nevertheless have either not at all, or at least very little, entered upon this way. That is why they have had to pass through ruder and more dangerous trials.

Who's Who?

(St. Ephrem, St. John Damascene, St. Bernard, St. Bernardine, St. Bonaventure, see above)

St. Francis de Sales, Bishop of Geneva and Doctor of the Church, lived from 1567-1622. His opinions on Mary are found in the Introduction to the Devout Life, Treatise on the Love of God and in over twenty of his published sermons. He strongly encouraged devotion to her as he practiced it himself.[10]

Here St. Louis begins his presentation of the four ways by which the lifestyle of true devotion leads a soul to divine union with Jesus. Contemplation, the highest form of prayer and an infused gift, is a fruit of true devotion to the Blessed Mother. She is able to make the cross we bear easier and more meritorious; and by offering our acts to the Lord she increases their value.[11] The contemplation of which St. John of the Cross and St. Teresa of Avila speak is possible through the lifestyle of true devotion. The easy way is presented as the very same way that Jesus took when coming into this world. He came directly through Mary. By not coming in any other way, He shows us the best way. To try to achieve divine union without the Mother of God is much more difficult. The imagery of these "other roads" is one of trial, uncertainty, fears, dryness and great effort. This is not to say that we will not have our own trials, but the difference with true devotion is that Mary sustains us during those trials, uncertainties, fears, and labors which makes our progress to Jesus all the more certain.

> *153. How is it, then, some of the faithful servants of Mary will say to me, that the faithful servants of this good Mother have so many occasions of suffering, nay, even more than others who are not so devout to her? They are contradicted, they are persecuted, they are calumniated, the world cannot endure them; or again, they walk in interior darkness and in deserts where there is not the least drop of the dew of Heaven. If this devotion to our Blessed Lady makes the road to Jesus easier, how is it that they who follow it are the most despised of men?*

St. Louis presents two questions here that he intends to answer: Why do Mary's servants suffer more than others? And, if this is supposed to be an easier road to Jesus, why is it so painful?

> *154. I reply that it is quite true that the most faithful servants of the Blessed Virgin, being also her greatest favorites, receive from her the greatest graces and favors of Heaven, which are crosses. But I maintain that it is also the servants of Mary who carry these crosses with more ease, more merit and more glory. That which would stay the progress of another a thousand times over, or perhaps would make him fall, does not once stop their steps, but rather enables them to advance because that good Mother, all full of grace and of the unction of the Holy Spirit, prepares her servants' crosses with so much maternal sweetness and pure love as to make them gladly acceptable, no matter how bitter they may be in themselves; and I believe that a person who wishes to be devout, and to live piously in Jesus Christ, and consequently to suffer persecutions and carry his cross daily, either will never carry*

great crosses, or will not carry them joyously or perseveringly, without a tender devotion to Our Lady, which is the sweetmeat and confection of crosses just as a person would not be able to eat unripe fruits without a great effort which he could hardly keep up, unless they had been preserved in sugar.

The answer to the two questions posed in the preceding paragraph lies in the cross of Christ. All authentic Christian spirituality takes us by the Cross to Jesus and transforms us into saints. St. Louis describes the experience of suffering these crosses as Mary's "greatest graces and favors of Heaven." These crosses (both interior and exterior sufferings) are made by Mary herself and she enables her devotees to bear these crosses exceedingly well, through her personal mediation.

Any soul truly striving for holiness cannot avoid crosses. The lifestyle of true devotion gives each one the capacity to bear whatever crosses God designs--both the large and the small, with joy and perseverance. As we recall from our previous discussion on patience, it is the love of the cross which marks a higher degree of patience. It is that love of suffering for the sake of God, for His glory and for the salvation of souls which separates the beginners in the spiritual life from the more advanced. This degree of patience is indicative of those who are reaching the higher degrees of holiness. Our Lady wants to lead us to the love of the cross and this high degree of holiness which eventually results in divine union with the Blessed Trinity.

Pope John Paul II states: "At the foot of the Cross there begins that special entrusting of humanity to the Mother of Christ, which in the history of the Church has been practiced and expressed in different ways. The same Apostle and Evangelist [John] after reporting the words addressed by Jesus on the Cross to his Mother and to himself, adds: 'And from that hour the disciple took her to his own home' (Jn. 19:27). This statement certainly means that the role of son was attributed to the disciple and that he assumed responsibility for the Mother of his beloved Master. And since Mary was given as a mother to him personally, the statement indicates, even though indirectly, everything expressed by the intimate relationship of a child with its mother. And all of this can be included in the word 'entrusting.' Such entrusting is the response to a person's love and in particular to the love of a mother."[12]

II. It Is A Short Way

155. This devotion to our Blessed Lady is a short road to find Jesus Christ, both because it is a road from which we do not stray, and because, as I have just said, it is a road we tread with joy and facility, and consequently with promptitude. We make more progress in a brief period of submission to and dependence on Mary than in whole years of following our own will and relying upon ourselves. A man obedient and submissive to Mary shall sing the signal victories which he shall gain over his enemies. (Prov. 21:28). They will try to hinder his advance, or to make him retrace his steps or fall; this is true. But with the support, the aid and the guidance of Mary, he shall advance with giant strides toward Jesus, without falling, without drawing back one step, without even slackening his pace, along the same path by which he knows (Ps. 18:6) that Jesus also came to us with giant strides and in the briefest space of time.

<u>Scriptures</u>

Proverbs 21:28 Douay: "A lying witness shall perish: an obedient man shall speak of victory."

Proverbs 21:28 NAB:"The false witness will perish, but he who listens will finally have his say."

Psalm 18:6 Douay: "He has pitched a tent there for the sun, which comes forth like the groom from his bridal chamber and, like a giant, joyfully runs its course."

Psalm 19:6 NAB: "[Wisdom] comes forth like a bridegroom from his chamber, and like an athlete joyfully runs its course.

St. Louis refers to these two Scripture passages to emphasize that obedience always leads to victory even if it requires perseverance in humility and silent waiting. Then, once the waiting is over, Mary leads the soul quickly and powerfully to Jesus and into the depths of holiness.

It does not take long to find Jesus through the practice of true devotion. St. Louis guarantees that "we make more progress in a brief period of submission to Mary" than by any other form of spirituality or exercises without her. The key to practicing this lifestyle is the renewed practice of submitting all things and depending entirely upon her to lead us to Jesus. This is most especially true when we experience the overwhelming recurrence of occasions of sin, temptations or sin itself and backslide in our progress. With Mary's help, however, in such occasions we make greater progress forward through grace, conversion and healing.

156. Why do you think that Jesus lived so few years on earth, and of those few years, spent nearly all of them in subjection and obedience to His Mother? The truth is that, being perfected in a short time (Wis. 4:13), He lived a long time--longer than Adam, whose fall He had come to repair, although the patriarch lived above nine hundred years. Jesus Christ lived a long time because He lived in complete subjection to His holy Mother, and closely united with her, in order that He might thus obey His Father. For (1) the Holy Spirit says that a man who honors his mother is like a man who lays up a treasure; that is to say, he who honors Mary, his Mother, to the extent of subjecting himself to her and obeying her in all things, will soon become exceedingly rich, because he is every day amassing treasures by the secret of that touchstone: "He who honors his mother is as one who lays up a treasure" (Ecclus. 3:5); (2) because, according to a mystical interpretation of the inspired text, "My old age is to be found in the mercy of the bosom" (Ps. 91:11), it is in the bosom of Mary, which has surrounded and engendered a perfect man (Jer. 31:22), and has had the capacity of containing Him whom the whole universe could neither contain nor comprehend—it is, I say, in the bosom of Mary that they who are youthful become elders in light, in holiness, in experience and in wisdom, and that we arrive in a few years at the fullness of the age of Jesus Christ."

Scriptures

Wisdom 4:13-14 Douay: "Being made perfect in a short space, he fulfilled a long time: for his soul pleased God: therefore he hastened to bring him out of the midst of iniquities: but the people see this, and understand not, nor lay up such things in their hearts:"

Wisdom 4:13-14 NAB: "Having become perfect in a short while, he reached the fullness of a long career; for his soul was pleasing to the Lord, therefore he sped him out of the midst of wickedness."

Ecclesiasticus 3:5 Douay: "And he that honoureth his mother is as one that layeth up a treasure."

Sirach 3:4 NAB: "…He stores up riches who reveres his mother."

Psalm 91:11 This old translation St. Louis/Fr. Faber employ has proved to be incorrect.[13] The Latin is: "senectus mea in misericordia uberi."

Psalm 91:11 Douay: "You have exalted my horn like the wild bull's; you have anointed me with rich oil."

Psalm 92:11 NAB: "You have given me the strength of a wild bull; you have poured rich oil upon me."

Jeremiah 31:22 Douay: "How long wilt thou be dissolute in deliciousness, O wandering daughter: for the Lord hath created a new thing upon the earth: A woman shall compass a man."

Jeremiah 31:22 NAB: "…The Lord has created a new thing upon the earth: the woman must encompass the man with devotion."

These Scriptures all support St. Louis' teaching that Mary makes the soul pleasing to God in a short time, God blesses those who are obedient to their mother—as He also commands in the 4th Commandment, and He creates a new spiritual motherhood for humanity by means of Mary. It is in her that souls grow rapidly—more rapidly than in the natural course of maturation.

St. Louis proposes that a young man or woman can attain divine wisdom quite quickly by practicing this lifestyle of true devotion based on the observation that a man who honors his mother becomes exceedingly rich.

This interpretation of Mary encompassing the Lord, 'the perfect man' in her womb, follows from St. Jerome who sees in this passage Mary's virginal conception of Jesus. He is already formed in her womb as the perfect man, since He has no sin according to his Divinity. After birth He will advance in "wisdom and grace" (cf. Luke 2:52) according to His humanity.[14]

The word "touchstone" is the translation from the French "la pierre philoso-phale"= the philosopher's stone. The existence of a philosopher's stone belonged to medieval alchemists who believed that somewhere there existed a stone whose powder could transmute metals into gold. Not only did it exist somewhere, but it was believed to be everywhere, it just had to be found. It could change metals into gold, but also had spiritual properties that could cure illnesses, prolong life and bring about spiritual revitalization. Thus, it was the means not only to wealth, but life itself.[15]

St. Louis refers analogously to Mary as the touchstone who makes men rich in grace. It is through her intercession with Jesus that healings occur, life is prolonged and spiritual conversions and holiness occur.

St. Louis proposes that a young man or woman can attain wisdom quite quickly by practicing the lifestyle of true devotion due to Our Lady's intervention. This short way is an accelerated way in which one quickly grows in illumination/self-knowledge, holiness, experience and wisdom in the ways of the interior life.

III. It Is A Perfect Way

157. This practice of devotion to our Blessed Lady is also a perfect path by which to go and unite ourselves to Jesus; because the divine Mary is the most perfect and the most holy of creatures, and because Jesus, who has come to us most perfectly, took no other road for His great and admirable journey. The most High, the Incomprehensible, the Inaccessible, He Who is, has willed to come to us, little worms of earth who are nothing. How has He done this? The Most High has come down to us perfectly and divinely, by the humble Mary, without losing anything of His divinity and sanctity. So it is by Mary that the very little ones are to ascend perfectly and divinely, without any fear, to the Most High. The Incomprehensible has allowed Himself to be comprehended and perfectly contained by the little Mary, without losing anything of His immensity. So also it is by the little Mary that we must let ourselves be contained and guided perfectly without any reserve. The Inaccessible has drawn near to us and has united Himself closely, perfectly and even personally to our humanity, by Mary, without losing anything of His majesty. So it is by Mary that we must draw near to God and unite ourselves perfectly and closely to His Majesty without fear of being repulsed. In a word, He Who is has willed to come to that which is not, and to make that which is not, become He Who is; and He has done this perfectly in giving himself and subjecting Himself entirely to the young Virgin Mary, without ceasing to be in time He who is from all eternity. In like manner, it is by Mary that we, who are nothing, can become like to God by grace and glory, by giving ourselves to her so perfectly and entirely as to be nothing in ourselves, but everything in her, without fear of delusion.

The way to divine union with Jesus through Mary is perfect because Mary is a perfect creature. Jesus did not lose anything by becoming man through her. His divine attributes were not lost passing through her womb. In a similar manner, we must allow ourselves to be contained in her also. In the process of our growing in grace we do so perfectly as we pass by Mary to the Father. We engage in the process with great humility and trust as we have already seen.

158. Make for me, if you will, a new road to go to Jesus and pave it with all the merits of the blessed, adorn it with all their heroic virtues, illuminate and embellish it with all the lights and beauties of the angels, and let all the angels and saints be there themselves, to escort, defend and sustain those who are ready to walk there; and yet in truth, in simple truth, I say boldly, and I repeat that I say truly, I would prefer to this new, perfect path the immaculate way of Mary. "He made my way blameless" (Ps. 17:33). It is the way without stain or spot, without original or actual sin, without shadow or darkness. When my sweet Jesus comes a second time on earth in His glory, as it is most certain He will do, to reign there, He will choose no other way for His journey than the divine Mary, by whom He came the first time so surely and so perfectly. But there will be a difference between His first and His last coming. The first time He came secretly and hiddenly; the second time He will come gloriously and resplendently. But both times He will have come perfectly, because both times He will have come by Mary. Alas! Here is a mystery which is not understood. "Here let all tongues be mute."

Scriptures

Psalm 17:32-33 Douay: "For who is God except the Lord? Who is a rock, save our God? The God who girded me with strength and kept my way unerring."
Psalm 18:32-33 NAB: "Truly, who is God except the Lord? Who but our God

is the rock? This God who girded me with might, kept my way unerring."

St. Louis quotes from this psalm transferring the idea that God who keeps me safe provides me with a sure way to Him. For St. Louis that sure and immaculate way is Mary, a way that cannot be sullied or corrupt when imitating her virtues and following her inspirations in humble and faithful obedience.

All other ways are less perfect—even those of the angels and saints, because Mary is the most perfect creature of all creatures, holy, immaculate and full of grace. St. Louis compares the two comings of Christ: the first time He came in secrecy and hiddenness as a tiny baby at Bethlehem. The second time He will come gloriously and resplendently. Both comings will be perfect as He uses the same means—Mary. How exactly this will work for the second coming remains a mystery.

IV. It Is A Secure Way

> 159. This devotion to our Blessed Lady is also a secure way to go to Jesus and to acquire perfection by uniting ourselves to Him. 1st) It is a secure way, because the practice which I am teaching is not new. Father Boudon, who died a short time ago in the odor of sanctity, says in a book which he composed on this devotion that it is so ancient that we cannot fix precisely the date of its beginning. It is, however, certain that for more than seven hundred years we find traces of it in the Church.
>
> St. Odilo, the Abbot of Cluny, who lived about the year 1040, was one of the first who publicly practiced it in France, as is told in his life.
>
> Peter Cardinal Damian relates that in the year 1016 Blessed Marino, his brother, made himself a slave of the Blessed Virgin in the presence of his director in a most edifying manner. He put a rope around his neck, took the discipline, and laid on the altar a sum of money, as a token of his devotedness and consecration to Our Lady; and he continued this devotion so faithfully during his whole life that he deserved to be visited and consoled at his death by his good Mistress, and to receive from her mouth the promise of paradise in recompense for his services.
>
> Caesarius Bollandus mentions an illustrious knight, Vautier de Birbac, a near relative of the Duke of Louvain, who about the year 1300 consecrated himself to the Blessed Virgin.
>
> This devotion was also practiced by several private individuals up to the seventeenth century, when it became public.

Who's Who?

Henri-Marie Boudon, who lived from 1624-1702, was an archdeacon of Evreux, France. The book to which St. Louis is referring is entitled <u>God Alone or the Holy Slavery of the Admirable Mother of God</u> which was published in 1674. In this book he defends the idea of the slavery of love towards Mary. He treats of her universal mediation and defends devotion to her.[16]

St. Odilo lived from 962-1049. He was the fifth abbot of Cluny in France. He speaks about Mary in his sermons especially as her virtues related to monastic life. St. Odilo's great contribution to the Cluniac monastic tradition is his prayer of consecration as a slave of Mary: "O most clement Virgin Mary, Mother of the Savior of all the ages, from today and henceforth, hold me in your services, and in all my affairs be with me as a most merciful advocate. From now on, after God, I choose nothing before you, and spontaneously I commit myself forever to your bondage as your slave."[17]

Peter Cardinal Damian, Doctor of the Church and Cardinal-Bishop of Ostia, was born in 1007 and died in 1072. He became a hermit at Fonte-Avellana and became renowned for his austere penances. He was outspoken on reform for the clergy. In 1057 he became the Cardinal-Bishop of Ostia and represented the Holy Father in many disputes. The reference to his brother is contained in the Opusc. 13 ad Desiderium abbatem cassinensem, c.4. Different dates appear in different translations of the <u>True Devotion</u>: TAN has the brother's consecration as 1016. <u>Le Traité</u> (Editions du Seuil) has 1076 which the Montfort Publications also follows. The latter date (1076) is incorrect since Peter Damian died in 1072.[18]

Caesarius of Heisterbach (Bollandus) was a German Cistercian monk born in 1170 and died around 1210-1240. He taught theology to Cistercian novices. He became known outside the monastery also and was a very popular writer of stories of saints and ascetical romances. He wrote that Mary protects Cistercian monks with her mantle. He wrote tracts and homilies on Mary.[19]

In these paragraphs St. Louis insists that the security of the lifestyle of true devotion is to be found in its long history of practice in the Church. He cites examples from various sources he had read in his study of Marian devotion. Many of these names remain obscure to the modern devotee of true devotion, but the main point of this list is to locate devotion to Mary and the holy slavery of love, within the history of the Church.

> *160. Father Simon de Roias, of the Order of the Most Holy Trinity, known as the Order of Redemption of Captives, and preacher of Philip III, made this devotion popular in Spain and Germany; and at the request of Philip III, obtained of Gregory XV ample indulgences for those who practiced it. Father de Los Rios, the Augustinian, devoted himself with his intimate friend, Father de Roias, to spreading this devotion throughout Spain and Germa-*

ny both by preaching and by writing. He composed a thick volume called Hierarchia Mariana, in which he treats with as much piety as learning of the antiquity, excellence and solidity of this devotion.

Who's Who?

Simon de Roias, Spanish Augustinian priest who lived from 1552-1624 propagated holy slavery to Mary in Spain. He founded the "Confraternity of the Slaves of the Virgin Mother of God and of her most holy name, Mary."[20]

Bartholomew de los Rios lived from 1580-1652. He was a Spanish Augustinian priest. The book to which St. Louis is referring (On Marian Hierarchy, book 6) was published in 1641.[21]

161. In the seventeenth century the Theatine Fathers established this devotion in Italy, Sicily and Savoy. Father Stanislaus Phalcius, the Jesuit, furthered this devotion wonderfully in Poland. Father de Los Rios, in his work just cited, quotes the names of princes, princesses, bishops and cardinals of different kingdoms, who embraced this devotion. Cornelius à Lapide, as praiseworthy for his piety as for his profound erudition, having been commissioned by several bishops and theologians to examine this devotion, did so with great thoroughness and deliberation, and praised it in a manner which we might have expected from his well-known piety; and many other distinguished persons have followed his example. The Jesuit Fathers, always zealous in the service of our Blessed Lady, in the name of the Sodalists of Cologne presented a little treatise on this devotion to Duke Ferdinand of Bavaria, who was then Archbishop of Cologne. He approved it, granted permission for its printing, and exhorted all the parish priests and religious of his diocese to promote this solid devotion as much as they could.

Who's Who?

Stanislaus Fenicki or "Phalacius" was a Jesuit priest who lived from 1592-1652. He spread devotion of holy slavery to Poland and published the book Slave of Mary in 1632.[22]

Cornelius à Lapide (van den Steen) lived from 1567-1637. He was asked to examine the orthodoxy of Fr. Fenicki's work on holy slavery—of which he rendered a positive account.[23]

162. Cardinal de Bérulle, whose memory is held in veneration throughout all France, was one of the most zealous in spreading

*this devotion in that country, in spite of all the calumnies and per-
secutions which he suffered from critics and freethinkers. They ac-
cused him of novelty and superstition. They wrote and published
a libel against him, in order to defame him; and they, or rather the
devil by their ministry, made use of a thousand artifices to hinder
his spreading the devotion in France. But that great and holy man
only answered their calumnies by his patience; and he met the
objections contained in their libel by a short treatise in which he
most convincingly refuted them. He showed them that the devotion was founded on the example of Jesus Christ, on the obligations which we have toward Him, and on the vows which we have
made in holy Baptism. It was chiefly by means of this last reason
that he shut his adversaries' mouths, making them see that this
consecration to the holy Virgin, and to Jesus Christ by her hands,
is nothing else than a perfect renewal of the vows and promises of
Baptism. He has said many beautiful things about this practice,
which can be read in his works.*

Who's Who?

Cardinal Pierre de Bérulle lived from 1575-1629. He was a founder of the
French school of spirituality and founder of the French Congregation of the Ora-
tory. He urged devotion to Mary emphasizing the internal rather than the external.
He supported the idea of holy slavery which was then popular in Spain as we have
seen above.[24]

*163. We may also see in Father Boudon's book the different
Popes who have approved this devotion, the theologians who have
examined it, the persecutions it has undergone and has overcome,
and the thousands of persons who have embraced it, without any
Pope ever having condemned it. Indeed, we can not see how it
could be condemned without overturning the foundations of
Christianity.*

*164. 2nd) This devotion is a secure means of going to Jesus
Christ, because it is the very characteristic of our Blessed Lady
to conduct us surely to Jesus, just as it is the very characteristic
of Jesus to conduct us surely to the Eternal Father. Spiritual persons, therefore, must not fall into the false belief that Mary can
be a hindrance to them in attaining divine union; for is it possible
that she who has found grace before God for the whole world in
general and for each one in particular, should be a hindrance to a*

soul in finding the great grace of union with Him? Can it be possible that she who has been full and superabounding with graces, so united and transformed into God that it has been a kind of necessity that He should be incarnate in her, should be a stumbling-block in the way of a soul's perfect union with God? It is quite true that the view of other creatures, however holy, may perhaps at certain times retard divine union. But this cannot be said of Mary, as I have remarked before and shall never weary of repeating. One reason why so few souls come to the fullness of the age of Jesus Christ is that Mary, who is as much as ever the Mother of the Son, and as much as ever the fruitful spouse of the Holy Spirit, is not sufficiently formed in their hearts. He who wishes to have the fruit well ripened and well formed must have the tree that produces it; he who wishes to have the fruit of life, Jesus Christ, must have the tree of life, which is Mary; he who wishes to have in himself the operation of the Holy Spirit must have His faithful and inseparable spouse, the divine Mary, who makes Him fertile and fruit-bearing, as we have said elsewhere.

St. Louis continues to treat of the security of this true devotion by posing a couple of rhetorical questions that emphasize the point: Can Mary be a hindrance in a soul's perfect union with God? The answer is, of course, no. People who are set on living the lifestyle of true devotion must not be deceived into thinking that Mary fails to lead them to Jesus. She is unlike any other creature. She is not content with drawing people to herself. He continues also with the imagery of Mary as the tree of life and Jesus is the fruit produced on that tree. One can't have the fruit without the tree; one can't have Jesus without Mary.

165. *Be persuaded, then, that the more you look at Mary in your prayers, contemplations, actions and sufferings, if not with a distinct and definite view, at least with a general and imperceptible one, the more perfectly will you find Jesus Christ, who is always, with Mary, great, powerful, active and incomprehensible—more than in Heaven or in any other creature. Thus, so far from the divine Mary, all absorbed in God, being an obstacle to the perfect in attaining union with God, there has never been up to this time, and there never will be, any creature who will aid us more efficaciously in this great work; either by the graces she will communicate to us for this purpose—for, as a saint has said, "No one can be filled with the thought of God except by her"—or by the protection she will afford us against the illusions and trickeries of the evil spirit.*

The more we consider Mary—whether directly or indirectly in our prayers—the more perfectly we will find Jesus as she leads us perfectly to Him. It is impossible for any other creature to bring us to the attainment of divine union. She obtains two gifts for us when we live the true devotion—(1) union with God; (2) protection from the illusions and tricks of Satan.

> *166. Where Mary is, there the evil spirit is not. One of the most infallible marks we can have of our being conducted by the good spirit is our being very devout to Mary, thinking often of her and speaking often of her. This last is the thought of a saint, who adds that as respiration is a certain sign the body is not dead, the frequent thought and loving invocation of Mary is a certain sign the soul is not dead by sin.*

Who's Who?

The "saint" who is mentioned in this paragraph and quoted in the preceding one is St. Germanus of Constantinople (see above).[25]

Here St. Louis presents Mary's protective action against the Evil One. Every inclination to Mary is an action of the Holy Spirit. The devil always leads us away from her. When we are drawn towards Mary, the Rosary, etc. we can be assured that is coming from God.

> *167. As it is Mary alone, says the Church (and the Holy Spirit who guides the Church), who makes all heresies come to naught— "Thou alone hast destroyed all heresies in the whole world"--we may be sure that, however critics may grumble, no faithful client of Mary will ever fall into heresy or illusions, at least formal ones. He may very well err materially, take falsehood for truth, and the evil spirit for the good; and yet he will do even this less readily than others. But sooner or later he will acknowledge his material fault and error; and when he knows it, he will not be in any way self-opinionated by continuing to believe and maintain what he had once thought true.*

The verse "thou alone hast destroyed all heresies in the whole world" is taken from one of the antiphons for morning prayer in the Office of the Blessed Virgin Mary—"Rejoice O Virgin Mary, thou alone hast destroyed all heresies in the world"[26] which men and women pray in addition to or instead of the Breviary.

No faithful child of Mary who lives the true devotion will ever fall into heresy. Because Mary leads us to Jesus who is all Truth she cannot at the same time lead us to a formal rejection of the Truth. We may make errors of judgment, be deceived by the temptations of the Evil One, but ultimately we cannot reject Jesus or the teachings of the Church as long as we are devoted to her.

168. Whoever, then, wishes to put aside the fear of illusion, which is the besetting timidity of men of prayer, and to advance in the way of perfection and surely and perfectly find Jesus Christ, let him embrace with great-heartedness—"with a great heart and willing mind" (2 Macc.1:3)—this devotion to our Blessed Lady which perhaps he has not known before; let him enter into this excellent way which was unknown to him and which I now point out: "I show you a more excellent way" (1 Cor. 12:31). It is a path trodden by Jesus Christ, the Incarnate Wisdom, our sole Head. One of His members cannot make a mistake in passing by the same road. It is an easy road, because of the fullness of the grace and unction of the Holy Spirit which fills it to overflowing. No one wearies there; no one walking there ever has to retrace his steps. It is a short road which leads us to Jesus in a little time. It is a perfect road, where there is no mud, no dust, not the least spot of sin. Lastly, it is a secure road, which conducts us to Jesus Christ and life eternal in a straight and secure manner, without turning to the right hand or to the left. Let us, then, set forth upon that road and walk there day and night, until we come to the fullness of the age of Jesus Christ (Eph. 4:13).

Scriptures

2 Maccabees 1:3 Douay: "And give you all a heart to worship him, and to do his will with a great heart, and a willing mind."

2 Maccabees 1:3 NAB: "May he give to all of you a heart to worship him and to do his will readily and generously."

1 Corinthians 12:31 NAB: "Strive eagerly for the greatest spiritual gifts. But I shall show you a still more excellent way."

Ephesians 4:13 NAB: "Until we all attain to the unity of faith and knowledge of the Son of God, to mature manhood, to the extent of the full stature of Christ."

Through these Scriptural references, St. Louis invites the reader to abandon all fear and give his heart over to Mary because it is the way of love which leads the soul to perfection and divine union with Jesus.

St. Louis states that the lifestyle of true devotion, especially in the beginner, conquers the fear of illusion and allows one to advance in the way of holiness. The fear of illusion in true devotion is the fear that devotion to Jesus through Mary will be a way of life without the anointing of the Holy Spirit. It is the fear that it will take a long time to arrive at holiness. It is the fear that it will invite many occasions of sin. And it is the fear that it may lead one away from salvation and Heaven. But the way of true devotion is the way of love which leads a soul without error into the heart of the love of the Blessed Trinity. In this paragraph, St. Louis recaps the four ways (easy, short, perfect and secure) encouraging us to persevere in order to arrive at holiness: a holiness which is unmistakable by this way.

Application of the Lifestyle of True Devotion

1. How does Mary lead me without obstacle to Divine Union with Jesus?
2. Has my devotion to Mary caused me greater suffering?
3. How can the cross be considered a favor from heaven?
4. How do I make more progress in the spiritual life by my submission to Mary than without her?
5. How does Mary keep me from straying from the path to Jesus?
6. Explain how Mary makes me wise in holiness in a short time by the practice of this devotion.
7. Comment on how Our Lady is "a perfect way" to Jesus.
8. What delusions is one capable of experiencing in the spiritual life that Mary prevents?
9. Who are some of the saints who have promoted going to Jesus by means of His mother?
10. How is it possible that Mary can be a hindrance to divine union with Jesus?
11. What other creature is there that will lead me to divine union with Jesus?
12. Why is it that no one can be simultaneously a heretic and a devotee to Mary?
13. To what illusions in the spiritual life are beginners (and those more advanced) subject?

Sixth Motive

It Gives Us Great Interior Liberty

169. This practice of devotion gives to those who make use of it faithfully a great interior liberty, which is the liberty of the children of God. (Rom 8:21). Since, by this devotion, we make ourselves slaves of Jesus Christ and consecrate ourselves entirely to Him in this capacity, our good Master, in recompense for the loving captivity in which we put ourselves, (1) takes from the soul all scruple and servile fear, which are capable only of cramping, imprisoning or confusing it; (2) He enlarges the heart with firm confidence in God, making it look upon Him as a Father; and (3) He inspires us with a tender and filial love.

Scriptures

Romans 8:19-21 NAB: "For creation awaits with eager expectation the revelation of the children of God; for creation was made subject to futility, not of its own accord but because of the one who subjected it, in hope that creation would be set free from slavery to corruption and share in the glorious freedom of the children of God."

St. Louis alludes to Romans 8 to remind us that we are no longer children of slavery, but children of God because the Holy Spirit has led us to the Father to love and know Him. In the same way, Mary, the Spouse of the Holy Spirit, leads us to the Father and perfects our human dignity.

The lifestyle of true devotion leads us to inner freedom and peace. As we have consecrated ourselves as slaves of Jesus through Mary, He blesses this consecration in three ways and leads us to a deeper love for the Father. Jesus reveals to us the Father in the following three ways: (1) He removes scrupulosity and fear of Him; (2) He gives us a personal relationship with God the Father and a greater trust in Him; and (3) He inspires us to love Him.

> *170. Without stopping to prove these truths with arguments, I shall be content to relate here what I have read in the life of Mother Agnes of Jesus, a Dominican nun of the convent of Langeac, in Auvergne, who died there in the odor of sanctity in the year 1634. When she was only seven years old, and was suffering from great spiritual anguish, she heard a voice which told her that if she wished to be delivered from her anguish, and to be protected against all her enemies, she was as quickly as possible to make herself the slave of Jesus and His most holy Mother. She had no sooner returned to the house than she gave herself up entirely to Jesus and His Mother in this capacity, although up to that time she did not so much as know what the devotion meant. Taking up an iron chain, she put it around her body and wore it until her death. After this, all her anguish and scruples ceased, and she experienced great peace and dilation of heart. This is what brought her to teach the devotion to many persons who made great progress in it--among others, Father Olier, the founder of St. Sulpice, as well as many priests and ecclesiastics of the same seminary. One day Our Lady appeared to her and put around her neck a chain of gold, to show her the joy she had at Mother Agnes' having made herself her Son's slave and her own; and St. Cecilia, who accompanied Our Lady in that apparition, said to the religious: "Happy are the faithful slaves of the Queen of Heaven; for they shall enjoy true liberty." "To serve thee is liberty."*

Who's Who?

Mother Agnes de Langeac was Prioress of the Dominican Sisters of the Convent of St. Catherine of Langeac, France. She was born December 17, 1602 and became a Dominican tertiary in of the Order of St. Dominic in 1621. She was influential in guiding Jean-Jacques Olier in the foundation of St. Sulpice Seminary. She died October 19, 1634. She was beatified by Pope John Paul II on November

20, 1994. She was favored by frequent visions of her guardian angel, the Virgin Mary, ecstasies and mortification. She had a special apostolate to pray for priests. Different editions of her Life appeared in 1655 and 1675. St. Louis would have been familiar with this biography from his time as librarian at St. Sulpice.[27]

St. Cecilia was an early Roman martyr and is the patron saint of musicians.

Application of the Lifestyle of True Devotion

1. How does the lifestyle of true devotion give me freedom to be a son or daughter of God? How does a child of God live?
2. What prevents me from experiencing inner peace?

Seventh Motive

It Procures Great Blessings For Our Neighbor

171. Another consideration which may bring us to embrace this practice is the great good which our neighbor receives from it. For by this practice we exercise charity toward him in an eminent manner, seeing that we give him by Mary's hands all that is most precious to ourselves—namely, the satisfactory and impetratory value of all our good works, without excepting the least good thought or the least little suffering. We agree that all the satisfactions we may have acquired, or may acquire up to the moment of our death, should be employed at Our Lady's will either for the conversion of sinners or for the deliverance of souls from Purgatory. Is this not loving our neighbor perfectly? Is this not being a true disciple of Jesus Christ, who is always to be recognized by his charity? (Jn. 13:35). Is this not the way to convert sinners, without any fear of vanity; and to deliver souls from Purgatory, with scarcely doing anything but what we are obliged to do by our state of life?

Scriptures

John 13:35: "This is how all will know that you are my disciples, if you have love for one another."

In citing John's Gospel, St. Louis implies that by giving all things over to Mary we increase in Christian charity and love. Our fundamental vocation is to love. Love of God and love of neighbor is the fulfillment of the Law. This practice is an intense way of loving one's neighbor.

The fruit of the lifestyle of true devotion is not only for ourselves. It is also a powerful means of obtaining blessings for our family and friends—especially those for whom we are most worried. When we surrender all of the demands for results of our prayers and good works into Mary's hands, she distributes them to our friends perfectly—both for the conversion and the healing of the living and for the repose of the souls for those who are in Purgatory. When we become overwhelmed by frequent requests for prayers, we can answer them all perfectly by giving those requests to Mary.

> *172. To understand the excellence of this motive, we must understand also how great a good it is to convert a sinner or to deliver a soul from Purgatory. It is an infinite good, greater than creating Heaven and earth; because we give to a soul the possession of God. If by this practice we deliver but one soul in our life from Purgatory, or convert but one sinner, would not that be enough to induce a truly charitable man to embrace it? But we must remark that, in as much as our good works pass through the hands of Mary, they receive an augmentation of purity, and consequently of merit, and of satisfactory and impetratory value. On this account they become more capable of solacing the souls in Purgatory and of converting sinners than if they did not pass through the virginal and liberal hands of Mary. It may be little that we give by Our Lady; but in truth, if it is given without self-will and with a disinterested charity, that little becomes very mighty to turn away the wrath of God and to draw down His mercy. It would be no wonder if, at the hour of death, it should be found that a person faithful to this practice should by means of it have delivered many souls from Purgatory and converted many sinners, though he should have done nothing more than the ordinary actions of his state of life. What joy at his judgment! What glory in his eternity!*

St. Louis stresses the infinite value of the spiritual works of mercy and what a noble duty it is to pray for the dead. The great good of saving souls can be accomplished by means of true devotion to Jesus through Mary simply by praying for the dead. These prayers are augmented when passed through Mary's hands and become more efficacious than if just coming directly from our own hands and our mixed motives for wanting to pray for people. The beauty of this lifestyle of true devotion is that all of these good works are accomplished according to our state in life, vocation, work, etc. It does not require extraordinary means or efforts. Our total self-donation to Mary accomplishes it all and she purifies and embellishes what little we may have to offer.

<u>Application of the Lifestyle of True Devotion</u>

1. How does the practice of this lifestyle help me to love my neighbor perfectly?

2. How do my ordinary actions convert sinners and deliver souls from purgatory when I practice true devotion?

Eighth Motive

<u>It Is An Admirable Means of Perseverance</u>

173. Lastly, that which in some sense most persuasively draws us to this devotion to Our Lady is that it is an admirable means of persevering and being faithful in virtue. Whence comes it that the majority of the conversions of sinners are not durable? Whence comes it that we relapse so easily into sin? Whence comes it that the greater part of the just, instead of advancing from virtue to virtue and acquiring new graces, often lose the little virtue and the little grace they have? This misfortune comes, as I have shown before, from the fact that man is so corrupt, so feeble and so inconstant, and yet trusts in himself, relies on his own strength and believes himself capable of safeguarding the treasure of his graces, virtues and merits. But by this devotion, we entrust all that we possess to the Blessed Virgin, who is faithful; we take her for the universal depositary of all our goods of nature and of grace. It is in her fidelity that we trust; it is on her power that we lean; it is on her mercy and charity that we build, in order that she may preserve and augment our virtues and merits, in spite of the devil, the world and the flesh, who put forth all their efforts to take them from us. We say to her as a good child to his mother, and a faithful servant to her mistress: "Keep that which is committed to your trust. (1 Tim. 6:20). My good Mother and Mistress, I acknowledge that up to this time I have, through your intercession, received more graces from God than I deserve; and my sad experience teaches me that I carry this treasure in a very frail vessel, and that I am too weak and too miserable to keep it safely of myself: 'I am very young and despised' (Ps. 118:141); I beseech you, therefore, receive in trust all that I possess, and keep it for me by your fidelity and power. If you keep it for me, I shall lose nothing; if you hold me up, I shall not fall; if you protect me, I shall be sheltered from my enemies."

<u>Scriptures</u>

1 Timothy 6:20 NAB: "O Timothy, guard what has been entrusted to you. Avoid profane babble and the absurdities of so-called knowledge."

Psalm 118:141 Douay: "I am mean and contemptible, but your precepts I have not forgotten."

Psalm 119:141 NAB: "Though belittled and despised, I do not forget your precepts."

Just as St. Paul encourages Timothy to keep the deposit of faith entrusted to him, St. Louis inspires the reader to believe that Mary keeps all that which is entrusted to her (namely, all the virtues, merits, etc. that have been given over to her). In the same way, the psalmist who loves God's promises makes a total surrender of everything to Him despite the hardships of fidelity.

The lifestyle of true devotion allows us more readily to persevere in virtue and decrease relapses into sin. St. Louis introduces this motive by posing three questions as to why we don't persevere after conversion or after the fervor of a retreat. He answers that we trust too much in our own strength. In true devotion, we trust not in ourselves but in Mary's faith, power and charity. She becomes the one who takes care of all of our natural goods and graces. She is their guardian and distributor. A depositary (from the Latin, "depositarius"= a trustee) is the one who takes care of the deposit.

St. Louis concludes this paragraph and interrupts his teaching to break into a prayer to Mary asking her to receive and safeguard all that he possesses.

> *174. Listen to what St. Bernard says in order to encourage us to adopt this practice: "When Mary holds you up, you do not fall; when she protects you, you need not fear; when she leads you, you do not tire; when she is favorable to you, you arrive at the harbor of safety." St. Bonaventure seems to say the same thing still more clearly. "The Blessed Virgin," he says, "is not only retained in the plenitude of the saints, but she also retains and keeps the saints in their plenitude, so that it may not diminish. She prevents their virtues from being dissipated, their merits from perishing, their graces from being lost, the devil from harming them, and even Our Lord from punishing them when they sin."*

St. Louis draws reinforcement to his teaching on perseverance aided by Mary's assistance by quoting selections from St. Bernard of Clairvaux and St. Bonaventure.

> *175. Our Blessed Lady is the faithful Virgin who by her fidelity to God repairs the losses which the faithless Eve has caused by her infidelity. It is she who obtains for those who attach themselves to her the graces of fidelity to God and perseverance. It is for this reason that a saint compares her to a firm anchor which holds her servants fast and hinders them from being shipwrecked in the agitated sea of this world, where so many persons perish simply through not being fastened to the anchor. "We fasten our souls," says he, "to thy hope, as to an abiding anchor." It is to her that the saints who have saved themselves have been the*

most attached and have done their best to attach others, in order to persevere in virtue. Happy, then, a thousand times happy, are the Christians who are now fastened faithfully and entirely to her, as to a firm anchor! The violence of the storms of this world will not make them founder, nor sink their heavenly treasures! Happy those who enter into Mary, as into the ark of Noah! The waters of the deluge of sin, which drown so great a portion of the world, shall do no harm to them; for "They who work in me shall not sin", says Mary, together with the Divine Wisdom. (Ecclus. 24:30). Blessed are the faithless children of the unhappy Eve, if only they attach themselves to the faithful Mother and Virgin who "remains always faithful and never belies herself." "She always loves those who love her" (Prov. 8;17)—not only with an affective love, but with an effectual and efficacious one, by hindering them, through a great abundance of graces, from drawing back in the pursuit of virtue, from falling in the road, and from losing the grace of her Son.

Scriptures

Ecclesiasticus 24:30 Douay: "He that hearkeneth to me, shall not be confounded: and they that work by me, shall not sin."

Sirach 24:21 NAB: "He who obeys me will not be put to shame, he who serves me will never fail."

2 Tim. 2:13 NAB: [applied to Mary] "If we are unfaithful he remains faithful, for he cannot deny himself."

Proverbs 8:17 Douay: "I love them that love me: and they that in the morning early watch for me, shall find me."

Proverbs 8:17 NAB: "Those who love me I also love, and those who seek me find me."

In these Scriptures, St. Louis demonstrates that the obedient servant of Mary triumphs, because Mary is always faithful to her promises. Her love for them keeps them from returning to sin and she moves them forward towards union with Jesus.

St. Louis quotes from St. John Damascene who presents Mary as an anchor which prevents her children from being shipwrecked in the stormy sea of this life. The goal of this lifestyle is not only to attach ourselves to Mary by true devotion as an anchor of safety, but also to get others attached to her that they may find that same safety. Mary is compared to Noah's ark because she saves us from the floodwaters of sin carrying us safely over the sea of chaos and into a new life to be experienced after the flood. Jesus is also in this Ark with us because He is in her womb. We find safety in His presence during the dangers of life.

Effectual—producing or capable of producing an intended effect; adequate.

Efficacious—effective as a means, measure, remedy, etc.; having or showing the desired result or effect.

Affective—causing emotion or feeling.

Mary in a sense "hinders" her children from returning to sin by giving them a great abundance of graces and by helping them to remain in a state of grace.

> *176. This good Mother, out of pure charity, always receives whatever we deposit with her—and what she has once received as depositary, she is obliged in justice, by virtue of the contract of trusteeship, to keep safe for us; just as a person with whom I had left a thousand dollars in trust would be under the obligation of keeping them safe for me, so that if, by his negligence, they were lost, he would in justice be responsible to me for them. But the faithful Mary cannot let anything which has been entrusted to her be lost through her negligence. Heaven and earth could pass away sooner than that she could be negligent and faithless to those who trust in her.*

She does not lose or misplace any of the graces and good works which we entrust to her. As depositary of graces, she is the safest location in heaven and on earth.

> *177. Poor children of Mary, your weakness is extreme, your inconstancy is great, your inward nature is very much corrupted. You are drawn (I grant it) from the same corrupt mass as all the children of Adam and Eve. Yet do not be discouraged because of that. Console yourselves and exult in having the secret which I teach you—a secret unknown to almost all Christians, even the most devout. Leave not your gold and silver in your coffers, which have already been broken open by the evil spirits who have robbed you. These coffers are too little, too weak, too old, to hold a treasure so precious and so great. Put not the pure and clear water of the fountain into your vessels, all spoilt and infected by sin. If the sin is there no longer, at least the odor of it is, and so the water will be spoilt. Put not your exquisite wines into your old casks, which have had bad wine in them; else even these wines will be spoilt and per- haps break the casks, and be spilled on the ground.*

178. Though you, predestinate souls, understand me well enough, I will speak yet more openly. Trust not the gold of your charity, the silver of your purity, the waters of your heavenly graces, nor the wines of your merits and virtues, to a torn sack, an old and broken coffer, a spoilt and corrupted vessel, like yourselves, else you will be stripped by the robbers—that is to say, the demons—who are seeking and watching night and day for the right time to do it; and you will infect by your own bad odor of self-love, self-confidence and self-will, every most pure thing which God has given you. Pour, pour into the bosom and the heart of Mary all your treasures, all your graces, all your virtues. She is a spiritual vessel, she is a vessel of honor, she is a singular vessel of devotion. Since God Himself has been shut up in person, with all His perfections, in that vessel, it has become altogether spiritual, and the spiritual abode of the most spiritual souls. It has become honorable and the throne of honor for the grandest abode of the most spiritual souls. It has become honorable and the throne of honor for the grandest princes of eternity. It has become wonderful in devotion, and a dwelling the most illustrious for sweetness, for graces and for virtues. It has become rich as a house of gold, strong as a tower of David, and pure as a tower of ivory.

St. Louis addresses the reader in numbers 177-178 and advises him not to trust in his own charity, purity, graces, merits and virtues, because of our sinful nature. He warns, too, that evil spirits are seeking to destroy all the virtues we have obtained. St. Louis describes these spirits as "robbers" who are on the prowl waiting for an opportunity to steal God's gifts. He states, rather, that one should entrust all these virtues and graces to Mary's care where they will be well safeguarded from these robbers. If God the Father entrusted His very Son to her care, so much more should we be able to entrust ourselves to her. The titles "spiritual vessel, vessel of honor, vessel of devotion, house of gold, tower of David and tower of ivory" come from the Litany of Loretto.

179. Oh, how happy is the man who has given everything to Mary, and has entrusted himself to Mary, and lost himself in her, in everything and for everything! He belongs all to Mary, and Mary belongs all to him. He can say boldly with David: "Mary is made for me" (Cf. Ps. 118:56); or with the beloved disciple: "I have taken her for my own"(Jn. 19:27); or with Jesus Christ: "All that I have is thine, and all that thou hast it Mine." (Jn 17:10).

Psalm 118:56 Douay: "This has been mine, that I have observed your precepts."

Psalm119:56 NAB: "This is my good fortune, for I have observed your precepts."

John 19:27 NAB: "And from that hour the disciple took her into his home."

John 17:10 NAB: "I do not pray for the world but for the ones you have given me, because they are yours, and everything of mine is yours and everything of yours is mine, and I have been glorified in them."

These Scriptures from both the Psalm and the Gospel of John reinforce St. Louis' point that the totality of belonging to Mary and surrendering everything over to her is a cause of tremendous joy.

St. Louis resumes his teaching that such a trust in Mary produces a great happiness, delight and relief to the soul.

> *180. If any critic who reads this shall take it into his head that I speak here exaggeratedly, and with an extravagance of devotion, alas! He does not understand me—either because he is a carnal man who has no relish for spiritual things; or because he is a worldling who cannot receive the Holy Spirit; or because he is proud and critical, condemning and despising whatever he does not understand himself. But the souls which are not born of blood, nor of flesh, nor of the will of man (Jn. 1:13), but of God and Mary, understand me and relish me--and it is for these that I also write.*

Scriptures

John 1:13 CCD: "But to as many as received him he gave the power of becoming sons of God; to those who believe in his name: Who were born not of blood, nor of the will of the flesh, nor of the will of man, but of God."

John 1:13 NAB: "But to those who did accept him he gave power to become children of God, to those who believe in his name, who were born not by natural generation nor by human choice nor by a man's decision but of God."

St. Louis warns in this brief digression that not everyone will be capable of living the true devotion—especially those who live according to the cravings of the senses; those preoccupied with conforming to the ways of the world; and the proud and critical whose opinions prevent the growth of faith and trust. But, St. Louis brings this teaching to those born of God who will understand and relish this teaching. We recall that this lifestyle is truly a gift from God and as such we give Him thanks for the gift and never cease to ask for it that the beauty and mystery of this gift will continue to unveil itself throughout our lifetime.

181. Nevertheless, I say now, both for the former and the latter, in returning from this digression, that the divine Mary, being the most gracious and liberal of all pure creatures, never lets herself be outdone in love and liberality. As a holy man said of her, for an egg she gives an ox; that is to say, for a little that is given to her, she gives much of what she has received from God. Hence, if a soul gives itself to her without reserve, she gives herself to that soul without reserve, if only we put our confidence in her without presumption, and on our side labor to acquire virtues and to bridle our passions.

The lifestyle of true devotion is filled with so many graces beyond our expectations. A person who gives himself entirely to the Blessed Mother will also receive from her all that she is and has. We receive so much more than we can possibly give her. All that we have to do is trust her and work to live virtuously and to avoid sin.

182. Then let the faithful servants of the Blessed Virgin say boldly with St. John Damascene, "Having confidence in you, O Mother of God, I shall be saved; being under your protection, I shall fear nothing; with your help I shall give battle to my enemies and put them to flight; for devotion to you is an arm of salvation which God gives to those whom it is his will to save."

St. Louis quotes St. John Damascene, which he has transcribed from the works of two French writers, that devotion to Mary is a strength God gives to His children for conquering evil and leading them to Jesus.

183. Of all the truths which I have been explaining with regard to our Blessed Lady and her children and servants, the Holy Spirit gives us an admirable figure in the Scriptures (Gen. 27). It is in the story of Jacob, who received the blessing of his father Isaac through the skill and pains of his mother Rebecca. This is the story as the Holy Spirit relates it. I will afterward add the explanation of it.

St. Louis introduces his interpretation of the story of Jacob and Esau from Genesis 27 and he will use this Biblical story to compare the children of God who are both the reprobate and the elect in relationship to their Mother, Mary.

<u>Application of the Lifestyle of True Devotion</u>

1. What are the ways in which the true devotion helps me to persevere in virtue?
2. Why does St. Louis compare Mary to Noah's ark in paragraph 175?
3. What makes Mary such a safe depository?

4. What makes me "defective" in keeping the graces I've received?
5. Why do some people not understand this lifestyle described by St. Louis?
6. How does Mary help me to "labor to acquire virtue" and "bridle my passions"?

Article One

Rebecca and Jacob

I. *The Biblical Narrative*

184. Esau having sold Jacob his birthright, Rebecca, the mother of the two brothers, who loved Jacob tenderly, secured this advantage of the birthright for him many years afterward by a stroke of skill most holy but most full of mystery. Isaac, feeling very old, and wishing to bless his children before he died, called his son Esau, who was his favorite, and commanded him to go out hunting and get him something to eat, in order that he might afterward bless him. Rebecca promptly informed Jacob of what had passed, and ordered him to go and take two kids from the flock. When he had given them to his mother, she prepared for Isaac what she knew he liked. She clothed Jacob in the garments of Esau, which she kept, and covered his hands and his neck with the skin of the kids, so that his father, who was blind, even though he heard Jacob's voice, might think by touching the skin of his hands that it was Esau. Isaac, having been surprised by the voice, which he thought was Jacob's voice, made him come near. Having touched the skins with which his hands were covered, he said that the voice truly was the voice of Jacob, but that the hands were the hands of Esau. After he had eaten, and, in kissing Jacob, had smelt the odor of his perfumed garments, he blessed him and wished for him the dew of Heaven and the fruitfulness of earth. He made him lord over all his brethren and finished his blessing with these words: "Cursed be he that curseth thee, and let him that blesseth thee be filled with blessings." Isaac had hardly finished these words when Esau entered, bringing with him what he had captured while out hunting in order that his father might eat it, and then bless him. The holy patriarch was surprised with an incredible astonishment when he understood what had happened. But, far from retracting what he had done, on the contrary he confirmed it, for he saw plainly that the finger of God was in the matter. Esau then uttered great cries, as the Holy Scripture says, and loudly accusing the deceitfulness of his brother, he asked his father if he had but one blessing. In this conduct of his, as the holy Fathers remark, Esau was the image of those who are only too glad to ally God with the world and would fain enjoy both the consolations of Heaven and the consolations of earth. At last Isaac, touched with the cries of Esau, blessed him, but with a blessing of the earth, subjecting him to his brother. This made him conceive such an envenomed hatred for Jacob that he waited only for his father's death in order to attempt to kill him. Nor would Jacob have escaped death if his dear mother Rebecca had not saved him from it by her efforts and by the good counsels which she gave him, and which he followed.

II. Interpretation

185. Before explaining this beautiful story, we must observe that, according to the holy Fathers and the interpreters of Scripture, Jacob, is the figure of Jesus Christ and the predestinate, and Esau that of the reprobate. We have but to examine the actions and conduct of each to be convinced of this.

<u>1st Esau, figure of the reprobate.</u>

(1) Esau, the elder, was strong and robust of body, adroit and skillful in drawing the bow and in taking much game in the chase. (2) He hardly ever stayed in the house; and putting no confidence in anything but his own strength and address, he worked only out of doors. (3) He took very few pains to please his mother Rebecca, and indeed did nothing for that end. (4) He was such a glutton and loved eating so much that he sold his birthright for a mess of pottage. (5) He was, like Cain, full of envy against his brother, and persecuted him beyond measure.

186. Now this is the daily conduct of the reprobate. They trust in their own strength and aptitude for temporal affairs. They are very strong, very able and very enlightened in earthly business; but very weak and very ignorant in heavenly things.

In this comparison between Jacob and Esau, St. Louis begins with the Esau figure of the reprobate—those who are damned. He presents the following description of them:

--They trust in their own strength and worldly affairs.
--They are very able-minded in human and business affairs.
--They are ignorant of the supernatural life.
--They avoid all interiority and cultivation of holiness.
--They have a condescending attitude toward religious people and things.
--They are indifferent to Marian devotion in general.

--They are opposed to the lifestyle of true devotion.

--They live a superficial devotional life and do not imitate Mary's virtues.

--They are given to sensual appetites and desires.

--They antagonize and persecute the predestinate

187. It is on this account that they are never at all, or at least very seldom, at their own homes—that is to say, in their own interior, which is the inward and essential house which God has given to every man, to live there, after His example; for God always dwells in Himself. The reprobate do not love retirement, nor spirituality, nor inward devotion; and they treat as little, or as bigots, or as savages, those who are interior or retired from the world, and who work more within than without.

188. The reprobate care next to nothing for devotion to our Blessed Lady, the Mother of the predestinate. It is true that they do not hate her formally. Indeed they sometimes praise her and say they love her, and even practice some devotion in her honor. Nevertheless, they cannot bear that we should love her tenderly, because they have not the tenderness of Jacob for her. They find much to say against the practices of devotion her good children and servants faithfully perform in order to gain her affection, because they do not think that devotion necessary to salvation; and they consider that, provided that they do not hate Our Lady formally or openly despise her devotion, they do enough. Moreover, they imagine that they are already in her good graces, and that, in fine, they are her servants, inasmuch as they recite and mumble certain prayers in her honor, without tenderness for her or amendment in themselves.

189. The reprobate sell their birthright, that is to say, the pleasures of paradise. They sell it for a pottage of lentils, that is to say, for the pleasures of the earth. They laugh, they eat, they drink, they amuse themselves, they gamble, they dance, and take no more pains than Esau did to render themselves worthy of the blessing of their Father. In a word, they think only of earth and they love earth only; they speak and act only for earth and for its pleasures, selling for one moment of enjoyment, for one vain puff of honor, for a morsel of hard metal, yellow or white, their Baptismal grace, their robe of innocence and their heavenly inheritance.

190. Finally, the reprobate daily hate and persecute the predestinate, openly and secretly. They feel the predestinate are a burden to them, they despise them, they criticize them, they ridicule them, they abuse them, they rob them, they cheat them, they impoverish them, they drive them away, they bring them low into the dust; while they themselves are making fortunes, are taking their pleasures, getting themselves into good positions, enriching themselves, becoming greater and living at their ease.

St. Louis' description of the characteristics of the reprobate is self-explanatory. This is the lifestyle to be avoided because of its contempt for Mary and the interior life. Rather, St. Louis extols the Jacob figure, who represents the predestinate and the true devotee of Mary. They behave in the following way:

2ⁿᵈ Jacob, figure of the Predestinate

(a) Conduct of Jacob

191. As to Jacob, the younger son, he was of a feeble constitution, meek and peaceful. He lived for the most part at home, in order to gain the good graces of his mother Rebecca, whom he loved tenderly. If he went abroad, it was not of his own will, nor through any confidence in his own will, but to obey his mother.

192. He loved and honored his mother. It was on this account that he kept at home. He was never so happy as when watching her. He avoided everything which could displease her, and did everything which he thought would please her; and this increased the love which Rebecca already had for him.

193. He was subject in all things to his dearest mother. He obeyed her entirely in all matters—promptly, without delaying, and lovingly, without complaining. At the least indication of her will, the little Jacob ran and worked; and he believed, without questioning, everything she said to him. For example, when she told him to fetch two kids in order that she might prepare something for his father Isaac to eat, Jacob did not reply that one was enough to make a dish for a single man, but did without argument what she told him to do.

194. He had great confidence in his dear mother. As he did not rely in the least on his own ability, he depended exclusively on her care and protection. He appealed to her in all his necessities, and consulted her in all his doubts. For example, when he asked if, instead of a blessing, he should not receive a curse from his father, he believed her and trusted her when she said that she would take the curse upon herself.

195. Lastly, he imitated as far as he could the virtues he saw in his mother. It seems as if one of his reasons for leading such a sedentary life at home was to imitate his dear mother, who was virtuous, and kept away from bad companions who corrupt the morals. By this means he made himself worthy of receiving the double blessing of his beloved father

(b) Conduct of the Predestinate

196. Such also is the conduct which the predestinate daily observe. They are sedentary and homekeepers with their Mother. In other words, they love retirement and are interior. They give themselves to prayer; but it is after the example and in the company of their Mother, the holy Virgin, the whole of whose glory is within, and who during her entire life loved retirement and prayer so much. It is true that they sometimes appear without, in the world; but it is in obedience to the will of God and that of their dear Mother, to fulfill, the duties of their state. However apparently important their outward works may be, they esteem still more highly those which they do within themselves, in their interior, in the company of the Blessed Virgin. For it is within that they accomplish the great work of their perfection, compared with which all their other works are but child's play. It is on this account that, while sometimes their brothers and sisters are working outwardly with such energy, success and skill, in the praise and with the approbation of the world, they on the contrary know by the light of the Holy Spirit that there is far more glory, more good and more joy in remaining hidden in retreat with Jesus Christ, their Model, in an entire and perfect subjection to their Mother, than to do of themselves wonders of nature and grace in the world, as so many Esaus and reprobates do. "Glory for God and riches for men are to be found in the house of Mary." (Cf. Ps 111:3). Lord Jesus, how sweet are Thy tabernacles! The sparrow has found a house to lodge in, and the turtledove a nest for her little ones. Oh, happy is the man who dwells in the house of Mary, where Thou wast the first to make Thy dwelling! It is in this house of the predestinate that he receives assistance from Thee alone, and that he has arranged in his heart the steps and ascents of all the virtues by which to raise himself to perfection in this vale of tears. "How lovely are Thy tabernacles. " (Ps. 83:2)

Psalm 111:3 Douay: "Wealth and riches shall be in his house; his generosity shall endure forever."

Psalm 112:3 NAB: "Wealth and riches shall be their homes; their prosperity shall endure forever."

Psalm 83:2 Douay: "How lovely is your dwelling place, O Lord of hosts!"

Psalm 84:2 NAB: "How lovely your dwelling, O Lord of hosts!"

St. Louis adapts these psalms to emphasize that union with Mary produces far greater riches and wealth than any other kind of spiritual exercise. Union with Mary is a holy union because it is in her that the Lord Jesus made His dwelling, by means of the Incarnation. St. Louis begins to outline the perfection of the predestinate in contrast to the corruption of the reprobate; that is, those who love devotion to Mary and those who despise it. This metaphor reinforces ideas already mentioned in this book. St. Louis continues these themes in the following paragraphs.

> 197. The predestinate tenderly love and truly honor our Blessed Lady as their good Mother and Mistress. They love her not only in word but in truth. They honor her not only outwardly but in the depths of their hearts. They avoid, like Jacob, everything which can displease her; and they practice with fervor whatever they think will make them find favor with her. They bring to her and give her, not two kids, as did Jacob to Rebecca, but their body and their soul, with all that depends on them, symbolized by the two kids of Jacob. They bring them to her: (1) that she may receive them as things which belong to her; (2) that she may kill them, that is, make them die to sin and self, by stripping them of their own skin and their own self-love, so as by this means to please Jesus, her Son, who wills not to have any for His disciples and friends but those who are dead to themselves: (3) that she may prepare them for the taste of our heavenly Father, and for His greatest glory, which she knows better than any other creature; and (4) that by her care and intercession this body and soul, thoroughly purified from every stain, thoroughly dead, thoroughly stripped and prepared, may be a delicate meat, worthy of the mouth and the blessing of our heavenly Father. Is this not what the predestinate do, who by way of testifying to Jesus and Mary an effective and courageous love, relish and practice the perfect consecration to Jesus Christ by the hands of Mary which we are now teaching them?
>
> The reprobate will tell us loudly enough that they love Jesus, and that they love and honor Mary; but it is not with their substance (Prov. 3:9), it is not to the extent of sacrificing their body with its senses, their soul with its passions, as the predestinate do.

Proverbs 3:9 Douay: "Honor the Lord with thy substance, and give him of the first of all thy fruits."

Psalm 3:9 NAB: "Honor the Lord with your wealth, with first fruits of all your produce."

St. Louis cites these Scriptures to illustrate that those who are not the true children of Mary (the condemned) do not give themselves entirely to her; although they may partially acknowledge her. The gift of self-donation to Jesus through Mary is a total gift of one's whole being which makes this consecration so unique. Mary prepares her children, body and soul, for the Heavenly Father, as St. Louis will describe further.

> *198. The predestinate are subject and obedient to our Blessed Lady as to their good Mother, after the example of Jesus Christ, who, of the three and thirty years He lived on earth, employed thirty to glorify God His Father by a perfect and entire subjection to His holy Mother. They obey Mary in following her counsels exactly as the little Jacob did those of Rebecca, who said to him: "My son, follow my counsels" (Gen. 27:8); or like the people at the marriage of Cana, to whom Our Lady said: "Whatever my Son shall say to you, that do." (Jn. 2:5). Jacob, for having obeyed his mother, received the blessings as it were miraculously, although naturally he would not have had it. The people at the marriage of Cana, for having followed Our Lady's counsel, were honored with the first miracle of Our Lord, who there changed the water into wine at the prayer of His holy Mother. In like manner, all those who, to the end of time, shall receive the blessing of our heavenly Father, and shall be honored with the wonders of God, shall only receive their graces as a result of their perfect obedience to Mary. The Esaus, on the contrary, lose their blessing through their want of subjection to the Blessed Virgin.*

Scriptures

Genesis 27:8 Douay: "Now my son, do what I tell you."
Genesis 27:8 NAB: "Now son, listen carefully to what I tell you."
John 2:5 NAB: "His mother said to the servers, "Do whatever he tells you."

Again, St. Louis has recourse to Sacred Scripture to emphasize total obedience to Mary who intercedes on their behalf and in their best interests. He maintains that there are many graces lost by disobedience to Mary.

> *199. The predestinate have also great confidence in the goodness and power of our Blessed Lady, their good Mother. They call incessantly for her help. They look upon her as their polar star, to*

lead them to a good port. They lay bare to her their troubles and their necessities with much openness of heart. They depend on her mercy and her gentleness, in order to obtain pardon of their sins through her intercession, or to taste her maternal sweetness in their troubles and weariness. They even throw themselves, hide themselves and lose themselves in an admirable manner in her loving and virginal bosom, that they may be enkindled there with the fire of pure love, that they may be cleansed there from their least stain, and fully find Jesus, who dwells there as on His most glorious throne. Oh, what happiness! "Think not," says Abbot Gueric, "that it is happier to dwell in Abraham's bosom than in Mary's; for it is in this last that Our Lord has placed His throne." The reprobate, on the contrary, put all their trust in themselves. They only eat, with the prodigal, what the swine eat. They eat earth like the toads, and, like the children of the world, they love only visible and external things. They have no relish for the sweetness of Mary's bosom. They have not the feeling of a certain resting-place and a sure confidence, which the predestinate feel in the holy Virgin, their good Mother. They are miserably attached to their outward hunger, as St. Gregory says, because they do not wish to taste the sweetness which is prepared within themselves, and within Jesus and Mary.

Who's Who?

Blessed Guerric of Igny died in 1157. He was a Cistercian monk and the second abbot of the Monastery of Igny, France. This reference is from his sermon on the Assumption of Mary. He writes also on her spiritual motherhood, holiness and action as mediatrix.[1]

Pope St. Gregory the Great lived from 540-604. He was elected pope in 590. He is a Doctor of the Church and an important pope in ensuring the supreme authority of the papacy and in restoring Rome after the devastating invasions, pillages and earthquakes of the 5th Century.[2]

A listing of some of the qualities identifying the predestinate and the reprobate include the following:

Predestinate	Reprobate
--Have confidence in Mary	--Trust only in themselves
--Seek her intercession	--Live only visible and external realities
--Hide nothing from her	--Given over to sensuality
--Call upon her mercy and love	--Attached to compulsions and sinful appetites
--Hide themselves in the love of her Immaculate Heart	--Disdain Mary's virtues
--Allow her to cleanse them	--Superficial devotion to Mary at best
--Imitate Mary's virtues	

200. Lastly, the predestinate keep the ways of our Blessed Lady, their good Mother; that is to say, they imitate her. It is on this point that they are truly happy and truly devout, and bear the infallible mark of their predestination, according to the words this good Mother speaks to them: Blessed are they who practice my virtues (Prov. 8:32), and with the help of divine grace walk in the footsteps of my life. During life they are happy in this world through the abundance of grace and sweetness which I impart to them from my fullness, and more abundantly to them than to others who do not imitate me so closely. They are happy in their death, which is mild and tranquil, and at which I am ordinarily present myself, that I may conduct them to the joys of eternity; for never has any one of my good servants been lost who imitated my virtues during life. The reprobate, on the contrary, are unhappy during their life, at their death and for eternity, because they do not imitate Our Lady in her virtues, but content themselves with sometimes being enrolled in her confraternities, reciting some prayers in her honor, or going through some other exterior devotion. O holy Virgin, my good Mother, how happy are those (I repeat it with the transports of my heart), how happy are those who, not letting themselves be seduced by a false devotion toward you, faithfully keep your ways, your counsels and your orders! But how unhappy and accursed are those who abuse your devotion, and keep not the commandments of your Son: "Cursed are all who fall from Thy commandments!" (Ps. 118:21).

Scriptures

Proverbs 8:32 Douay: "Now therefore, ye children, hear me: Blessed are they that keep my ways."

Proverbs 8:32-33 NAB: "So now, O children, listen to me; instruction and wisdom do not reject! Happy the man who obeys me, and happy those who keep my ways..."

Psalm 118:21 Douay: "You rebuke the accursed proud, who turn away from your commands."

Psalm 119: 21 NAB: "With a curse you rebuke the proud who stray from your commands."

St. Louis refers to Proverbs to announce God's blessings upon those who imitate the virtues of the Blessed Mother by means of this devotion and on the contrary, he demonstrates that those who abuse this devotion will receive a curse and not a blessing. Those who practice the lifestyle of true devotion and imitate Mary's virtues experience the following:

--There is no conflict for them between their exterior activity and their interior devotion.

--They have love and honor for Mary.

--They make the total self-donation to Mary of their body and soul.

--This self-donation is complete; not partial or withholding something.

--They are subject and obedient to Mary.

--They live their interior lives in union with Mary.

--They obtain God's blessings by obedience to Mary.

--They have confidence in Mary's goodness and power.

--They prefer lives of hiddenness in the Immaculate Heart of Mary.

--They live in imitation of Mary's virtues.

Application of the Lifestyle of True Devotion

1. Explain the difference between the reprobate and the elect.
2. What is the orientation of the reprobate and the elect towards Mary?
3. What is Mary's action on behalf of the elect?

Article Two

The Blessed Virgin and Her Slaves of Love

201. Let us now turn to look at the charitable duties which our Blessed Lady, as the best of all mothers, fulfills for the faithful servants who have given themselves to her after the manner I have described, and according to the figure of Jacob.

St. Louis now presents five points indicating how Mary fulfills her divine motherhood and takes care of her children following the interpretation of the Jacob/Esau story in the preceding paragraphs.

I. She Loves Them

She loves them: " I love those who love me." (Prov. 8:17). She loves them: (1) because she is their true Mother, and a mother always loves her child, the fruit of her womb; (2) out of gratitude, because they effectively love her as their good Mother; (3) because, as they are predestinate, God loves them: "Jacob I have loved, but Esau I have hated" (Rom. 9:13); (4) because they are entirely consecrated to her, and are her portion and her inheritance: "Let thy inheritance be in Israel." (Ecclus. 24:13).

Scriptures

Proverbs 8:17 Douay: "I love them that love me; and they that in the morning early watch for me, shall find me."

Proverbs 8:17 NAB: "Those who love me I also love, and those who seek me find me."

Romans 9:13 NAB: "As it is written, I loved Jacob, but hated Esau."

Ecclesiasticus 24:13 Douay: "And he said to me: Let thy dwelling be in Jacob, and thy inheritance in Israel, and take root in my elect."

Sirach 24:8 NAB: "Then the Creator of all gave me his command, and he who formed me chose the spot for my tent, saying, 'In Jacob make your dwelling, in Israel your inheritance.'"

St. Louis cites these Scriptures to emphasize Mary's love for her children and her vocation to motherhood.

This paragraph examines the question: *why* does Mary love her children? She loves them because she is a true mother; not just a symbolic mother. She loves them because they love her and because God loves them.

> *202. She loves them tenderly, and more tenderly than all other mothers put together. Throw, if you can, all the natural love which all the mothers of the world have for their children into the heart of one mother for one only child. Surely that mother will love that child immensely. Nevertheless, it is true that Mary loves her children still more tenderly than that mother would love that child of hers. She loves them not only with affection but with efficacy. Her love for them is active and effective, like that of Rebecca for Jacob, and far beyond it. See what this good Mother, of whom Rebecca was but the type, does to obtain for her children the blessing of our heavenly Father.*

This paragraph examines the question: *how* does Mary love her children? She loves them with a tenderness that surpasses natural motherhood because she is full of grace. And she loves with an efficacy which is very powerful because she is the Queen of heaven and earth.

> *203. 1st) She is on the lookout, as Rebecca was, for favorable occasions to do them good, to advance and enrich them. She sees clearly all good and evil, all prosperous and adverse fortunes, the blessings and the cursings of God; and then she so disposes things from afar that she may exempt her servants from all sorts of evils, and obtain for them all sorts of blessings; so that if there is a good fortune to make by the fidelity of a creature to any high employment, it is certain that Mary will procure that good fortune for some of her true children and servants, and will give them the grace to go through with it faithfully: "She herself takes care of our interests," says a certain saint.*

Mary is ever vigilant to do good things for her children, to obtain for them occasions for growing in grace, to enrich them in virtues and to protect them from evil. Those who practice this lifestyle receive her constant help throughout the day in ways perhaps they will never know in this life. It is similar to little children who do not appreciate what their mother does for them. Consequently, our attitude then should be one of thanksgiving to her at the end of every day even when we don't see her hand directly involved in things. We know by faith that she is involved in every aspect of our lives.

> *204. 2ⁿᵈ) She also gives them good counsels, as Rebecca did to Jacob: "My Son, follow my counsels." (Gen 27:8). Among other counsels, she inspires them to bring her the two kids, that is to say, their body and soul, and to consecrate them to her, so that she may make of them a dish agreeable to God; and she inspires them to do everything which Jesus Christ her Son has taught by his words and his examples. If it is not by herself that she gives these counsels, it is by the ministry of angels, who have no greater honor or pleasure than to descend to earth to obey any of her commands, and to help any of her servants.*

Scriptures

Genesis 27: 8 Douay: "Now my son, do what I tell you."
Genesis 27:8 NAB: "Now, son, listen carefully to what I tell you."
In this passage from the Rebecca/Jacob account, St. Louis highlights again the active role of Mother and son. That is, Mary encourages us to listen to her and follow her counsels. The true devotee patiently listens to her and follows those counsels after careful discernment and in obedience to her and the Church.

Mary advises her children. She advises them how to surrender their body and soul to Jesus. She advises them how to be obedient to the Gospel and the teachings of the Church and her counsel cannot contradict the Gospel and Church teaching. This is an area of discernment which grows over time. Her children also grow in a devotion and an appreciation for the angels, the messengers of God, who work to strengthen their conscience.

> *205. 3ʳᵈ) When they have brought to her and consecrated to her their body and soul, and all that depends on them, without excepting anything, what does that good Mother do? Just what Rebecca did of old with the two kids Jacob brought her: (1) She kills them, makes them die to the life of the old Adam. (2) She flays and strips them of their natural skin, their natural inclinations, their self-love, their own will and all attachment to creatures. (3) She cleanses them of their spots, their vilenesses and their sins. (4) She dresses them to the taste of God, and for His greatest glory; and as it is Mary alone who knows perfectly what the divine taste is, and what the greatest glory of the Most High is, it is Mary*

alone who, without making any mistake, can adapt and dress our body and soul for that taste infinitely exalted, and for that glory infinitely hidden.

Mary leads her children through a developmental growth in holiness as they daily exercise the lifestyle of true devotion. This growth process includes:

Repentance--the person develops a new fervor for the Sacrament of Reconciliation. He or she desires to turn away from sin more and more and to live in grace. The desire to receive the Sacrament should not proceed from a false humility, but from a humble recognition of the virtue of purity and holiness that Mary is obtaining for him.

Mortification--the child of Mary develops a greater desire to "die to self"— that is to rid oneself of all the sinful inclinations and motivations that have obscured doing everything for God's will alone. He or she desires to mortify all of the senses, to reduce and control immediate gratification. This grace Mary obtains for us to detach us from earthly and worldly desires (not necessities).

Purification--the person desires to be purified through the trials and crosses that occur in life and to unite his or her sufferings with Jesus. He desires not to complain against those trials, but to see in everything God's holy will and divine providence. Mary obtains this virtue of faith and trust in God and not in ourselves.

Formation--the child of Mary desires to be formed or "clothed" in virtue; especially the virtues of Mary with which she clothes him. The formation in virtue requires the constant attentiveness to exercise the virtues and to pray to acquire them by the intercession of the Blessed Virgin. Mary obtains for us a share in her virtues.

> *206. 4ᵗʰ) This good Mother, having received the perfect offering which we make to her of ourselves and our merits and satisfactions, by the devotion I am describing, strips us of our worldly garments; she cleanses us and so makes us worthy to appear before our heavenly Father. (1) She clothes us in the clean, new, precious and perfumed garments of Esau the elder—that is, of Jesus Christ her Son—which she keeps in her house, that is, which she has in her own power, inasmuch as she is the treasurer and universal dispenser of the merits and virtues of her Son, which she gives and communicates to whom she wills, when she wills, as she wills, and in such quantity as she wills; as we have seen before. (2) She covers the neck and the hands of her servants with the skins of the kids she has killed; that is to say, she adorns them with the merits and value of their own actions. She kills and mortifies, it is true, all that is impure and imperfect in them, but she neither loses nor dissipates one atom of the good which grace has done there. On the contrary, she preserves and*

*augments it, to make it the ornament and the strength of their
neck and their hands; that is to say, to fortify them and help them
carry the yoke of the Lord, which is worn upon the neck, and to
work great things for the glory of God and the salvation of their
poor brethren. (3) She bestows a new perfume and a new grace
upon their garments and adornments in communicating to them
her own garments, that is, her merits and virtues, which she be-
queathed to them by her testament when she died; as said a holy
religious of the last century, who died in the odor of sanctity,
and learnt this by revelation. Thus all her domestics, faithful
servants and slaves, are doubly clad in the garments of her Son
and in her own: "All her domestics are clothed in double clothing." (Prov. 31:21). It is on this account that they have nothing
to fear from the cold of Jesus Christ, who is white as snow—a
cold which the reprobate, all naked and stripped of the merits of
Jesus and Mary, cannot for one moment bear.*

<u>Scriptures</u>

Proverbs 31:21 Douay: "She shall not fear for her house in the cold of snow:
for all her domestics are clothed with double garments."

Proverbs 31:21 NAB: "She fears not the snow for her household; all her
charges are doubly clad."

St. Louis quotes from Proverbs the special blessing of graces that devotees
of Mary receive. They receive a double portion and should not fear that they will
lack anything, because her care is so all encompassing. She anticipates every
need and every desire and fulfills it perfectly in accord with the Father's will for
that individual soul.

Mary clothes us in the graces of Jesus. She brings to perfection the merits of
all that has been offered up to Him by our sacrifices and prayers. She adds her
own merits and virtues to augment ours so that her children may be beautifully
dressed and protected. The imagery of clothing is not just poetic; it describes
the protection of her Immaculate Mantle which she wraps around us to protect
us from the Evil One and the darts of temptations that come to us. Like a shield,
her clothing over us protects our fragile body and soul. On another level of understanding, her clothing us is like being invested with a religious habit. Just as
those in religious life are clothed in the habit of their order, so are we who are
consecrated to her clothed in the "habit" of her virtues, graces and protection.
This clothing is symbolically manifested externally by the wearing of scapulars,
miraculous medals, etc.

*207. 5th) Finally, she enables them to obtain the blessing of
our heavenly Father, though being but the youngest born and indeed only adopted children, they have no natural right to have it.*

With these garments all new, most precious and of most fragrant odor, and with their body and soul well prepared and dressed, they draw near with confidence to the Father's bed of repose. He understands and distinguishes their voice, which is the voice of the sinner; He touches their hands, covered with skins; He smells the good odor of their clothes; He eats with joy of that which Mary their mother has dressed for Him. He recognizes in them the merits and the good odor of His Son and of His holy Mother, and so: First, He gives them His double blessing, the blessing of the "dew of Heaven" (Gen. 27:28), that is to say, of divine grace, which is the seed of glory: "He hath blessed us with spiritual blessings in Christ" (Eph. 1:3): and then the blessing "of the fat of the earth" (Gen. 27:28); that is to say, the good Father gives them their daily bread, and a sufficient abundance of the goods of this world. Secondly, he makes them masters of their other brethren, the reprobate. But this primacy is not always apparent in this world, which passes in an instant (1 Cor. 7:31), and where the reprobate are often masters. "How long shall sinners glory? Shall they utter and speak iniquity?" (Ps. 93:3-4). "I have seen the wicked highly exalted and lifted up." (Ps. 36:35). But it is nevertheless a true primacy; and it will appear manifestly in the other world for all eternity, where the just, as the Holy Spirit says, "shall reign over the nations and command them." (Wis. 3:8). Thirdly, His Majesty, not content with blessing them in their person and their goods, blesses also those who shall bless them and curses those who shall curse and persecute them.

Scriptures

Genesis 27:28 NAB: "May God give to you the dew of the heavens and of the fertility of the earth abundance of grain and wine."

Ephesians 1:3-4 NAB: "Blessed be the God and Father of Our Lord Jesus Christ, who has blessed us in Christ with every spiritual blessing in the heavens, as he chose us in him, before the foundation of the world to be holy and without blemish before him."

1 Corinthians 7:31 NAB: "For the world in its present form is passing away."

Psalm 93(94):3-4 NAB: "How long, Lord, shall the wicked, how long shall the wicked glory? How long will they mouth haughty speeches, go on boasting, all these evildoers?"

Psalm 36:35 Douay: " I saw a wicked man, fierce, and stalwart as a flourishing, age-old tree."

Palm 37:35 NAB:"I have seen ruthless scoundrels, strong as flourishing cedars."

Wisdom 3:8 Douay: "They shall judge nations, and rule over people, and their Lord shall reign for ever."

Wisdom 3:8 NAB: "They shall judge nations and rule over peoples, and the Lord shall be their King forever."

In these many Scripture passages from the Old and New Testament, St. Louis simply reveals aspects of the Father's blessing that Mary obtains for her children. These blessings include: life, the grace of Christ necessary for salvation, their material needs on earth, their ultimate triumph over evil, and eventually eternal life in Heaven.

Mary presents her children to the Father in Heaven. He recognizes in them their special consecration to Jesus through her. He:

(1) Blesses them to provide for both their spiritual and material needs.

(2) He makes them conquerors over the ungodly.

(3) He extends His blessing upon those whom they love and His protection against their enemies.

II.   *She Fosters and Nurtures Them.*

208.   The second charitable duty which our Blessed Lady fulfills toward her faithful servants is that she furnishes them with everything, both for their body and for their soul. She gives them double clothing, as we have just seen. She gives them to eat of the most exquisite meats of the table of God; for she gives them to eat of the bread of life, which she herself has formed (Ecclus. 24:26). My dear children, she says, under the name of Divine Wisdom, be filled with my generations; that is to say, with Jesus, the fruit of life, whom I have brought into the world for you. (Prov. 9:5). Come, she repeats to them in another place, eat my bread, which is Jesus, and drink the wine of His love, which I have mixed for you. (Canticles 5:1). As it is Mary who is the treasurer and dispenser of the gifts and graces of the Most High, she gives a good portion, and indeed the best portion, to nourish and maintain her children and her servants. They are fattened on the Living Bread, they are inebriated with the wine which brings forth virgins. (Zach. 9:17). They are borne at the bosom of Mary. (Is.66:12). They have such facility in carrying the yoke of Jesus Christ that they feel almost nothing of its weight; the oil of devotion has made it soften and decay: "And the yoke shall putrefy in the presence of the oil." (Is. 10:27).

Ecclesiasticus 24:26 Douay:"Come over to me, all ye that desire me, and be filled with my fruits."

Sirach 24:18 NAB: "Come to me, all you that yearn for me, and be filled with my fruits."

Proverbs 9:5 NAB: "Come, eat of my food, and drink of the wine I have mixed!"

Cantlicles 5:1 Douay: "I am come into my garden O, my sister, my spouse, I have gathered my myrrh, with my aromatical spices: I have eaten the honeycomb with my honey. I have drunk my wine with my milk:..."

Songs 5:1 NAB: "I have come to my garden, my sister, my bride; I gather my myrrh and my spices, I eat my honey and my sweetmeats, I drink my wine and my milk."

Zechariah 9:17 CCD: " For what is the good thing of him and what is his beautiful thing, but the corn of the elect, and wine springing forth virgins?"

Zechariah 9:17 NAB: "For what wealth is theirs, and what beauty! Grain that makes the youths flourish, and new wine, the maidens!"

Isaiah 66:12 CCD: "For thus saith the Lord: Behold I will bring upon her as it were a river of peace, and as an overflowing torrent the glory of the Gentiles, which you shall suck; you shall be carried at the breasts, and upon the knees they shall caress you."

Isaiah 66:12 NAB: "For thus says the Lord: Lo, I will spread prosperity over her like a river, and the wealth of the nations like an overflowing torrent. As nurslings, you shall be carried in her arms, and fondled in her lap..."

Isaiah 10:27 CCD: "And it shall come to pass in that day, that his burden shall be taken away from off thy shoulder, and his yoke from off thy neck, and the yoke shall putrefy at the presence of the oil."

Isaiah 10:27 NAB: "On that day, His burden shall be taken from your shoulder, and his yoke shattered from your neck."

St. Louis makes beautiful allusions with these Scripture passages to Mary feeding her children. She feeds them on the Eucharist. The body and blood of Jesus is formed in her womb by means of the Incarnation before it became sacramentally present to the world. She forms religious vocations and nurtures them. She herself personally intervenes in their formation and she renews them in zeal. Mary provides out of her charity for the bodies and souls of her children. She leads them especially to the Mass and reception of the Eucharist. Every vocation finds its nourishment in her and from her and she feeds them with the best of milk: "the bread of life and the cup of eternal salvation."

III.   *She Conducts and Directs Them*

209. The third good which Our Lady does for her servants is that she conducts and directs them according to the will of her Divine Son. Rebecca guided her little Jacob, and gave him good advice from time to time; either to draw upon him the blessing of his father or to avert from him the hatred and persecutions of his brother Esau. Mary, who is the Star of the Sea, leads all her faithful servants into a safe harbor. She shows them the paths of eternal life. She makes them avoid the dangerous places. She conducts them by her hand along the path of justice. She steadies them when they are about to fall; she lifts them up when they have fallen. She reproves them like a charitable mother when they fail; and sometimes she even lovingly chastises them. Can a child obedient to Mary, his foster-Mother and his enlightened guide, go astray in the paths of eternity? "If you follow her," says St. Bernard, "you cannot wander from the road." Fear not, therefore, that a true child of Mary can be deceived by the evil one, or fall into any formal heresy. There where the guidance of Mary is, neither the evil spirit with his illusions, nor the heretics with their subtleties, can ever come.

Mary keeps her chosen souls within the Divine Will of Jesus Christ. Mary teaches them to do good and to avoid evil. The lifestyle of true devotion cannot be opposed to God's will for an individual soul since it consists in the daily renewal of the baptismal promises, imitation of Mary's virtues and the complete donation of one's self to her in order to be completely conformed to Jesus Christ. This does not mean that temptations will not occur, but the grace to resist those temptations and to recognize them increases through true devotion.

IV.   *She Defends and Protects Them.*

210. The fourth good office which Our Lady renders to her children and faithful servants is to protect and defend them against their enemies. Rebecca, by her cares and artifices, delivered Jacob from all the dangers in which he found himself, and particularly from the death which his brother Esau would have inflicted on him because of the envy and hatred which he bore him; as Cain did of old to his brother Abel. Mary, the good Mother of the predestinate, hides them under the wings of her protection, as a hen hides her chickens. She speaks, she stoops down to them, she condescends to all their weaknesses. To secure them from the hawk and vulture, she puts herself round about them, and accompanies them "like an army in battle array." (Canticle 6:3). Shall a man who has an army of a hundred thousand soldiers around him fear his enemies? A faithful servant of Mary, surrounded by her protection and her imperial power, has still less to fear. This good Mother and powerful Princess of the Heavens would rather dispatch battalions of millions of angels to assist one of her servants than that it should ever be said that a faithful servant of Mary, who trusted in her, had had to succumb to the malice, the number and the vehemence of his enemies.

Scriptures

Canticles 6:3 CCD: "Thou art beautiful, O my love, sweet and comely as Jerusalem: terrible as an army set in array."

Songs 6:4 NAB: "You are as beautiful as Tirzah my beloved, as lovely as Jerusalem, as awe-inspiring as bannered troops."

St. Louis uses this Scripture to portray the image of Mary gathering her children under her protection against the wiles of the enemy. She shields them from his attacks placing her body between her children and the Enemy.

Mary protects her children. She personally ensures their safety by wrapping her Immaculate Mantle around them. She hides them from their enemies. In the spiritual warfare of good and evil she claims her children as her army and is thus able to hide them from death. St. Louis presents two images of birds of prey: the hawk who attacks living things, and the vulture which attacks dying things. She protects us from the hawk who would destroy us when we're alive in a state of grace, and she protects us from the vulture who would destroy us when we have been gravely wounded by sin and the loss of grace. In addition, Mary has millions of angels at her command to protect her children in this spiritual warfare.

V.   *She Intercedes For Them*

211. Lastly, the fifth and greatest good which Mary procures for her faithful clients is to intercede for them with her Son, to appease Him by her prayers, to unite them to Him in a most intimate union, and to keep them unshaken in that union. Rebecca made Jacob draw near to his father's bed. The good man touched him, embraced him, and even kissed him with joy, being content and satisfied with the well-dressed viands which the boy had brought him; and having smelt with much contentment the exquisite perfume of his garments, he cried out: "Behold the odor of my son, which is like the odor of a full field that the Lord hath blessed." (Gen. 27:27). This odor of the full field which charms the heart of the Father is nothing else than the odor of the virtues and merits of Mary, who is a field full of grace where God the Father has sown His only Son, as grain of the wheat of the elect. Oh, how welcome to Jesus Christ, the Father of the world to come, is a child perfumed with the good odor of Mary! (Is. 9:6). Oh, how promptly and how perfectly is such a child united to his Lord! But we have shown this at length already.

Scriptures

Gen. 27:27 NAB: "Ah, the fragrance of my son is like the fragrance of a field that the Lord has blessed!"

Isaiah 9:6 CCD: " For a Child is born to us, and a son is given to us, and the government is upon his shoulder: and his name shall be called, Wonderful, Counselor, God the Mighty, the Father of the world to come, the Prince of peace."

Isaiah 9:6 NAB: "For a child is born to us, a son is given us; upon his shoulder dominion rests. They name him Wonder-Counselor, God-Hero, Father-Forever, Prince of Peace."

In these Scriptures St. Louis alludes to Mary's role as mediatrix and intercessor. Her children take on her perfume which became a pleasing odor to the Father in Heaven and to Jesus Christ His Son.

Mary intercedes for her children with her Son to lead them into divine union with Him. She also preserves them in grace lest they be tempted to choose sin. Mary is constantly vigilant with her children to protect and defend them without ever sleeping or losing her vigilance.

212. Furthermore, after Mary has heaped her favors upon her children and faithful servants, and has obtained for them the blessing of the heavenly Father and union with Jesus Christ, she preserves them in Jesus and Jesus in them. She takes care of them, watches over them always, for fear they should lose the grace of God and fall into the snares of their enemies. "She retains the saints in their fullness," and makes them persevere to the end, as we have seen. This is the interpretation of the story of Jacob and Esau, that great and ancient figure of predestination and reprobation, so unknown and so full of mysteries.

The lifestyle of true devotion is also one which involves the preservation of graces received so that the child of Mary lives in a state of equilibrium; that is, there are not states of frequent fluctuation between mortal sin and grace. It may take time during the initial formation process of purification to reach this equilibrium so one ought not be discouraged but keep his eyes focused on the Mother who brings this about. This paragraph concludes St. Louis' application of the Jacob/Esau parallel with the predestinate/reprobate and true/false devotees of Mary.

Application of the Lifestyle of True Devotion

1. Why does Mary love her children? Why does she love you?
2. How does Mary love her children? How does she love you?
3. What are the ways and how often do you thank Mary for the occasions on which she has procured special graces for you?
4. In what way did Mary first inspire you to make the consecration to Jesus through her?
5. How has Mary led me to repentance, mortification, purification and formation?
6. In what ways does Mary dress me in the virtues of her Son?
7. How does Mary obtain God's blessing for me and for my descendants?
8. How has Mary intervened in my life to furnish me with what I needed for body and soul?
9. Explain how Mary keeps me in the divine will of her Son, Jesus.
10. How does Mary defend and protect me in the spiritual warfare? When do I seek her protection?
11. Why is intercession the greatest good that Mary performs for her children?

Chapter III

Wonderful Effects of This Devotion

213. My dear brother, be sure that if you are faithful to the interior and exterior practices of this devotion which I will point out, the following effects will take place in your soul.

Now begins St. Louis' treatment of seven effects one will experience when he consecrates himself to Jesus through Mary. As we practice the lifestyle of true devotion we will notice these effects taking place in our soul. The effects lead us progressively away from self-love ultimately to a life glorifying God. This way of living is, of course, how Mary lived.

– First Effect –

<u>Knowledge and Contempt of Self</u>

By the light which the Holy Spirit will give you through His dear spouse, Mary, you will understand your own evil, your corruption and your incapacity for anything good. In consequence of this knowledge, you will despise yourself. You will think of yourself only with horror. You will regard yourself as a snail that spoils everything with its slime; or a toad, that poisons everything with its venom; or as a spiteful serpent seeking only to deceive. In other words, the humble Mary will communicate to you a portion of her profound humility, which will make you despise yourself—despise nobody else, but love to be despised yourself.

St. Louis introduces the first of seven effects which takes place in the person who practices the lifestyle of true devotion. The idea of despising oneself should not be seen in the modern psychological light of low self-esteem or neurosis, but in the spiritual sense of humility. We recognize that our desire to do evil is quite strong and that without God's grace we would have no hope for salvation or goodness. "Without me you can do nothing" (John 15:5). Humility leads us to truth about our relationship with God. One of the first effects then is the gift of Mary's humility. We see in ourselves our great capacity for corruption, destruction and deception. This is where we would be without God's grace which St. Louis vividly describes us as snails, toads and snakes—the lowest life forms not created in God's image and likeness.

1. How has sharing in Mary's humility helped me realize how much I need grace in my life?
2. When do I experience this increased self- knowledge?

--Second Effect--

Participation in Mary's Faith

214. Our Blessed Lady will give you also a portion of her faith, which was the greatest of all faiths that ever were on earth, greater than the faith of all the patriarchs, prophets, apostles and saints put together. Now that she is reigning in Heaven, she no longer exercises this faith, because she sees all things clearly in God by the light of glory. Nevertheless, with the consent of the Most High, in entering into glory she did not lose her faith. She kept it for her faithful servants in the Church militant. The more, then, that you gain the favor of that august Princess and faithful Virgin, the more will you act by pure faith; a pure faith which will make you care hardly at all about sensible consolations and extraordinary favors; a lively faith animated by charity, which will enable you to perform all your actions from the motive of pure love; a faith firm and immovable as a rock, through which you will rest quiet and constant in the midst of storms and hurricanes; a faith active and piercing, which like a mysterious pass-key, will give you entrance into all the mysteries of Jesus, into the last ends of man, and into the Heart of God Himself; a courageous faith, which will enable you to undertake and carry out without hesitation great things for God and for the salvation of souls; lastly, a faith which will be your blazing torch, your divine life, your hidden treasure of divine wisdom and your omnipotent arm; which you will use to enlighten those who are in the darkness of the shadow of death, to inflame those who are lukewarm and who have need of the heated gold of charity, to give life to those who are dead in sin, to touch and overthrow, by your meek and powerful words, the hearts of marble and the cedars of Lebanon; and finally, to resist the devil and all the enemies of salvation.

Mary allows her children to share in her profound faith. The more one advances in the lifestyle of true devotion, the more one lives by faith. "We walk by faith, not by sight" (2 Corinthians 5:7). This faith will purify us of doing things in order to be recognized and appreciated. When there are troubles in our lives and those of our families and/or parishioners we will be able to maintain an interior recollection and peace rooted in the belief that "all things work for good for those who love God" (Romans 8:28). This faith will obtain for us a greater understanding of the Scriptures and a more courageous zeal to serve the Lord. This faith will enhance our preaching the Gospel and living and evangelizing an authentic Christian witness in the midst of an ungodly and irreligious world. This faith will aid priests in the conversion of the most hardened sinners. And, it will give us the capacity to recognize the Evil One working against us and how to be victorious over him united with Mary's faith. As this faith grows, the devotee will notice, however, a concomitant growth in darkness, meaning, that the sensible consolations may steadily diminish. Living by faith means not knowing always what God is doing, but believing and trusting in His Divine Providence. It takes courage to persevere in faith because we do not have the light of absolute certainty.

Application of the Lifestyle of True Devotion

1. What does it mean that Mary has kept her faith for you?
2. How do I feel about pure faith without sensible consolations?
3. What are the effects of participating in Mary's faith?

--Third Effect—

Deliverance From Scruples, Cares And Fears

215. This Mother of fair love (Ecclesiasticus 24:24) will take away from your heart all scruple and all disorder of servile fear. She will open and enlarge it to run the way of her Son's commandments (Ps. 118:32) with the holy liberty of the children of God. She will introduce into it pure love, of which she has the treasure, so that you shall no longer be guided by fear, as hitherto, in your dealings with the God of charity, but by love alone. You will look on Him as your good Father, whom you will be incessantly trying to please, and with whom you will converse confidently, as a child with its tender father. If, unfortunately, you offend Him, you will at once humble yourself before Him. You will ask His pardon with great lowliness, but at the same time you will stretch your hand out to Him with simplicity, and you will raise yourself up lovingly, without trouble or disquietude, and go on your way to Him without discouragement.

<u>Scriptures</u>

Ecclesiasticus 24:24 CCD: "I am the mother of fair love, and of fear, and of knowledge, and of holy hope."

[Ecclesiasticus 24:24: "ego mater pulchrae dilectionis et timoris et agnitionis et sanctae spei.]

This verse appears in some ancient Greek manuscripts and has made its way into the Latin translation and into Mary's praises in the Litany of Loreto, but it is not universally accepted in most Biblical translations. The reader will find a modern English translation of this passage as:

Sirach 24:17 NAB: "I bud forth delights like the vine, my blossoms become fruit fair and rich."

Psalm 118:32 CCD: "I will run the way of your commands when you give me a docile heart."

Psalm 119:32 NAB: "I will run the way of your commands, for you open my docile heart."

St. Louis employs these Scriptures to speak of how Mary changes the hearts of her children so that their hearts (that is, their capacity to love God) will increase to the point that there is no longer any fear of God, worry, or lack of trust.

St. Louis states that one of the effects of the lifestyle of true devotion is a conversion from doing things for God out of fear of punishment to a desire to do all things for God with love so that ultimately one can be motivated by love alone. Another aspect of this devotion is that one will recover from mortal sin without the anguish of heart and approach the Sacrament of Reconciliation and the Father with loving trust. Mary leads the soul to Jesus who leads us to the heart of the Father. The consecration to Mary leads to knowledge of the Father and that means a more personal knowledge of God who is love.

<u>Application of the Lifestyle of True Devotion</u>

1. When were the times I have been afraid of God?
2. How has Mary changed my fear of God to love of Him?
3. What is scrupulosity? To what degree do I suffer from it?

--Fourth Effect-
<u>Great Confidence in God and Mary</u>

216. Our Blessed Lady will fill you with great confidence in God and in herself: (1) because you will not be approaching Jesus by yourself, but always by that good Mother: (2) because, as you have given her all your merits, graces and satisfactions to dispose of at her will, she will communicate to you her virtues and will clothe you in her merits, so that you will be able to say to God with confidence: "Behold Mary Thy handmaid; be it done unto me according to Thy word" (Lk. 1:38); (3) because, as you have given yourself entirely to her, body and soul, she, who is liberal with the liberal, and more liberal even than the liberal, will in return give herself to you in a marvelous but real manner, so that you may say to her with assurance: " I am thine, holy Virgin; save me" (Cf. Ps. 118:94) or as I have said before, with the beloved disciple: "I have taken thee, holy Mother, for my own." You may also say with St. Bonaventure: "My loving and redeeming Mistress, I will have confidence and will not fear, because you are my strength and my praise in the Lord...I am altogether yours and all that I have belongs to you!" And in another place: "O glorious Virgin, blessed above all created things! I will put you as a seal upon my heart, because your love is as strong as death." "Lord, my heart and my eyes have no right to extol themselves, or to be proud, or to seek great and wonderful things. Yet even at that, I am not humble; but I have lifted up and encouraged my soul by confidence; I am like a child, weaned from the pleasures of earth and resting on its mother's lap; and it is on that lap that all good things come to me." (Cf. Ps. 130:1-2). What will still further increase your confidence in her is that you will have less confidence in yourself. You have given her in trust all you have of good about you, that she may have it and keep it; and so all the trust you once had in yourself has become an increase of confidence in her, who is your treasure. Oh, what confidence and what consolation is this for a soul who can say that the treasure of God, where He was pleased to put all He had most precious, is his own treasure also! It was a saint who said she is a treasure of the Lord.

Scriptures

Luke 1:38: "Behold I am the handmaid of the Lord. May it be done unto me according to your word."

Psalm 118:94 CCD: "I am yours; save me, for I have sought your precepts."

Psalm 119:94 NAB: "I am yours; save me, for I cherish your precepts."

Psalm 130:1-2 CCD: "Lord, my heart is not proud, nor are my eyes haughty; I busy not myself with great things, nor with things too sublime for me. Nay rather, I have stilled and quieted my soul like a weaned child. Like a weaned child on its mother's lap so is my soul within me.'

Psalm 131:1-2 NAB: "Lord, my heart is not proud; nor are my eyes haughty. I do not busy myself with great matters, with things too sublime for me. Rather, I have stilled my soul, hushed it like a weaned child. Like a weaned child on its

179

mother's lap, so is my soul within me."

These Scriptures again speak of total trust in Mary's intercession and role in forming us into saints. As true devotion grows in the soul, so too does one's trust in Mary and one's desire to surrender more and more to her care. This is not done automatically on the day of the consecration, but grows over time as one enters more deeply into the lifestyle of true devotion and an understanding of its graces and power.

<u>Who's Who?</u>

The saint to which he is referring is Raymond Jordan (Raymondus Jordanus). Raymond Jordan, whose pen name was Idiota (the Greek means "private"), was a Frenchman who belonged to the Canons Regular of St. Augustine and in fact was prior at Uzès, France and then Abbot of Selles-sur-Cher, France where he died. He wrote six books of "Meditations," a "Treatise on the Blessed Virgin," and a "Treatise on the Religious Life." He is believed to have lived sometime in the 14th Century.[3]

St. Louis speaks about an inverse relationship in this effect of true devotion involving confidence in Mary. The more one decreases in trust in himself, the more one increases in confidence and trust in Mary. Because everything has been entrusted to her in confidence she will increase what we have given away. Growing in this lifestyle means constantly having to trust Mary more and more. The temptation will be to turn back to ourselves and to trust in our own strength. While we are required to cooperate daily with grace, we may discern obstacles that seem larger than ever which will require a deeper and stronger trust in Mary.

<u>Application of the Lifestyle of True Devotion</u>

1. How has my confidence in Mary increased and confidence in my own strength decreased?
2. Do I complain that God doesn't hear my prayers or listen to me?
3. How has the lifestyle of true devotion led me to a greater trust in God's providence for my life?

--Fifth Effect--

<u>Communication of the Soul and Spirit of Mary</u>

217. The soul of our Blessed Lady will communicate itself to you, to glorify the Lord. Her spirit will enter into the place of yours, to rejoice in God her salvation, provided only that you are faithful to the practices of this devotion. [As St. Ambrose says:] "Let the soul of Mary be in each of us to glorify the Lord: let the spirit of Mary be in each of us to rejoice in God." Ah! When will the happy time come, said a holy man of our own days who was all absorbed in Mary--Ah! When will the happy time come when the divine Mary will be established Mistress and Queen of all hearts, in order that she may subject them fully to the empire of her great and holy Jesus? When will souls breathe Mary as the body breathes air? When that time comes, wonderful things will happen in those lowly places where the Holy Spirit, finding His dear spouse, as it were, reproduced, in souls, shall come in with abundance, and fill them to overflowing with His gifts, and particularly with the gift of wisdom, to work miracles of grace. My dear brother, when will that happy time, that age of Mary, come, when many souls, chosen and procured from the Most High by Mary, shall lose themselves in the abyss of her interior, shall become living copies of Mary, to love and glorify Jesus? That time will not come until men shall know and practice this devotion which I am teaching. "That Thy reign may come, let the reign of Mary come."

Who's Who?

St. Ambrose was born around the year 340 and died 397. He was consecrated bishop of Milan, Italy in 374. He was a prolific writer and defender of the Church against the prevailing heresy of Arianism. His writings on Mary are contained in many of his biblical commentaries.[4]

When Mary communicates her spirit to her children it will infuse her children with a spirit to praise God just as she praises Him in her Magnificat. By practicing the lifestyle of true devotion we begin to experience a deeper praise of God in our own soul. This lifestyle introduces a new era in the Church. It will surpass the era of the Charismatic Renewal of the 20th Century because it will be the era of the Holy Spirit and Mary together operating in the lives of souls with an increase of charisms. Where Mary is, there the Holy Spirit comes in search of His Spouse. His coming will augment the charismatic gifts and her presence in the soul, by means of this consecration, will purify the charisms and augment them. The "spirit of Mary" or the "essence" of Mary is to love Jesus and give glory to the Father through the power of the Holy Spirit.

Application of the Lifestyle of True Devotion

1. What does it mean to say that Mary is the Queen of my heart?
2. What does it mean to be lost in the abyss of Mary's interior?
3. How has the communication of Mary's spirit to me changed the way I pray?

--Sixth Effect--

<u>Transformation of the Faithful Soul by Mary Into the Likeness of Jesus Christ</u>

218. If Mary, who is the tree of life, is well cultivated in our soul by fidelity to the practices of this devotion, she will bear her fruit in her own time, and her fruit is none other than Jesus Christ. How many devout souls do I see who seek Jesus Christ, some by one way or by one practice, and others by other ways and other practices; and oftentimes, after they have toiled much throughout the night, they say, "We have toiled all night, and have taken nothing!" (Lk. 5:5). We may say to them: "You have labored much and gained little"; Jesus is yet feeble in you. But by that immaculate way of Mary and that divine practice which I am teaching, we toil during the day, we toil in a holy place, we toil but little. There is no night in Mary, because there is no sin or even the slightest shade. Mary is a holy place, and the holy of holies where saints are formed and molded.

<u>Scriptures</u>

Luke 5:5 CCD: "And Simon answered and said to him, "Master, the whole night through we have toiled and have taken nothing; but at thy word I will lower the net."

Luke 5:5 NAB: "Simon said in reply, 'Master, we have worked hard all night and have caught nothing, but at your command I will lower the nets.'"

St. Louis refers to the Gospel of Luke to emphasize that just as the Apostles toiled all night without the Lord and then caught an abundant harvest after His instruction, so too the man or woman without Mary will toil with frustration in the spiritual life until he or she receives the Blessed Mother's instruction and care.

The lifestyle of true devotion bears fruit in our soul most particularly Jesus Himself. For those who seek the imitation of Christ, St. Louis maintains that his teaching on the true devotion is the best way.

Night is a metaphor for sin; lack of faith, etc. There is no "night" in Mary. We do not find sin by means of her; we do not find lack of faith by means of her; we do not find our labors in vain when we labor by her, nor do we find discouragement, frustration, tiredness or failure by means of her. The lifestyle of true devotion forms saints in Mary because she transforms her faithful children into her one perfect Child, Jesus. This transformation is unique and personal for each man and woman consecrated to her.

219. Take notice, if you please, that I say the saints are mold-ed in Mary. There is a great difference between making a figure in relief by blows of hammer and chisel, and making a figure by throwing it into a mold. Statuaries and sculptors labor much to make figures in the first manner; but to make them in the second manner, they work little and do their work quickly. St. Augustine calls our Blessed Lady "the mold of God"—the mold fit to cast and mold gods. He who is cast in this mold is presently formed and molded in Jesus Christ and Jesus Christ in him. At a slight expense and in a short time he will become God, because he has been cast in the same mold which has formed a God.

220. It seems to me that I can very aptly compare directors and devout persons, who wish to form Jesus Christ in themselves or others by practices different from this one, to sculptors who trust in their own professional skill, ingenuity or art, and so give an infinity of hammerings and chiselings to a hard stone or a piece of badly polished wood, to make an image of Jesus Christ out of it. Sometimes they do not succeed in giving anything like the natural expression of Jesus, either from having no knowledge or experience of the Person of Jesus, or from some blow awkwardly given which has spoiled the work. But those who embrace the secret of grace which I am revealing to them I may rightly compare to founders and casters who have discovered the beautiful mold of Mary, where Jesus was naturally and divinely formed; and without trusting in their own skill, but only in the goodness of the mold, they cast themselves and lose themselves in Mary, to become the faithful portraits of Jesus Christ.

221. Oh, beautiful and true comparison! But who will comprehend it? I desire that you may, my dear brother. But remember that we cast in a mold only what is melted and liquid; that is to say, you must destroy and melt down in yourself the old Adam to become the new one in Mary.

St. Louis makes here a comparison between a piece of art that is formed by means of a sculptor and a mold. He likens the sculpture to human effort and enterprise and the mold to passive formation in Mary. She is the cast of the perfect mold for Jesus and reproduces every child in that same perfect way. Many times our desires and labors for sanctity are based on our idea of copying some other saint and what he or she did, which we learn to our disappointment bears little fruit. With Mary as the mold she forms us according to God's divine purpose as long as we cooperate with those graces necessary for that conformity.

Sculpture (Self)	versus	Mold (Mary)

Sculpture (Self)	Mold (Mary)
--requires much labor	--little labor, just cooperation and grace
--one trusts in his own skill	--trust in the goodness of the
--potential for ruining the work;	mold itself (Mary)
not becoming holy.	--the content is destroyed and refashioned perfectly.
--He has no experience of what the end product will look like. He doesn't know how to make himself into a saint.	

This is a comparison between those who try to form themselves (or others in the case of spiritual directors) into Jesus like a sculptor by human effort and toil and those who allow Mary to mold them into Jesus. In order for the molding process to be effective, the old self must be "melted" down and reformed. This melting down requires death to sinful behavior, thought patterns, words, vices, imperfections, lack of prayer, inadequate spiritual life, etc.—all those aspects mentioned earlier in the formation process of the spiritual life where Mary forms her children.

Application of the Lifestyle of True Devotion

1. How does Mary transform me more and more into Jesus Christ?
2. How has my spiritual life been one of toiling in the night without Mary?
3. Do I believe that Mary wants to form me into a saint?

--Seventh Effect—

The Greater Glory of God

222. By this practice, faithfully observed, you will give Jesus more glory in a month than by any other practice, however difficult, in many years; and I give you the following reasons for it:

1ˢᵗ) Because, doing your actions by our Blessed Lady, as this practice teaches you, you abandon your own intentions and operations, although good and known, to lose yourself, so to speak, in the intentions of the Blessed Virgin, although they are unknown. Thus you enter by participation into the sublimity of her intentions, which are so pure that she gives more glory to God by the least of her actions—for example, in twirling her distaff or pointing her needle—than St. Lawrence by his cruel martyrdom on the gridiron, or even all the saints by all their heroic actions put together. It was thus that, during her sojourn here below, she acquired such an unspeakable aggregate of graces and merits that it were easier

*to count the stars of the firmament, the drops of water in the sea
or the grains of sand upon its shore, than her merits and graces.
Thus it was that she gave more glory to God than all the angels
and saints have given Him or ever will give Him. O prodigy of a
Mary! Thou canst not help but do prodigies of grace in souls that
wish to lose themselves altogether in thee!*

Who's Who?

St. Lawrence died in the year 258. He was one of the seven deacons of Rome, believed to have been born in Spain. He died during Emperor Valerian's persecution. He was martyred by being burned alive on a hot iron or grill.[5]

St. Louis introduces this last effect of true devotion by stating that the practice that he is recommending (doing all things by, with, in and for Mary in order to do it by, with, in and for Jesus) gives more glory to God than any other. He lists four reasons for this: The first is in the abandonment of our own intentions to those of the Blessed Virgin---even when we don't know what are her intentions. This abandonment obtains for our own intentions a greater purity. Mary, as the prodigy of God's work will produce a prodigy of graces in our soul.

> *223. 2ⁿᵈ) Because the soul in this practice counts as nothing
> whatever it thinks or does of itself, and puts its trust and takes its
> pleasures only in the dispositions of Mary, when it approaches
> Jesus or even speaks to Him. Thus it practices humility far more
> than the souls who act of themselves and trust, with however im-
> perceptible a complacency, in their own dispositions. But if the
> soul acts more humbly, it therefore more highly glorifies God, who
> is perfectly glorified only by the humble and those that are little
> and lowly in heart.*

The lifestyle of true devotion is truly one of great humility and this virtue typifies it. All that the person trusts and enjoys is handed over to Mary for her to take to Jesus. Such humility and surrender glorifies the Father more than the slightest trace of pride in one's own natural abilities, gifts and actions. The second reason why this lifestyle gives greater glory to God is the depth of humility practiced.

> *224. 3ʳᵈ) Because our Blessed Lady, being pleased, out of
> great charity to receive the present of our actions in her virginal
> hands, gives them an admirable beauty and splendor. Moreover,
> she offers them herself to Jesus Christ, and it is evident that Our
> Lord is thus more glorified by them than if we offered them by our
> own criminal hands.*

Mary beautifies all our actions entrusted to her and delivers them personally to her Son who takes delight in receiving anything from His mother. The third reason why this lifestyle gives greater glory to God is that Mary beautifies everything we give her to take to the Father.

> *225. 4ᵗʰ) Lastly, because you never think of Mary without Mary's thinking of God for you. You never praise or honor Mary without Mary's praising and honoring God with you. Mary is altogether relative to God; and indeed, I might well call her the relation to God. She only exists with reference to God. She is the echo of God that says nothing, repeats nothing, but God. If you say "Mary," she says, "God." St. Elizabeth praised Mary, and called her blessed, because she had believed. Mary, the faithful echo of God, at once intoned: "My soul doth magnify the Lord." (Lk. 1:46). That which Mary did then, she does daily now. When we praise her, love her, honor her or give anything to her, it is God who is praised, God who is loved, God who is glorified, and it is to God that we give, through Mary and in Mary.*

Scriptures

Luke 1:46 CCD: " And Mary said, My soul magnifies the Lord,"
Luke 1:46 NAB: "And Mary said, 'My soul proclaims the greatness of the Lord'"

Mary exists in relation to God, always pointing and referring all things to Him—especially our prayers. She is the "echo of God." All prayers invoking her intercession are referred to the Father.

Our lifestyle of true devotion does not terminate in Mary, but is a Magnificat through her for the glory of God the Father, Son and Holy Spirit. The fourth reason why this devotion gives greater glory to God is that our act of humility in going to Mary is not a detraction from God but an amplification of glory as Mary relays and augments everything we give to Him. She increases the little we have to offer, thus rendering Him greater glory.

Application of the Lifestyle of True Devotion

1. How do I daily abandon my intentions into Mary's intentions? What do I say? How do I remember to do it?
2. How do I take pleasure in Mary's dispositions and not in my own? What obstacles do I encounter trying to practice this?
3. Why does it please Mary to receive my intentions into her hands?
4. What does St. Louis mean in paragraph #225 that Mary is the "echo of God"?

Chapter IV

Particular Practices Of This Devotion

– Article One –

Exterior Practices

226. Although what is essential in this devotion consists in the interior, we must not fail to unite to the inward practice certain external observances. "We must do the one, yet not leave the other undone" (Mt. 23:23); because the outward practices, well performed, aid the inward ones; and because they remind man, who is always guided by his senses, of what he has done or ought to do; and also because they are suitable for edifying our neighbor, who sees them; these are things which inward practices cannot do. Let no worldling, then, or critic, intrude here to say that because true devotion is in the heart, we must avoid external devotion; or that devotion ought to be hidden, and that there may be vanity in showing it. I answer, with my Master, that men should see our good works, that they may glorify our Father who is in Heaven. (Mt 5:16); not, as St. Gregory says, that we ought to perform our actions and exterior devotions to please men and get praise—that would be vanity; but that we should sometimes do them before men with the view of pleasing God, and glorifying Him thereby, without caring either for the contempt or the praise of men. I will allude only briefly to some exterior practices, which I call "exterior" not because we do not perform them interiorly, but because they have something outward about them to distinguish them from those which are purely inward.

Scriptures

Matthew 23:23 NAB: "Woe to you, scribes and Pharisees, you hypocrites. You pay tithes of mint and dill and cummin, and have neglected the weightier things of the law: judgment and mercy and fidelity. But these you should have done, without neglecting the others."

Matthew 5:16 NAB: "Just so, your light must shine before others, that they may see your good deeds and glorify your heavenly Father."

St. Louis refers to Matthew's Gospel to illustrate that one must observe all the practices of the "law." Similarly, both the interior and exterior recommendations of true devotion are complementary and support each other. There is value to the exterior in that it gives witness to God the Father, edifies believer and nonbeliever and fulfills the virtue of religion.

The essence of the lifestyle of true devotion is interior. Yet, the interior life is preserved and cultivated by healthy exterior practices and devotions. These actions are, of course, performed with humility, not to impress one's neighbor or to gain praise and flattery, but to give glory to the Father.

<u>Application of the Lifestyle of True Devotion</u>

1. What is the essential aspect of this devotion?
2. Of what do the external practices remind us?
3. How do exterior practices give praise to God? How can they be detrimental?

I.   <u>Preparatory Exercises and Consecration</u>

227. Those who wish to enter into this particular devotion, which is not at present erected into a confraternity (though that were to be wished), after having, as I said in the first part of this preparation for the reign of Jesus Christ, employed twelve days at least in ridding themselves of the spirit of the world, which is contrary to the spirit of Jesus Christ, should employ three weeks in filling themselves with Jesus Christ by the holy Virgin. They can follow this order:

In this section St. Louis points out that the consecration should not be taken lightly, but should be entered into with sufficient preparation and detachment from the things of the world. It is interesting to note that the time period of twelve days is a significantly long period of time to rid oneself of the influences of the world, which reflects upon the deeply ingrained effects of the world on our soul. The following paragraphs specify his program for this preparation.

228. During the first week they should offer up all their prayers and pious actions to ask for a knowledge of themselves and contrition for their sins; and they should do this in a spirit of humility. For that end they can, if they choose, meditate on what I have said before of our inward corruption. They can look upon themselves during the six days of this week as snails, crawling things, toads, swine, serpents and unclean animals; or they can reflect on these three considerations of St. Bernard: the vileness of our origin, the dishonors of our present state, and our ending as the food of worms. They should pray Our Lord and the Holy Spirit to enlighten them; and for that end they might use the ejaculations, "Lord, that I may see!" (Lk. 18:41); or "May I know myself!"; or "Come, Holy Spirit," together with the Litany of the Holy Spirit and the prayer which follows, as indicated in the first part of this work. They should have recourse to the Blessed Virgin and ask her to grant them this immense grace, which must be the foundation of all the others; for this end, they should say daily the Ave Maris Stella and the Litany of the Blessed Virgin.

<u>Scriptures</u>

Luke 18:41 CCD: " 'What wouldst thou have me do for thee?' and he said, 'Lord, that I may see.'"

Luke 18:41 NAB: " 'What do you want me to do for you?' He replied, 'Lord, please let me see.'"

The first week begins with praying for self-knowledge in order to recognize that without God's grace and the sanctifying grace from our baptism, we are no better than the animals. Our baptism has given us a tremendous dignity and nobility as sons and daughters of God. St. Louis encourages us to invoke the Holy Spirit for self-knowledge and the Blessed Mother to obtain for us the graces of insight to recognize our mixed motivations, pride and selfishness.

Pope John Paul II speaks eloquently of the action of the Holy Spirit coming to convict us of sin when he states: "Here we wish to concentrate our attention principally on this mission of the Holy Spirit, which is 'to convince the world concerning sin,' but at the same time respecting the general context of Jesus' words in the upper room. The Holy Spirit, who takes from the Son the work of the Redemption of the world, by this very fact, takes the task of the salvific 'convincing of sin.' This convincing is in permanent reference to 'righteousness': that is to say to definitive salvation in God, to the fulfillment of the economy that has as its center the crucified and glorified Christ. And this salvific economy of God in a certain sense removes man from 'judgment,' that is from damnation which has been inflicted on the sin of Satan, 'the prince of this world,' the one who because of his sin has become 'the ruler of this world of darkness.' And here we see that, through this reference to 'judgment,' vast horizons open up for understanding 'sin' and also 'righteousness.' The Holy Spirit, by showing sin against the background of Christ's cross in the economy of salvation (one could say 'sin saved'), enables us to understand how his mission is also 'to convince' of the sin that has already been definitively judged ('sin condemned').[6]

We implore the Holy Spirit to convict us of how we have strayed from God's plan of holiness for us and ask Our Lady to get us back on course.

> *229. During the second week they should apply themselves, in all their prayers and works each day, to know the Blessed Virgin. They should ask this knowledge of the Holy Spirit; they should read and meditate on what we have said about it. For this intention they should recite, as in the first week, the Litany of the Holy Spirit and the Ave Maris Stella, and in addition a Rosary daily, or if not a whole Rosary, at least the beads.*

We continue the second week invoking the Holy Spirit for the knowledge of His Spouse, the Blessed Virgin Mary. The combination of prayers to the Holy Spirit and the rosary brings us into a greater knowledge of Mary and of her participation in God's plan of salvation for us. The Rosary introduces us into the life of Jesus and Mary in the Gospel. In union with the mysteries of our faith we pray to change our lives, save souls, reconcile sinners and raise the dead.

> *230. They should apply themselves during the third week to know Jesus Christ. They can meditate upon what we have said about Him, and say the prayer of St. Augustine which they will find in the beginning of the second part of this treatise. They can, with the same saint, repeat a hundred times a day: "Lord, that I may know Thee!" or; "Lord, that I may see Who Thou art!" They should recite, as in the preceding weeks, the Litany of the Holy Spirit and the Ave Maris Stella, and should add daily the Litany of the Holy Name of Jesus.*

The prayer of St. Augustine is found in paragraph #67 above.

Continuing into the third week, the invocation to the Holy Spirit and intercession of the Blessed Virgin Mary leads us to know Jesus. Mary and the overshadowing of the Holy Spirit bring Jesus into the world and will bring a greater knowledge and love of Him into our souls. Knowledge of Jesus brings us to the "experience" of Jesus in the Sacraments: particularly the Eucharist and Reconciliation that we may truly experience His healing power.

> *231. At the end of the three weeks they should go to Confession and Communion, with the intention of giving themselves to Jesus Christ in the quality of slaves of love, by the hands of Mary. After Communion, which they should try to make according to the method given further on, they should recite the formula of the consecration, which they will also find further on. They ought to write it, or have it written unless they have a printed copy of it; and they should sign it the same day on which they have made it.*

On the day of consecration we receive the Sacrament of Reconciliation and Holy Communion with the intention at Mass to become a slave of love to Jesus through Mary. Having received Jesus in the Eucharist, who makes Himself a slave of love in the Host for us, we now pray for the grace to be able to give ourselves entirely back to Him as slaves of love. We do this by Mary whose own total surrender brought Jesus into the world for us.

> *232. It would be well also that on that day they should pay some tribute to Jesus Christ and our Blessed Lady, either as a penance for their past unfaithfulness to the vows of their Baptism, or as a testi-*

mony of their dependence on the dominion of Jesus and Mary. This tribute ought to be according to the devotion and ability of each one, such as a fast, a mortification, an alms or a candle. If they had but a pin to give in homage, and gave it with a good heart, it would be enough for Jesus, who looks only at the good will.

As an outward sign of this interior devotion, St. Louis recommends some kind of tribute or offering to Jesus and Mary as a witness to our consecration. The purity of intention in that offering is the most important aspect. It is a significant external reminder or souvenir of the beautiful day of our consecration.

233. Once a year at least, and on the same day, they should renew the same consecration, observing the same practices during the three weeks. They might also, once a month or even once a day renew all they have done, in these few words: "I am all Thine and all that I have is Thine, O most loving Jesus, through Mary, Thy most holy Mother."

St. Louis recommends the annual renewal of this offering with the same three-week preparation period and the daily renewal of the consecration prayer. The daily renewal is best said at the beginning and/or the end of the day.

Application of the Lifestyle of True Devotion

1. Why is it important to prepare carefully for this consecration? Why do I need to rid myself of the spirit of the world? How does the spirit of the world influence me?
2. What is the goal of the first week of preparation?
3. What is the goal of the second week?
4. What is the goal of the third week?
5. What do I do on the day of consecration both interiorly and exteriorly?
6. What "tribute" did I offer to Jesus and Mary?
7. Do I renew my consecration annually with the three-week preparation?
8. Do I remember to say the prayer daily? Or, especially on Sundays and Holy Days?

II.   Recitation of the Little Crown of the Blessed Virgin.

234. They may recite every day of their life—without however, making a burden of it—the Little Crown of the Blessed Virgin, composed of three Our Fathers and twelve Hail Marys, in honor of Our Lady's twelve privileges and grandeurs. This is a very ancient practice and it has its foundation in Holy Scripture. St. John saw a woman crowned with twelve stars, clothed with the sun, and with the moon under her feet (Apoc. 12:1); and this woman, according to the interpreters, was the most holy Virgin.

<u>Scriptures</u>

Revelation 12:1 NAB: "A great sign appeared in the sky, a woman clothed with the sun, with the moon under her feet, and on her head a crown of twelve stars."

The Scripture reference to Revelation is based on St. John's mystical vision of the woman clothed with the sun which is interpreted to be both Mary and the Church.

St. Louis adapts his version of the Little Crown from Fr. François Paré's work <u>The Triple Crown of the Blessed Virgin,</u> which was published in the year 1630.[7] The "ancient practice" refers to various titles given to Our Lady in the Church's liturgy which he has combined to form this beautiful prayer.

> *235. There are many ways of saying this Crown well, but it would take too long to enter upon them. The Holy Spirit will teach them to those who are the most faithful to this devotion. Nevertheless, to say it quite simply, we should begin by saying: "Grant that I may praise thee, holy Virgin; give me strength against thy enemies." After that, we should say the Apostles' Creed, then an Our Father with four Hail Marys and then one Glory be to the Father; then another Our Father, four Hail Marys, and Glory be to the Father, and so on with the rest; and at the end we should say the Sub Tuum Praesidium ("We fly to thy patronage...").*

St. Louis instructs that the Crown should begin with the invitatory: "Grant that I may praise thee..." which is a 9th Century antiphon from the Office of the Assumption of the Blessed Virgin Mary from the breviary.[8] He then advises it should end with the prayer: "We fly to thy patronage, O holy Mother of God; despise not our petitions in our necessities, but deliver us always from all dangers, O glorious and blessed Virgin." This final prayer to Mary is indeed very ancient dating back to the 3rd Century.[9] Both the opening and closing invocations to Our Lady emphasize her protection and assistance.

<u>Application of the Lifestyle of True Devotion</u>

1. St. Louis singles out the Little Crown as one of the external devotions. What   are Mary's twelve privileges and grandeurs?

III. The Wearing of Little Chains

236. It is a most glorious and praiseworthy thing, and very use-ful to those who have thus made themselves slaves of Jesus in Mary, that they should wear, as a sign of their loving slavery, little iron chains, blessed with the proper blessing. It is perfectly true that these external insignia are not essential, and a person who has em-braced this devotion may very well go without them; nevertheless, I cannot refrain from warmly praising those who, after having shaken off the shameful chains of the slavery of the devil, in which Origi-nal Sin, and perhaps actual sin, had bound them, have voluntarily surrendered themselves to the glorious slavery of Jesus Christ, and glory with St. Paul in being in chains for Christ (Eph. 3:1; Philem. 9), chains a thousand times more glorious and precious, though of iron, than all the golden ornaments of emperors.

Scriptures

Ephesians 3:1 NAB: "Because of this, I, Paul, a prisoner of Christ Jesus for you Gentiles— "

Philemon 9 NAB: "I rather urge you out of love, being as I am, Paul an old man, and now also a prisoner for Christ Jesus."

This external sign, although not a necessary one, is an expression of belonging to Jesus through Mary as a slave of love. It is similar to the wedding ring which one wears as a sign of one's "love and fidelity" to the spouse. For St. Louis this new chain represents the rejection of our former slavery to sin and the new-found slavery to love and serves as a reminder of such wholehearted belonging to Jesus through Mary as he discussed in the section on servitude and slavery.

237. Once there was nothing more infamous on earth than the cross, and now that wood is the most glorious boast of Christian-ity. Let us say the same of the irons of slavery. There was noth-ing more ignominious among the ancients; there is nothing more shameful even now among the heathens. But among Christians, there is nothing more illustrious than the chains of Jesus; for they unchain us and preserve us from the infamous fetters of sin and the devil. They set us at liberty and chain us to Jesus and Mary; not by compulsion and constraint, like galley-slaves, but by char-ity and love, like children. "I will draw them to Me," says God by the mouth of the prophet, "by the chains of love." (Osee 11:14*). These chains are as strong as death (Canticles 8:6), and in a cer-tain sense even stronger than death in those who are faithful in carrying these glorious chains to their death. For though death *destroys their bodies by bringing them to corruption, it does not destroy the chains of their slavery, which, being of iron, do not corrode so easily. Perhaps, on the day of the resurrection of the body, at the last judgment, these chains shall be around their bones, and shall be a part of their glory, and be transmuted into chains of light and splendor. Happy then, a thousand times happy, the illustrious slaves of Jesus who wear their chains even to the tomb!*

<u>Scriptures</u>

*The Hosea (Osee) text should read 11:4 (not verse 14).[10] This same text is printed correctly in paragraph 241.

Osee 11:4 CCD: "I will draw them with the cords of Adam, with the bands of love; and I will be to them as one that taketh off the yoke on their jaws: and I put his meat to him that he might eat."

Hosea 11:4 NAB: "I drew them with human cords, with bands of love;…"

Canticles 8:6 Douay: "Put me as a seal upon thy heart, as a seal upon thy arm, for love is strong as death, jealousy as hard as hell, the lamps thereof are fire and flames."

Song of Songs 8:6 NAB: "Set me as a seal on your heart, as a seal on your arm; for stern as death is love, relentless as the nether world is devotion; its flames are a blazing fire."

These Scriptures reinforce the symbol of chains as of binding love, not as of human degradation and oppression.

The symbol of the chains of slavery has undergone the same transformation as did the crucifix. Once each of these represented the worst in humanity. Now the cross is seen as the sign of our salvation and the chain as a symbol of love for him or her who belongs whole-heartedly and totally to the Lord and to His Mother. We are chained to Love Itself. It is free donation of the self to God, not an imprisonment to Him.

Because chains do not decompose after death, they represent and symbolize the strength of the true devotion to Jesus through Mary perduring even after death. St. Louis presents a beautiful image of the resurrected and glorified body wearing the chains as an everlasting symbol of fidelity and love.

238. The following are the reasons for wearing these little chains:

First, to remind the Christian of the vows and promises of his Baptism, of the perfect renewal he has made of them by this devotion, and of the strict obligation under which he is to be faithful to them. As man, who shapes his course more often by the senses than by pure faith, easily forgets his obligations toward God unless he has some outward thing to remind him of them, these little chains serve marvelously to remind the Christian of the chains of sin and the slavery of the devil from which Baptism has delivered him, and of the dependence on Jesus which he has vowed to Him in Baptism, and of the ratification of it which he has made by the renewal of his vows. One of the reasons why so few Christians think of their baptismal vows, and live with as much license as if they had promised no more to God than the heathen, is that they do not wear any external sign to remind them of their vows.

239. Secondly, to show that we are not ashamed of the servitude and slavery of Jesus Christ, and that we renounce the slavery of the world, of sin and of the devil. Thirdly, to protect ourselves against the chains of sin and of the devil; for we must wear either "the chains of sinners or the chains of charity and salvation."

240. O my dear brother, let us break the chains of sin and sinners, of the world and worldliness, of the devil and his ministers; and let us cast far from us their depressing yoke. (Ps. 2:3). Let us put our feet, to use the terms of the Holy Spirit, into His glorious fetters and our necks into His chains. (Ecclesiasticus 6:25). Let us shoulder and carry the Divine Wisdom [that is, Jesus Christ] and let us never weary of His chains (Ecclus. 6:26). You will remark that the Holy Spirit, before saying these words, prepares a soul for them, lest it should reject His important counsel. See His words: "Hearken, My son, and receive a counsel of understanding and reject not My counsel." (Ecclus.6:24).

Scriptures

Psalm 2:3 Douay: "Let us break their fetters and cast their bonds from us!"
Psalm 2:3 NAB: "Let us break their shackles and cast off their chains!"
Ecclesiasticus 6:24-26 Douay: "Give ear, my son, and take wise counsel, and cast not away my advice. Put thy feet into her fetters, and thy neck into her chains: Bow down thy shoulder, and bear her, and be not grieved with her bands."
Sirach 6:24-26 NAB: "Listen, my son, and heed my advice; refuse not my counsel. Put your feet into her fetters, and your neck under her yoke. Stoop your shoulders and carry her and be not irked at her bonds."
St. Louis uses these Scriptures to urge the devotee to abandon the chains of sin and the world and to put on the chains of love, to become a slave of love of the Holy Spirit.

241. You would wish, my very dear friend, that I should here unite myself to the Holy Spirit to give you the same counsel as His: "His chains are chains of salvation." (Ecclus. 6:31). As Jesus

Christ on the cross must draw all to Himself, whether they will it or not, He will draw the reprobate by the chains of their sins, that He may chain them like galley-slaves and devils to His eternal anger and revengeful justice. But He will, and particularly in these latter times, draw the predestinate by the chains of charity: "I will draw all things to Myself" (Jn. 12:32); "I will draw them with the bands of love."(Osec. 11:4).

<u>Scriptures</u>

Ecclesiasticus 6:31 Douay: " For in her is the beauty of life, and her bands are a healthful binding."

Ecclesiasticus 6:31 VULGATE: "Decor enim vitae est in illa et vincula illius netura salutaris."

Sirach 6:31 NAB: "You will wear her as your robe of glory, bear her as your splendid crown."

John 12:32: "'And when I am lifted up from the earth, I will draw everyone to myself.'" NAB

Hosea 11:4 See above

St. Louis alludes to the fact that Jesus draws everyone to Himself with love and that we should willingly be chained to Him with our love.

In summary, the reasons for wearing the chains of love include:
1. They remind us of our baptismal vows and promises and that the lifestyle of true devotion recalls these promises. The chains are a necessary reminder for us lest we forget those promises. On the other hand, they remind us of our former way of life when we were chained to sin and how Jesus has set us free.
2. The chains remind us that we have renounced the world, the flesh and the devil.
3. The chains remind us that we are protected from sin and the devil as they symbolize the deeper reality of our renunciation of sin and the devil in those same baptismal promises and that we have consecrated ourselves to Our Lady who strengthens us to be faithful to those promises.

242. These loving slaves of Jesus Christ, "the chained of Christ" (Ephesians 3:1; Philemon 9), can wear their chains on their feet or on their arms, around their body or around their neck. Father Vincent Caraffa, seventh Superior General of the Jesuits, who died in the odor of sanctity in the year 1643, used to wear an iron band around his feet as a mark of his servitude; and he said that his only regret was that he could not publicly drag a chain. Mother Agnes of Jesus, of whom we have spoken before, used to wear an iron chain

196

around her body. Others have worn it around their neck in penance for the pearl necklaces which they had worn in the world; while others have worn it around their arms to remind themselves, in their manual labors, that they were slaves of Jesus Christ.

Scriptures

See #236 above.

Who's Who?

Fr. Vincent Caraffa was born May 5, 1585 and died June 6, 1649. St. Louis' date is taken from Fr. Boudon's Holy Slavery which contained the wrong date of death.[11] Fr. Caraffa was the Seventh General Superior of the Jesuits and was Superior General at the time of the martyrdom of St. Isaac Jogues and St. Jean de Brébeuf, the North American martyrs. His own death occurred as a result of caring for victims of the plague that raged in Rome from 1648-1649.[12]

Mother Agnes of Jesus of Langeac is the Dominican Prioress who was mentioned previously in paragraph #170 above.

Each of these is an example of those who wore the chains and advanced in holiness as a result of this exterior sign of holy slavery of love. The exterior signs, however, are not essential to this devotion, but reinforce the interior practice of total abandonment to Jesus through Mary. One becomes holy then, not by the chain, but by the practice of the interior dispositions of total self-abandonment to Jesus through Mary that it signifies.

Application of the Lifestyle of True Devotion

1. What is the symbolism of wearing a type of chain?
2. What are the chains of sin that (did) afflict my life?
3. What external symbol do I wear as a sign that I am a slave of love to Jesus through Mary?

IV.   Special Devotion to the Mystery of the Incarnation

243. Those who undertake this holy slavery should have a special devotion to the great mystery of the Incarnation of the Word (March 25th). Indeed, the Incarnation is the mystery proper of this practice, inasmuch as it is a devotion inspired by the Holy Spirit: first, to honor and imitate the ineffable dependence which God the Son was pleased to have on Mary, for His Father's glory and our salvation—which dependence particularly appears in this mystery wherein Jesus is a captive and a slave in the bosom of the divine Mary, and depends on her for all things; secondly, to thank God for the incomparable graces He has given Mary, and particularly for having chosen her to be His most holy Mother, which choice was made in this mystery. These are the two principal ends of the slavery of Jesus in Mary.

Once again St. Louis highlights the supreme dignity of the mystery of the Annunciation and the Incarnation when the angel Gabriel appears to Mary and reveals God's plan to her seeking her consent. St. Louis states that such a devotion to this mystery of the faith is truly an inspiration of the Holy Spirit Who recalls that sacred event. This mystery recalls some of the key points of the true devotion: dependence upon Mary in imitation of Jesus; the holy slavery of love and total trust in Mary's care. The second aspect of honoring this mystery of faith is to praise and thank God the Father for His divine plan.

244. Have the goodness to observe that I generally say, "the slave of Jesus in Mary," "the slavery of Jesus in Mary." I might, in good truth, as many have done before, say the "slave of Mary," "the slavery of the holy Virgin"; but I think it better to say "the slave of Jesus in Mary," as Father Tronson, Superior General of the Seminary of St. Sulpice, renowned for his rare prudence and consummate piety, counseled to an ecclesiastic who consulted him on the subject. The following were the reasons:

In this paragraph St. Louis searches for the best mode of expressing this true devotion which he appropriately calls the slavery of Jesus in Mary so that proper relationship between the individual and Jesus is established. Mary is the means of perfecting the relationship between the soul and Jesus.

245. First, as we are living in an age of intellectual pride, and there are all around us numbers of puffed up scholars and conceited and critical spirits who have plenty to say against the best established and most solid practices of piety, it is better for us not to give them any needless occasion of criticism. Hence it is better for us to say, "the slavery of Jesus in Mary," and call ourselves the slaves of Jesus Christ rather than the slaves of Mary taking the denomination of our devotion rather from its last End, which is Jesus Christ, than from the road and the means to the end, which is Mary; though I repeat that in truth we may do either, as I have done myself. For example, a man who goes from Orleans to Tours by way of Amboise may very well say that he is going to Amboise, or that he is going to Tours; that he is a traveler to Amboise and a traveler to Tours; with this difference, however, that Amboise is but his straight road to Tours and that Tours is only the last end and term of his journey.

The reason for such precision in language is to avoid any needless criticism from those who are opposed to mentioning Mary in a soul's relationship with Jesus. St. Louis repeats here and in earlier places that Mary is just a means to arrive at the goal who is Jesus.

> *246. A second reason is that the principal mystery we celebrate and honor in this devotion is the mystery of the Incarnation, wherein we can see Jesus only in Mary, and incarnate in her bosom. Hence it is more to the purpose to speak of the slavery of Jesus in Mary and of Jesus residing and reigning in Mary, according to that beautiful prayer of so many great men: "O Jesus, living in Mary, come and live in us in Thy spirit of sanctity," etc.*

The second reason St. Louis presents for honoring the Incarnation is that this is the first time we "see" Jesus. And we see Him in His Mother's womb. Hence, he concludes, we speak of slavery of Jesus in Mary because He is literally "in" Mary where He resides in all His Kingly glory and majesty, even as child in her womb.

The full text of the prayer is: "O Jesus living in Mary, Come and live in Thy servants, In the spirit of Thy holiness, In the fullness of Thy might, In the truth of Thy virtues, In the perfection of Thy ways, In the communion of Thy mysteries; Subdue every hostile power, In Thy spirit, for the glory of the Father. Amen."

This popular prayer first appeared in one of Fr. Olier's works in 1655 which he adapted from Fr. Condren.[13]

> *247. Another reason is that this manner of speaking sets forth still more the intimate union between Jesus and Mary. They are so intimately united that the one is altogether in the other. Jesus is altogether in Mary and Mary is altogether in Jesus; or rather, she exists no more, but Jesus alone is in her, and it were easier to separate the light from the sun than Mary from Jesus; so that we might call Our Lord, "Jesus of Mary, " and our Blessed Lady, "Mary of Jesus."*

St. Louis continues with his third reason for speaking of "the slavery of Jesus in Mary." While Jesus is literally "in" Mary by reason of the Incarnation and pregnancy, Mary is by total surrender to the Father's will "in" Jesus. Her will has joined itself to the Father's will. It is reminiscent of what St. Paul will later say, "It is no longer I who live but Christ who lives in me" (Galatians 2:20). The union of Mary and Jesus is greater than any other union between a soul and Jesus because of the unique nature of the Incarnation and pregnancy. They belong to each other by a bond of love which can't be broken.

> *248. Time would not permit me to stop now to explain the excellences and grandeurs of the mystery of Jesus living and reign-*

ing in Mary; in other words, of the Incarnation of the Word. I will content myself with saying these few words: We have here the first mystery of Jesus Christ—the most hidden, the most exalted and the least known. It is in this mystery that Jesus, in His Mother's womb—which is for that very reason called by the saints "the cabinet of the secrets of God"—has, in concert with Mary, chosen all the elect. It is in this mystery that He has wrought all the other mysteries of His life by the acceptance which He made of them. "When he cometh into the world, He saith: ...Behold, I come to do Thy will, O God." Hence this mystery is an abridgement of all mysteries and contains the will and grace of all. Finally, this mystery is the throne of mercy, of the liberality and the glory of God. It is the throne of His mercy for us because, as we cannot approach Jesus but through Mary, we can see Jesus and speak to Him only by means of her. Jesus, who always hears His dear Mother, always grants His grace and mercy to poor sinners. "Let us go therefore with confidence to the throne of grace." (Heb. 4:16). It is the throne of His liberality toward Mary, because while the New Adam dwelt in that true terrestrial paradise, He worked so many miracles in secret that neither angels nor men can comprehend them. It is on this account that the saints call Mary the "magnificence of God"—as if God were magnificent only in Mary. (Is. 33:21). It is the throne of His glory for His Father, because it is in Mary that Jesus Christ has calmed His Father, angered against men, and that He has made restitution of the glory which sin ravished from Him, and that, by the sacrifice He made of His own will and of Himself, He has given Him more glory than ever the sacrifices of the Old Law could give—an infinite glory, which He had never before received from man.

Scriptures

Hebrews 10:5-9 NAB: "For this reason when he came into the world he said: 'Sacrifice and offering you did not desire, but a body you prepared for me; holocausts and sin offerings you took no delight in. Then I said, 'As is written of me in the scroll, behold, I come to do your will, O God. First he says, 'Sacrifices and offerings, holocausts and sin offerings, you neither desired nor delighted in.' These are offered according to the law. Then he says, 'Behold, I come to do your will.' He takes away the first to establish the second."

Hebrews 4:16 NAB: "So let us confidently approach the throne of grace to receive mercy and to find grace for timely help."

Isaiah 33:21 Douay: "Because only there our Lord is magnificent: a place of rivers, very broad and spacious streams: no ship with oars shall pass by it, neither shall the great galley pass through it."

Isaiah 33:22 NAB: "Indeed the Lord will be there with us, majestic; yes, the Lord our judge, the Lord our lawgiver, the Lord our king, he it is who will save us."

St. Louis refers to Hebrews and Isaiah to demonstrate that the mystery of the Incarnation reflects so beautifully the priority of Jesus' mission in coming to earth to teach us of the importance of obedience to God. We in turn find in Him a sympathetic and compassionate high priest who suffered just as we do, and it is through His sufferings and conquering thereof that we find salvation.

It is by means of this mystery of the Incarnation upon which all subsequent mysteries of His earthly ministry depend. The Incarnation is the first and most mysterious of mysteries because that which occurs during those nine months of gestation is hidden and unknown to the world. St. Louis states that, in Mary's womb, the predestined are chosen and the mystery of salvation history begins to take shape as Jesus' human body takes shape. Here "in utero" God's mercy is taking shape and it is by means of Mary, the mother, that we have access to this divine child in her womb. It is from Mary's womb that God's glory will be restored and where already a perfect sacrifice has occurred because Jesus has stripped himself of glory in order to become man. (Cf. Philippians 2:6-11.)

Application of the Lifestyle of True Devotion

1. Why is the Feast of the Annunciation central to St. Louis' theology of true devotion?
2. How has my lifestyle of true devotion given me a greater love for that Holy Day?
3. On which day of the year do I renew my consecration? How do I honor Jesus and Mary on this feast day?
4. How does the mystery of the Incarnation encompass all the other mysteries of our salvation?

V. Devotion to the Hail Mary and the Rosary

> 249. Those who adopt this slavery ought also to have a great devotion to saying the Hail Mary (the Angelic Salutation). Few Christians, however enlightened, know the real value, merit, excellence, and necessity of the Hail Mary. It was necessary for the Blessed Virgin to appear several times to great and enlightened saints to show them the merit of it. She did so to St. Dominic, St. John Capistrano and Blessed Alan de la Roche. They have composed entire works on the wonders and efficacy of that prayer for converting souls. They have loudly proclaimed and openly preached that, salvation having begun with the Hail Mary, the

salvation of each one of us in particular is attached to that prayer. They tell us that it is that prayer which made the dry and barren earth bring forth the fruit of life; and that it is that prayer well said which makes the word of God germinate in our souls, and bring forth Jesus Christ, the Fruit of Life. They tell us that the Hail Mary is a heavenly dew for watering the earth, which is the soul, to make it bring forth its fruit in season; and that a soul which is not watered by that prayer bears no fruit, and brings forth only thorns and brambles, and is ready to be cursed.

Who's Who?

Fr. Louis Tronson (1622-1700) became the 3rd Superior of St. Sulpice Seminary in Paris in 1676. It is possible de Montfort is referring to himself as the "ecclesiastic."

St. Dominic (mentioned above in #42) was born in 1170 in Calaroga, Castile Spain. He died August 6, 1221. According to legend, in the year 1208, Our Lady appeared to St. Dominic who was frustrated at his lack of success while preaching against the Albigensian heretics in Southern France. She said to him: "Wonder not that you have obtained so little fruit by your labors, you have spent them on barren soil, not yet watered with the dew of Divine Grace. When God willed to renew the face of the earth He began by sending down on it the fertilizing rain of the Angelic Salutation. Therefore preach my Psalter composed of 150 Angelic Salutations and 15 Our Fathers and you will obtain an abundant harvest."[14]

Through his preaching and teaching and praying the rosary he found great success in the conversion of heretics.

St. John Capistran was born in Capistrano, Italy 1385 and died October 23, 1456. He became a Franciscan Friar. He was mostly known for propagating devotion to the Holy Name of Jesus and was a student and friend of St. Bernardine of Siena and was engaged with him in the reform of the Franciscan Order. His many writings concerned the heresies of his day.[15]

Alan de la Roche was born in Brittany, France in 1428 and died in Zwolle, Holland September 8, 1475. He joined the Dominican order in 1450. Called the "Apostle of the Rosary," he founded the first confraternity of the Rosary at Douai in 1470 and labored for the establishment and restoration of devotion to the Rosary. He wrote extensively on many legends associated with the Rosary especially as it related to St. Dominic.[16] It is Alan de la Roche who first wrote about the revival of the Rosary being attributed to St. Dominic. The historical accuracy of the revelations to St. Dominic that de la Roche describes is contested.[17]

St. Louis states that our salvation is rooted in the "Hail Mary." Just as the greeting by the angel Gabriel brought forth fruitfulness from the womb of the Virgin, so, too, does the praying of the Rosary bring forth fruit in our lives.

Pope John Paul II speaks about the fruitfulness of holiness which occurs in the soul of those who pray the Rosary in the Introduction to his apostolic letter <u>Rosarium Virginis Mariae:</u>

"The Rosary of the Virgin Mary, which gradually took form in the second millennium under the guidance of the Spirit of God, is a prayer loved by countless Saints and encouraged by the Magisterium. Simple yet profound, it still remains, at the dawn of this third millennium, a prayer of great significance, destined to bring forth a harvest of holiness. It blends easily into the spiritual journey of the Christian life, which, after two thousand years, has lost none of the freshness of its beginnings and feels drawn by the Spirit of God to 'set out into the deep' (duc in altum!) in order once more to proclaim, and even cry out, before the world that Jesus Christ is Lord and Savior, 'the way, and the truth and the life' (Jn 14:6), 'the goal of human history and the point on which the desires of history and civilization turn.'"[18]

The praying of the Rosary for the true devotee of Mary is a powerful means of attaining sanctity and brings one daily into the mystery and beauty of the lives of Jesus and Mary. And we never pray it alone because Mary joins us in response to our request to: "pray for us now…"

250. Listen to what Our Lady revealed to Blessed Alan de la Roche, as he has recorded in his book on the dignity of the Rosary: "Know, my son, and make all others know, that it is a probable and proximate sign of eternal damnation to have an aversion, a lukewarmness, or a negligence in saying the Angelic Salutation, which has repaired the whole world." These words are at once ter- rible and consoling, and we should find it hard to believe them if we had not that holy man for a guarantee, and St. Dominic before him, and many great men since. But we have also the experience of several ages; for it has always been remarked that those who wear the outward sign of reprobation, like all impious heretics and proud worldlings, hate or despise the Hail Mary and the Rosary. Heretics still learn and say the Our Father, but not the Hail Mary nor the Rosary. They abhor it; they would rather wear a serpent than a Rosary. The proud also, although Catholics, have the same inclinations as their father Lucifer; and so have only contempt or indifference for the Hail Mary, and look at the Rosary as at a devotion which is good only for the ignorant and for those who cannot read. On the contrary, it is an equally universal experi- ence that those who have otherwise great marks of predestination about them love and relish the Hail Mary, and delight in saying it. We always see that the more a man is of God, the more he likes that prayer. This is what Our Lady also said to Blessed Alan, after the words which I have just quoted.

St. Louis cites Alan de La Roche's book <u>On the Dignity of the Rosary</u> to extend his position on the Hail Mary as a prayer of the predestinate (the saved). Those who are chosen have a particular devotion to this prayer. The reprobate (the damned), the proud (who refuse humility), heretics and worldlings have an aversion to the Hail Mary. He maintains, however, that the more one grows in the knowledge and love of God, the more one grows to love the Hail Mary because it is by means of the angelic salutation that God's plan of salvation is announced to the world.

> *251. I do not know how it is, nor why, but nevertheless I know well that it is true; nor have I any better secret of knowing whether a person is for God than to examine if he likes to say the Hail Mary and the Rosary. I say, if he likes; for it may happen that a person may be under some natural inability to say it, or even a supernatural one; yet, nevertheless, he likes it always, and always inspires the same liking in others.*

St. Louis uses one's love for or avoidance of praying the Rosary as an instrument of discernment. Those who are operating in the Holy Spirit are inclined to pray it. On the other hand, he states that there are those who have a natural inability to pray it which would be manifested in various mental inabilities to concentrate or focus. Of interest is his reference to those who exhibit a supernatural inability to pray the Rosary. This could be the effect of supernatural influences opposed to devotion to Mary; that is, fallen angels or evil spirits. This "better secret" for discernment should not be glossed over casually, but should be put to the test.

> *252. O predestinate souls, slaves of Jesus in Mary, learn that the Hail Mary is the most beautiful of all prayers after the Our Father. It is the most perfect compliment which you can give to Mary, because it is the compliment which the Most High sent her by an archangel, in order to win her heart; and it was so powerful over her heart by the secret charms of which it is so full, that in spite of her profound humility she gave her consent to the Incarnation of the Word. It is by this compliment also that you will infallibly win her heart, if you say it as you ought.*

> *253. The Hail Mary well said—that is, with attention, devotion, and modesty—is, according to the saints, the enemy of the devil which puts him to flight, and the hammer which crushes him. It is the sanctification of the soul, the joy of the angels, the melody of the predestinate, the canticle of the New Testament, the pleasure of Mary, and the glory of the Most Holy Trinity. The Hail Mary is a heavenly dew which fertilizes the soul. It is the chaste and loving kiss which we give to Mary. It is a vermilion rose which we present to her; a precious pearl we offer her; a chalice of divine ambrosial nectar which we proffer to her. All these are comparisons of the saints.*

204

254. I pray you urgently, by the love I bear you in Jesus and Mary, not to content yourselves with saying the Little Crown of the Blessed Virgin, but to say five decades, or even, if you have time, fifteen decades of the Rosary every day. At the moment of your death you will bless the day and the hour in which you followed my advice. Having thus sown in the blessings of Jesus and Mary, you will reap eternal blessings in heaven. "He who soweth in blessings, shall also reap blessings"(2 Cor. 9:6).

<u>Scriptures</u>

2 Corinthians 9:6 NAB: "Consider this: whoever sows sparingly will also reap sparingly, and whoever sows bountifully will also reap bountifully."

St. Louis cites 2 Corinthians to remind the devotee that God makes every grace abundant for us so that whatever we do in His name may be fruitful. Therefore one ought to do as much as possible to produce as much of an abundant harvest as possible.

St. Louis directly addresses the predestinate souls and encourages them to charm the heart of the Blessed Mother by praying well the Hail Mary. In such a way the Archangel Gabriel appealed to her soul.

Three characteristics describe how to pray the Rosary well:
1) with attention;
2) with devotion;
3) with modesty.

In the hands of the attentive, devoted and modest person the Rosary becomes a powerful weapon against the snares of the Devil. St. Louis exhorts the devout soul to pray the full Rosary daily (if possible) because it is such a powerful means for obtaining graces and glorifying God.

<u>Application of the Lifestyle of True Devotion</u>

1. Do I pray the Rosary faithfully every day?
2. Have I read the papal encyclicals on the Rosary? St. Louis de Montfort's <u>The</u> <u>Secret</u> of the Rosary?
3. What difficulties, temptations, distractions, do I experience when praying the Rosary?
4. What do I need to do in order to pray the Rosary with "attention, devotion and modesty"?

VI.   <u>Devotion to the Magnificat</u>

255. To thank God for the graces He has given to Our Lady, those who adopt this devotion will often say the Magnificat, as

Blessed Mary d'Oignies did, and many other saints. It is the only prayer, the only work, which the holy Virgin composed or rather which Jesus composed in her; for He spoke by her mouth. It is the greatest sacrifice of praise which God ever received from a pure creature in the law of grace. It is, on the one hand, the most humble and grateful, and on the other hand, the most sublime and exalted, of all canticles. There are in that canticle mysteries so great and hidden that the angels do not know them. The pious and erudite Gerson employed a great part of his life in composing works upon the most difficult subjects; and yet it was only at the close of his career, and even with trembling, that he undertook to comment on the Magnificat, so as to crown all his other works. He wrote a folio volume on it, bringing forward many admirable things about that beautiful and divine canticle. Among other things, he says that Our Lady often repeated it herself, and especially for thanksgiving after Communion. The learned Benzonius [Rutilio], in explaining the Magnificat, relates many miracles wrought by virtue of it, and says that the devils tremble and fly when they hear these words: "He hath showed might in his arm; He hath scattered the proud in the conceit of their heart" (Lk. 1:51).

Scriptures

Luke 1:51 CCD: "He has shown might with his arm; he has scattered the proud in the conceit of their heart."

Luke 1:51 NAB: "He has shown might with his arm, dispersed the arrogant of mind and heart."

St. Louis refers to Mary's Magnificat in Luke Chapter 1. It is such a powerful prayer resounding from Jesus and Mary together during her pregnancy that even the demons fly from it. The demons fly when we pray it too because of their pride and refusal to submit (in humility) to God. The virtue of obedience to the Father's will is repeated throughout this work as is the imitation of Mary's humility. By humility one will receive countless blessings and graces and will be drawn by the Lord to a deeper experience of His holiness.

Who's Who?

Blessed Marie d'Oignies was born around 1177 in Nivelles, Belgium and died June 23, 1213 at Oignies, Belgium. She was married at age 14, convinced her husband to live together celibately and turned their home into a leper hospice. She eventually became a recluse in a cell near the church of Oignies where she had many mystical experiences. She had a devotion to praying for the souls in Purgatory, receiving visions of St. John the Evangelist, her guardian angel, ecstasies, prophesies and had visions of the Blessed Sacrament. She may have been a stigmatist as wounds were found on her body after her death.[19]

Jean le Charlier de Gerson (1363-1429) was the Chancellor of the University of Paris in 1395. He was well known as a writer on mysticism. He wrote on the Incarnation and also a twelve-part work on the Magnificat entitled Collectorium super Magnificat. Following St. Bernard he promoted Mary as Queen of heaven, mistress of the angels, advocate and mediatrix, Virgin most merciful and Mother of mercy. Of note, Gerson also promoted devotion to St. Joseph.[20]

Benzonio Rutilio died in 1613 and was a bishop of Loretto. The text to which St. Louis refers is taken from Dissertations and Commentary on the Magnificat, 5th Book.[21]

St. Louis describes the Magnificat as the prayer which Jesus Himself inspires from the womb of Mary as "the greatest sacrifice of praise" because of its humility, purity and truthfulness. He also recommends it as a beautiful prayer to say after Communion at Mass in thanksgiving. This would be a most fitting moment to give praise to the Father with Mary for the marvels He has worked in the soul, viz., Jesus present in the Eucharist.

Application of the Lifestyle of True Devotion

1. What makes the Magnificat such a "sacrifice of praise"?
2. Do I meditate upon the words of this prayer?
3. Do I pray the Liturgy of the Hours?
4. Do I pray this prayer after Communion?
5. Why would devils fly at the sound of this prayer?

VII.   Contempt of and Flight from the World

> 256. Those faithful servants of Mary who adopt this devotion ought always greatly to despise, to hate and to eschew the corrupted world, and to make use of those practices of contempt of the world which we have given in the first part of this treatise.

The lifestyle of true devotion opposes a worldly lifestyle. Those who choose to consecrate themselves to Jesus through Mary cannot live according to the world, the flesh and the Devil. The "world" represents all that which is opposed to God and seeking first His kingdom. The world is dominated by Satan, whom Jesus describes as "prince of this world" who tries to destroy the Kingdom of God. Every Christian, but especially the devotees of Mary, strive to live "in the world, but not of the world," meaning that while we live in a world surrounded by evil and corruption, we do not adopt those values. Rather, we adopt the values of the Gospel as Jesus teaches us. And we live out those values in imitation of His Mother Mary. True devotion requires seeking first the kingdom of God through the mediation of His Queen.

Application of the Lifestyle of True Devotion

1. What do I do to fly from the world?
2. What does it mean to be "in the world but not of the world"?
3. Where do I go for greater prayer, silence and solitude?
4. How has my living the true devotion increased my desire for hiddenness, silence and recollection?

--Article Two—

Interior Practices

257. Besides the external practices of the devotion which we have been describing so far, and which we must not omit through negligence or contempt, so far as the state and condition of each one will allow him to observe them, there are some very sanctifying interior practices for those whom the Holy Spirit calls to high perfection. These may be expressed in four words: to do all our actions by Mary, with Mary, in Mary and for Mary; so that we may do them all the more perfectly by Jesus, with Jesus, in Jesus and for Jesus.

St. Louis introduces the interior practices of this lifestyle by reminding the devotee that it is the Holy Spirit Himself who calls souls to this high degree of holiness. There are four key means by which one progresses in holiness which he details in the following paragraphs. These four ways are to do all things through Mary so that that one may do them more perfectly for Jesus.

1. All by Mary

258. We must do all our actions by Mary; that is to say, we must obey her in all things, and in all things conduct ourselves by her spirit, which is the Holy Spirit of God. "Those who are led by the Spirit of God are the children of God." (Rom. 8:14). Those who are led by the spirit of Mary are the children of Mary, and consequently the children of God, as we have shown; and among so many clients of the Blessed Virgin, none are true or faithful but those who are led by her spirit. I have said that the spirit of Mary was the Spirit of God, because she was never led by her own

208

spirit, but always by the Spirit of God, who has rendered Himself so completely master of her that He has become her own spirit. It is on this account that St. Ambrose says: "Let the soul of Mary be in each of us to magnify the Lord, and the spirit of Mary be in each of us to rejoice in God." A soul is happy indeed when, like the good Jesuit lay-brother, Alphonse Rodriguez, who died in the odor of sanctity, it is all possessed and overruled by the spirit of Mary, a spirit meek and strong, zealous and prudent, humble and courageous, pure and fruitful.

Scriptures

Romans 8:14: "For those who are led by the Spirit of God are children of God."

St. Louis cites this quotation from Romans to emphasize the spiritual motherhood of Mary and that we become both the children of the Father and her children. And as children of God (and Mary) we are no longer slaves of sin and fear.

Who's Who?

St. Ambrose (see #217 above)

St. Alphonsus Rodriguez S.J., was born at Segovia, Spain July 25, 1532 and died at Majorca October 31,1617. Given to a life of prayer and mortification after the death of his wife and children, he became a Jesuit lay brother at the age of forty and served as porter at the college of Majorca for forty-six years. According to popular legend, he was known as the author of the "Little Office of the Immaculate Conception," and while this authorship cannot be proven, he did promote its use. He left manuscripts entitled "Spiritual Works" which are known for their simple, yet profound, spiritual knowledge. He was beatified in 1825 and canonized on September 6, 1887.[22]

We must obey Mary in all things which means to be obedient to the Holy Spirit, for it is to this same Holy Spirit that she is obedient. Mary's spirit is typified by meekness, strength, zeal, prudence, humility, courage, purity and fruitfulness. These are the particular virtues that we try to emulate in practicing the lifestyle of true devotion.

Quoting St. Ambrose, St. Louis emphasizes that a lifestyle of abiding in Mary's spirit allows us to magnify and rejoice in the Lord in a unique way through her mediation.

259. In order that the soul may let itself be led by Mary's spirit, it must first of all renounce its own spirit and its own lights and wills before it does anything. For example: It should do so before prayers, before saying or hearing Mass and before communicating; because the darkness of our own spirit, and the malice of our own will and operation, if we follow them, however good they may appear to us, will be an obstacle to the spirit of Mary. Secondly, we must deliver ourselves to the spirit of Mary to be moved and influenced by it in the manner she chooses. We must put ourselves and leave ourselves in her virginal hands, like a tool in the grasp of a workman, like a lute in the hands of a skillful player. We must lose ourselves and abandon ourselves to her, like a stone one throws into the sea. This can be done simply, and in an instant, by one glance of the mind, by one little movement of the will, or even verbally, in saying, for example, "I renounce myself, I give myself to thee, my dear Mother." We may not, perhaps, feel any sensible sweetness in this act of union, but it is not on that account the less real. It is just as if we were to say with equal sincerity, though without any sensible change in ourselves, what—may it please God—we never shall say: "I give myself to the devil"; we should not the less truly belong to the devil because we did not feel we belonged to him. Thirdly, we must from time to time, both during and after the action, renew the same act of offering and of union. The more often we do so, the sooner we shall be sanctified, and attain to union with Jesus Christ, which always follows necessarily on our union with Mary, because the spirit of Mary is the spirit of Jesus.

The process of being led by Mary's spirit is developed in three stages:

1) One must renounce his own spirit and will. Our self-will can be deceptive in that we do not always know what is best for us and we are drawn towards things that appear to be good, but in fact may be dangerous to our soul. Therefore one is not to trust too much in his own inspirations, but to discern carefully with Mary what course of action to take. This discernment is done best before praying and receiving the Eucharist when the soul is in a state of grace and in communication with God.

2) One must surrender patiently to her action in one's soul. St. Louis speaks of a complete abandonment of trust to her. This requires of us a great deal of patience as she directs us along the path of holiness which many times is in spiritual darkness. That is why St. Louis says that we may not feel that anything is happening in our interior or with our lives, but as long as we stay united with Mary, she will lead us directly to Jesus even in spiritual dryness. One must be careful at this stage not to quit the true devotion.

3) One must often renew this act of renunciation and surrender both before and after the sacrifice is made. St. Louis stresses that divine union is always possible for the soul that is in union with Mary. Divine union is the highest degree of union possible for us on earth. The lifestyle of true devotion can take us to great holiness and we must trust that Our Lady knows what she is doing with us.

<u>Application of the Lifestyle of True Devotion</u>

1. How do I obey Mary in all things?
2. How do I behave according to her spirit of meekness, zeal, prudence, humility, courage, purity and fruitfulness?
3. What does it mean to renounce my own spirit?
4. What is the significance of not experiencing any sensible consolation in uniting ourselves with Mary's spirit?
5. What accelerates the attainment of union with Jesus Christ in this devotion?

II. <u>All with Mary</u>

260. We must do all our actions with Mary; that is to say, we must in all our actions regard Mary as an accomplished model of every virtue and perfection which the Holy Spirit has formed in a pure creature for us to imitate according to our little measure. We must therefore in every action consider how Mary has done it, or how she would have done it, had she been in our place. For that end we must examine and meditate on the great virtues which she practiced during her life, and particularly, first of all, her lively faith, by which she believed without hesitation the angel's word, and believed faithfully and constantly up to the foot of the cross; secondly, her profound humility, which made her hide herself, hold her peace, submit to everything, and put herself the last of all; and, thirdly, her altogether divine purity, which never has had, and never can have, its equal under Heaven; and so on with all of her other virtues. Let us remember, I repeat, that Mary is the great and exclusive mold of God, proper to making living images of God at small cost and in a little time; and that a soul which has found that mold, and has lost itself in it, is presently changed into Jesus Christ, whom that mold represents to the life.

This second interior practice involves doing everything in imitation of Mary's virtues. In order to do this one must meditate frequently on her virtues, but especially on three of them which St. Louis repeats frequently:

1) Faith—Mary shows us how to live by faith in the Word of God expressed in the Scriptures and in the teachings of the Church.

2) Humility—Mary shows us how to live a life hidden from public acclaim and worldliness; how to desire and practice interior recollection; how to trust in Divine Providence in every moment of our lives; and, how to seek the lowest place to be exalted according to God's will.

3) Purity--- Mary shows us how to observe chastity according to our state of life and how to practice the beatitude: "Blessed are the pure of heart, for they shall see God."

One ought not be discouraged when considering the imitation of Mary's virtues because the process of virtue formation in a soul takes time and repetition. But with Mary's help we can make swift progress in acquiring virtues that may seem far beyond our reach.

Application of the Lifestyle of True Devotion

1.   How do I put into practice the imitation of Mary's virtues?
2.   When do I meditate upon Mary's life and virtues?

III. All in Mary

> *261. We must do our actions in Mary. Thoroughly to understand this practice, we must first know that our Blessed Lady is the true terrestrial paradise of the New Adam, and that the ancient paradise was but a figure of her. There are, then, in this earthly paradise, riches, beauties, rarities and inexplicable sweetnesses, which Jesus Christ, the New Adam, has left there; it was in this paradise that He took His complacence for nine months, worked His wonders and displayed His riches with the magnificence of a God. This most holy place is composed only of a virginal and immaculate earth, of which the New Adam was formed, and on which he was nourished, without any spot or stain, by the operation of the Holy Spirit, who dwelt there. It is in this earthly paradise that there is the true tree of life, which has borne Jesus Christ, the Fruit of Life, and the tree of the knowledge of good and evil, which has given light unto the world. There are in this divine place trees planted by the hand of God, and watered by his divine unction, which have borne and daily bear fruits of a divine taste. There are flowerbeds adorned with beautiful and varied blossoms of virtues, diffusing odors which delight the very angels. There are meadows green with hope, impregnable towers of strength, and the most charming houses of confidence. It is only the Holy Spirit who can make us know the hidden truth of these figures of material things. There is in this place an air of perfect purity; a fair sun, without shadow, of the Divinity; a fair day, without night, of the Sacred Humanity; a continual burning furnace of love, where all the iron that is cast into it is changed by excessive heat, to gold. There is a river of humility which springs from the earth, and which, dividing itself into four branches, waters all that enchanted place; and these are the four cardinal virtues.*

This third interior practice focuses on the purity and beauty of Mary's Immaculate Heart and is one of the most poetic pieces in the <u>True Devotion</u>. St. Louis compares Mary to a new Garden of Eden. There is in her a new beauty brought about by the very fact that Jesus dwelt in her for nine months. To do all our actions in Mary then, means to place ourselves spiritually in her life, virtues, ongoing fruitfulness, hope, strength, confidence, and purity. In Mary we breathe in the Divinity of Christ and His humanity. In Mary our love is constantly being purified. In Mary we drink abundantly of her humility, prudence, temperance, fortitude, and justice. In the lifestyle of true devotion we do things "in Mary" which is synonymous with doing them in beauty. All of our actions are eventually transformed into beauty when we do them in her Immaculate Heart. It takes prayer and trust to recognize this truth, but this is what we gain when we give ourselves totally to her and she gives herself totally to us.

Vocabulary

Complacence = a feeling of quiet pleasure.

> *262. The Holy Spirit, by the mouth of the Fathers, also styles the Blessed Virgin the Eastern Gate, by which the High Priest, Jesus Christ, enters the world and leaves it. (Ezech. 44:2-3). By it He came the first time, and by it He will come the second. The sanctuary of the divinity, the repose of the Most Holy Trinity, the throne of God, the city of God, the altar of God, the temple of God, the world of God—all these different epithets and encomiums are most substantially pure with reference to the different marvels and graces which the Most High has wrought in Mary. Oh, what riches! What glory! What pleasure! What happiness, to be able to enter into and dwell in Mary, where the Most High has set up the throne of His supreme glory!*

Scriptures

Ezekiel 44:2-3 NAB: "He said to me: This gate is to remain closed; it is not to be opened for anyone to enter by it; since the Lord, the God of Israel, has entered by it, it shall remain closed. Only the prince may sit down in it to eat his meal in the presence of the Lord. He must enter by way of the vestibule of the gate, and leave by the same way."

St. Louis employs this Scripture from Ezekiel which describes the closed gate of the Temple. He, following the Church Fathers, interprets it to mean that Mary is the gate whose body is the "closed gate" by which the high priest alone, Jesus Christ, enters. Nobody else may gain entrance to the Temple in Jerusalem, but now in Mary all those who are devoted to her by means of the consecration gain access to her interior and the interior in which Jesus Christ dwelt as man.

St. Louis continues to support his statement of the holiness of Mary because of Jesus' presence in her. He compares her to the closed gate of the Temple of Jerusalem which is closed signifying God's presence within the Temple. In the same way God's presence within Mary has consecrated her.

Vocabulary

Epithet = a word added to the name of a person to describe a characteristic attribute.
Encomium = a formal expression of high praise; like a eulogy.

> *263. But how difficult it is for sinners like ourselves to have the permission, the capacity and the light to enter into a place so high and so holy, which is guarded, not by one of the Cherubim like the old earthly paradise (Gen 3:24), but by the Holy Spirit Himself, who is its absolute master. He Himself has said of it: "My sister, My spouse, is a garden enclosed, a garden enclosed, a fountain sealed up." (Canticles 4:12). Mary is shut, Mary is sealed. The miserable children of Adam and Eve, driven from the earthly paradise, cannot enter into this one except by a particular grace of the Holy Spirit, which they must merit.*

Scriptures

Genesis 3:24 NAB: "When [God] expelled the man, he settled him east of the garden of Eden; and he stationed the cherubim and the fiery revolving sword, to guard the way to the tree of life."
Canticles 4:12 CCD: "My sister, my spouse, is a garden enclosed, a garden enclosed, a fountain sealed up."
Songs of Songs 4:12 NAB: "You are an enclosed garden, my sister, my bride, an enclosed garden, a fountain sealed."
These Scriptures are used to refer to Mary as the closed gate, the enclosed garden who is guarded by angels. Strangers and sinners may not enter there; only those who have received permission may gain admittance into her Immaculate Heart.
St. Louis continues with the idea of the closed gate of the temple and the enclosed garden of the virgin bride, Mary. Entry into this enclosed garden, this closed gate, or the Immaculate Heart of Mary is obtained by a special gift of the Holy Spirit. The lifestyle of true devotion, while available to everybody, will not be understood by everybody, nor desired by everybody. One must pray for and seek this gift. There is a continuous action within the Immaculate Heart. This action is one of on-going surrender so that one's interior is marked by a complacency, peace, confidence, assurance and total self-giving; in sum, love. These latter virtues mark

214

the arrival of the grace of true devotion, which is not a consecration made once upon a time or a book once read, but a lifestyle to be lived and renewed daily.

> *264. After we have obtained this illustrious grace by our fidelity, we must remain in the fair interior of Mary with complacency, repose there in peace, lean our weight there in confidence, hide ourselves there with assurance, and lose ourselves there without reserve. Thus, in that virginal bosom, (1) the soul shall be nourished with the milk of grace and maternal mercy; (2) it shall be delivered from its troubles, fears and scruples; (3) it shall be in safety against all its enemies—the world, the devil and sin—who never have entrance there. It is on this account that Mary says that they who work in her shall not sin (Ecclus. 24:30); that is to say, those who dwell in Mary in spirit shall fall into no considerable fault. Lastly, (4) the soul shall be formed in Jesus Christ and Jesus Christ in it, because her bosom is, as the holy Fathers say, the chamber of the divine sacraments, where Jesus Christ and all the elect have been formed. "This man and that man is born in her."*

Scriptures

Ecclesiasticus 24:30 Douay: "He that hearkeneth to me, shall not be confounded: and they that work by me, shall not sin."

Sirach 24:21 NAB: "He who obeys me will not be put to shame, he who serves me will never fail."

Concerning the quotation from the last line of the above paragraph cf. Psalm 86:5 Douay: "And of Sion they shall say: "One and all were born in her; and he who has established her is the Most High Lord."

Psalm 87:5 NAB: "But of Zion is must be said: "They all were born here. The Most High confirms this; the Lord notes in the register of the peoples: 'This one was born here.'

In these Scriptures St. Louis emphasizes the security and safety of being in Mary through obedience to her and the promise and guarantee of her motherly protection. The person who has entrusted himself to the Immaculate Heart of Mary experiences nourishment and sustenance from the grace of her motherly loving kindness. He experiences a relief from fears and scrupulosity. He experiences protection from all those forces opposed to God, for a heart entrusted totally to Mary cannot at the same time admit God's enemies into its interior. They won't remain and die in grave mortal sin. And the devotee is formed into Jesus, as we have previously seen.

Application of the Lifestyle of True Devotion

    1.   How does performing all my thoughts, words and actions "in Mary" reflect paradise on earth?

    2.   When I pray, do I ask the angels to grant me admittance to the Immaculate Heart of Mary?

    3.   What are the four effects of doing all things "in Mary" as St. Louis illustrates in paragraph #264?

IV.   <u>All for Mary</u>

> *265. Finally we must do all our actions for Mary. As we have given ourselves up entirely to her service, it is but just to do everything for her as servants and slaves. It is not that we take her for the last end of our services, for that is Jesus Christ alone; but we take her for our proximate end, our mysterious means and our easy way to go to Him. Like good servants and slaves, we must not remain idle, but, supported by her protection, we must undertake and achieve great things for this august sovereign. We must defend her privileges when they are disputed; we must stand up for her glory when it is attacked; we must draw all the world, if we can, to her service, and to this true and solid devotion; we must speak and cry out against those who abuse her devotion to outrage her Son, and we must at the same time establish this veritable devotion; we must pretend to no recompense for our little services, except the honor or belonging to so sweet a Queen, and the happiness of being united through her to Jesus her Son by an indissoluble tie, in time and in eternity. Glory to Jesus in Mary! Glory to Mary in Jesus! Glory to God alone!*

All one's actions are done for Mary because we have consecrated ourselves to her service like knights to a queen "like the eyes of a servant on the hand of her mistress…" (Psalm 123:2). Such tender attention to the Queen gives pleasure to Jesus. St. Louis encourages her devotees to undertake great things for Mary. Such chivalry includes:

--defending her privileges;

--defending her reputation;

--promoting the lifestyle of true devotion;

--defending the true devotion from its enemies;

--establishing true devotion without self-interest or self-aggrandizement.

Here one is also reminded of Our Lady's request at Fatima where she asked the children to pray in reparation for the five sins that pierce her Immaculate Heart. These include: (1) sins against her Immaculate Conception; (2) sins against her Perpetual Virginity; (3) sins against her Divine Maternity; (4) sins of those who try publicly to implant in children's hearts indifference, contempt and hatred against our Immaculate Mother; and (5) the sins of those who directly insult her in her sacred images.

<u>Application of the Lifestyle of True Devotion</u>

1. How am I doing all things "for Mary"?
2. What works am I undertaking for her?
3. How am I promoting the lifestyle of true devotion to Jesus through Mary?

V. <u>Manner of Practicing This Devotion When We Go to Holy Communion</u>

> *266. (1) You must humble yourself most profoundly before God. (2) You must renounce your corrupt interior and your dispositions, however good your self-love may make them look. (3) You must renew your consecration by saying: "I am all thine, my dear Mistress, with all that I have." (4) You must implore that good Mother to lend you her heart, that you may receive her Son there with the same dispositions as her own. You will explain to her that it touches her Son's glory to be put into a heart so sullied and so inconstant as yours, which would not fail either to lessen His glory or to destroy it. But if she will come and dwell with you, in order to receive her Son, she can do so by the dominion which she has over all hearts; and her Son will be well received by her, without stain, without danger of being outraged or unnoticed: "God is in the midst thereof, it shall not be moved." (Ps. 45:6). You will tell her confidently that all you have given her of your goods is little enough to honor her; but that by Holy Communion you wish to make her the same present as the Eternal Father gave her, and that you will honor her more by that than if you gave her all the goods in the world; and finally, that Jesus, who loves her in a most special manner, still desires to take His pleasure and repose in her, even in your soul, though it be far filthier and poorer than the stable where He did not hesitate to come, simply because she was there. You will ask her for her heart, by these tender words: "I take thee for my all. Give me thy heart, O Mary."*

<u>Scriptures</u>

Psalm 45:6 Douay: "God is in its midst; it shall not be disturbed; God will help it at the break of dawn."

Psalm 46:6 NAB: "God is in its midst; it shall not be shaken; God will help it at break of day."

St. Louis quotes from Psalm 46 which refers to the City of God. This City,

Jerusalem, and in this context Mary, is where God dwells. God dwells there with power, majesty and glory. In the Eucharist Jesus comes to dwell in the person who invites Mary into his soul, and there Jesus comes with power, majesty and glory in that sacrament.

The last quotation is an adaptation of John 19:27: " Then he said to the disciple, 'Behold your mother.' And from that hour the disciple took her into his home." And Proverbs 23:26: "My son, give me your heart, and let your eyes keep to my ways."

These final Scriptures emphasize the total self-donation of the soul to Mary and of Mary to the soul.

St. Louis culminates this treatment of true devotion with the Eucharist. He explains how to practice the lifestyle of true devotion to Jesus by Mary as it involves the reception of Jesus in the Eucharist. He states that Mary makes the reception of Holy Communion a true experience of heaven on earth. His treatment includes guides to practicing this devotion before, during and after Communion.

In order to be well-disposed to receive the Eucharist, St. Louis proposes that a person prepare himself by:

--humility
--renunciation of self-love
--renewal of the formula of consecration
--asking for Mary's dispositions of heart in order to receive her Son worthily.

Application of the Lifestyle of True Devotion

1. What are the four ways St. Louis recommends to prepare for Holy Communion?
2. What is the best way to honor Mary at Communion?

2nd At Holy Communion

> 267. After the Our Father, just before receiving Jesus Christ, you say three times: "Lord, I am not worthy." Say the first one to the Eternal Father, telling Him you are not worthy, because of your evil thoughts and ingratitude toward so good a Father, to receive His only Son; but that He is to behold Mary, His handmaid—"Behold the handmaid of the Lord" (Lk. 1:38)—who acts for you and who gives you a singular confidence and hope with his Majesty: "For thou singularly hast settled me in hope." (Ps. 4:10).

Scriptures

Luke 1:38 NAB: "Behold, I am the handmaid of the Lord."
Psalm 4:9 Douay: " As soon as I lie down, I fall peacefully asleep, for you

218

alone, O Lord, bring security to my dwelling."

Psalm 4: 9 NAB: "In peace I shall both lie down and sleep, for you alone, Lord, make me secure."

The quotation from Luke is from the scene of the Annunciation and in this context represents the soul who has become a slave of love to the Father's will in imitation of Mary's humility, love and self-sacrifice. The soul asks the Father to behold Mary's virtues in him. The hope of taking on Mary's virtues is not a vain or useless hope, but one that is very fruitful.

Before receiving Communion we express our unworthiness to receive the Lord because we have sinned with our thoughts. Nevertheless, we ask the Father to look upon Mary who is acting on our behalf as the "handmaid of the Lord" and can bring purity to our thoughts. St. Louis mentions saying the "Lord, I am not worthy" three times (in honor of the Trinity) because that was the method in the Tridentine Mass of St. Louis' time. Currently, in the Mass of Paul VI it is recited one time only.

> *268. You will say to the Son: "Lord, I am not worthy"; telling Him that you are not worthy to receive Him because of your idle and evil words and your infidelity to His service; but that nevertheless you pray Him to have pity on you, because you are about to bring Him into the house of His own Mother and yours, and that you will not let Him go without His coming to lodge with her: "I held Him; and I will not let Him go, till I bring him into my Mother's house and into the chamber of her that bore me." (Canticles 3:4). You will pray to Him to rise, and come to the place of His repose and into the ark of His sanctification: "Arise, Lord, into Thy resting place: Thou and the ark which Thou has sanctified." (Ps. 131:8). Tell Him you put no confidence at all in your own merits, your own strength and your own preparations, as Esau did; but that you trust only in Mary, your dear Mother, as the little Jacob did in Rebecca. Tell Him that, sinner and Esau that you are, you dare to approach His sanctity, supported and adorned as you are with the virtues of His holy Mother.*

Scriptures

Canticle of Canticles 3:4 Douay: "When I had passed by them, I found him whom my soul loveth: I held him: and I will not let him go, till I bring him into my mother's house, and into the chamber of her that bore me."

Song of Songs 3:4 NAB: "I had hardly left them when I found him whom my heart loves. I took hold of him and would not let him go till I should bring him to the home of my mother, to the room of my parent."

Psalm 131:8 CCD: "Advance, O Lord, to your resting place, you and the ark of your majesty."

Psalm 132:8 NAB: "Arise, Lord come to your resting place, you and your majestic ark."

In these Scriptures the communicant invites Jesus to come into his soul because in there He will find their mother who dwells mystically within by means of the consecration to her. The Lord Jesus finally finds a suitable dwelling place in the soul of the person consecrated to Mary and is urged to arise and take His rest therein.

At the reception of Holy Communion one prays in reparation for one's unworthiness on account of the sins of one's words. St. Louis resumes the idea that now that the soul has been consecrated to Mary, and she now abides therein, Jesus will be eager to dwell in that soul because Mary is there. The devotee's soul has become more beautiful because of Mary's presence. The soul presents itself with humility claiming no rights of its own, but only those of the Mother of the Son.

> *269. You will say to the Holy Spirit: "Lord, I am not worthy"; telling Him that you are not worthy to receive this masterpiece of His charity, because of the lukewarmness and iniquity of your actions, and because of your resistance to His inpsirations; but that all your confidence is in Mary, His faithful spouse. You will say, with St. Bernard: "She is my greatest security; she is the source of all my hope." You can even pray Him to come Himself in Mary, His inseparable spouse, telling Him that her bosom is as pure and her heart as burning as ever; and that, without His descent into your soul, neither Jesus nor Mary will be formed nor worthily lodged.*

Here one prays in reparation for his unworthiness because he has sinned by deeds of commission and omission and by failing to respond to grace. St. Louis advises the devotee to invoke the Holy Spirit to come to His spouse from whom He cannot "bear" to be separated. The perfect reception of Jesus and Mary requires the action of the Holy Spirit. At Communion St. Louis encourages us to pray in reparation to each person of the Blessed Trinity for sins of our thoughts, words and deeds. Each person of the Trinity is irresistibly drawn to the soul consecrated to Mary seeing her presence therein.

Application of the Lifestyle of True Devotion

1. How does Mary help purify my thoughts, words and deeds when I receive the Eucharist?

> *270. After Holy Communion, inwardly recollected and holding your eyes shut, you will introduce Jesus into the heart of Mary. You will give Him to His Mother, who will receive Him lovingly, will place Him honorably, will adore Him profoundly, will love Him perfectly, will embrace Him closely, and will render to Him, in spirit and in truth, many homages which are unknown to us in our thick darkness.*

The period after the reception of the Eucharist is a time of profound meditation and silence. It is a time to introduce Jesus to Mary who will receive Him in our soul perfectly and in accord with His divine majesty. St. Louis presents several ideas for meditation in the following paragraphs including:

--giving Jesus over to His Mother;
--humble silence and adoration of the Mother and Son meeting in one's soul;
--silent praise;
--prayers for the coming of the Kingdom of God.;
--prayers for the gift of wisdom, love, forgiveness, etc.

The Holy Spirit will lead the soul to a deep meditation if the soul lends itself to this true devotion. The key to this meditation is humility, silence, time and interior recollection. The gift of contemplation and divine union can occur through the lifestyle of true devotion.

> *271. Or else you will keep yourself profoundly humbled in your heart, in the presence of Jesus residing in Mary. Or else you will sit like a slave at the gate of the King's palace, where He is speaking with the Queen; and while they talk to each other without need of you, you will go in spirit to Heaven and over all the earth, praying all creatures to thank, adore and love Jesus and Mary in your place: "Come, let us adore." (Ps. 94:6).*

Scriptures

Psalm 94:6 CCD: "Come, let us bow down in worship, let us kneel before the Lord who made us."

Psalm 95:6 NAB: "Enter, let us bow down in worship; let us kneel before the Lord who made us."

St. Louis applies this psalm to the moment of adoration that takes place in a soul who has consecrated himself to Mary when Jesus and Mary "meet" in that soul during Holy Communion. That encounter is one of great adoration and loving reverence.

St. Louis recommends quiet adoration and awe in the presence of Jesus and

Mary. For St. Louis this period after Communion, filled with the loving exchange between Mother and Son in the depths of one's soul, causes one to be zealous for proclaiming Jesus to the world.

> *272. Or else you will yourself ask of Jesus, in union with Mary, the coming of His kingdom on earth, through His holy Mother; or you will sue for divine wisdom, or for divine love, for the pardon of your sins, or for some other grace; but always by Mary and in Mary; saying, while you look, aside at yourself: "Lord, look not at my sins"*; "but let Your eyes look at nothing in me but the virtues and merits of Mary."[Adaptation of Psalm 16:2 in reference to Mary] And then, remembering your sins, you will add: "It is I who have committed these sins" (cf. Matt. 13:28); or you will say: "Deliver me from the unjust and deceitful man" (Ps. 42:1); or else: "My Jesus, You must increase in my soul, and I must decrease"(Jn 3:30); Mary, you must increase within me, and I must be still less than I have been. "O Jesus and Mary, increase in me, and multiply yourselves outside in others also." (cf. Gen 1:22ff.)*

<u>Scriptures</u>

*This phrase is from the first priestly prayer before Communion. The Latin of the Tridentine Mass reads: "Ne respicias, Domine, peccata mea." The modern English translation reads: "By your holy body and blood free me from all my sins, and from every evil."

Psalm 16:2 CCD: "From you let my judgment come; your eyes behold what is right."

Psalm 17:2 NAB: "From you let my vindication come; your eyes see what is right."

Matthew 13:28 NAB: "He answered, 'An enemy has done this.' His slaves said to him, 'Do you want us to go and pull them up?'"

Psalm 43:1 NAB: "Grant me justice, God; defend me from a faithless people; from the deceitful and unjust rescue me."

Psalm 42:1 CCD: "Do me justice, O God, and fight my fight against a faithless people; from the deceitful and impious man rescue me."

John 3:30 NAB: "He must increase; I must decrease."

Gen 1:22ff NAB: "And God blessed them [the great sea monsters], saying, "Be fertile, multiply, and fill the water of the seas; and let the birds multiply on the earth." This Chapter continues with the creation of man and woman, made in the image and likeness of God, with the same commandment to "be fertile and multiply; fill the earth and subdue it. Have dominion over the fish of the sea, the birds of the air, and all the living things that move on the earth."

Each of these Scriptures represents an act of humility for one's sinfulness in the presence of the Almighty in the soul during Holy Communion. There is also the inclination of the soul to become more and more hidden that the life of Christ within it may shine forth more brightly and fully.

St. Louis uses this time after Communion as a moment to ask Jesus for graces (always in union with Mary), for forgiveness of sins, and also for Mary's spirit to increase in us and for our self-will and pride to decrease, and for Jesus and Mary to increase in us in order that we may bear supernatural life in other souls. In our lifestyle of true devotion we must learn to use the time after Communion fruitfully and not to rush through it. Too often we are distracted at Mass and what is going on around us and waste the occasion for so many graces. Let us learn to become more prayerful and more contemplative with Mary in Jesus within us.

> *273. There are an infinity of other thoughts which the Holy Spirit furnishes, and will furnish you, if you are thoroughly interior, mortified and faithful to this grand and sublime devotion which I have been teaching you. But always remember that the more you allow Mary to act in your Communion, the more Jesus will be glorified; and you will allow Mary to act for Jesus and Jesus to act in Mary in the measure that you humble yourself and listen to them in peace and in silence, without troubling yourself about seeing, tasting or feeling; for the just man lives throughout on faith, and particularly in Holy Communion, which is an action of faith: "My just man liveth by faith." (Heb. 10:38).*

Scriptures

Hebrews 10:38 CCD: "Now my just one lives by faith. But if he draws back, he will not please my soul."

Hebrews 10:38 NAB: "'But my just one shall live by faith, and if he draws back I take no pleasure in him.'"

St. Louis refers to Hebrews to emphasize that the practice of true devotion to Jesus through Mary is an act of faith. This faith must persevere many times in darkness, but the devotee's faith is augmented by Mary's faith and virtues and by her motherly intercession. Once one has begun to live the true devotion one should persevere and not become inconstant (as the false devotees mentioned earlier) despite the lack of sensible consolations. Those who draw back will lose grace; those who remain constant will bear fruit abundantly because Mary makes all things fruitful. Through her the Author of life has come into the world and by her He shall return in glory.

St. Louis concludes this section and his entire treatment on true devotion to Jesus through Mary, by emphasizing the centrality of the Eucharist. The present post-Communion reflections are but samples. The key to obtaining holiness through the lifestyle of true devotion is to practice it as an interior devotion with mortification and faithfulness. It must be practiced with great humility and without searching for spiritual consolations. By true devotion, with trust in Mary's care to lead us directly to Jesus and in the reception of the Eucharist we trust that she will bring us into divine union with Him, the Beloved of our soul.

Application of the Lifestyle of True Devotion

1. How is Jesus glorified all the more when I receive Him in the Eucharist?
2. Why is the pursuit of consolations at Communion a distraction?
3. How can I prevent being distracted at Communion?

Index

Scriptural Index

END NOTES
Part One Introduction

[1] Pope John Paul II <u>Rosarium Virginis Mariae</u>.(Vatican City: Italy, October 16, 2002)

[2] Pope John Paul II. <u>Gift and Mystery: On the 50th Anniversary of My Priestly Ordination</u> (New York: Doubleday, 1996), 28-29.

[3] St. Louis de Montfort, <u>True Devotion to Mary</u>, trans. Fr. Frederick Faber (Rockford, IL: TAN Books and Publishers, Inc., 1985), 22-23.

Preliminary Remarks
Chapter One

[1] St. Louis Marie Grignion de Montfort <u>True Devotion</u> (Bay Shore, NY: Montfort Publications, 1996).

[2] Galatians 2:20.

[3] Pope Paul VI <u>Marialis Cultus</u>. (Vatican City: Italy) February 2, 1974 #25.

[4] Ibid., #26.

[5] St. Louis Marie Grignion de Montfort. <u>True Devotion to Mary</u> (Rockford, IL: TAN Books and Publishers, Inc.), 1985. #7 no. 2.

[6] Michael O'Carroll, C.S.Sp."St. Bonaventure" in <u>Theotokos: A Theological Encyclopedia of the Blessed Virgin Mary</u>. (Wilmington, DE: Michael Glazier, Inc., 1982) 84-85.

[7] Luigi Gambero "St. Bonaventure." <u>Mary in the Middle Ages</u>. trans. Thomas Buffer (San Francisco CA: Ignatius Press, 2005), 206-215.

[8] "St. Augustine Doctor of the Church (354-430)" in <u>Theotokos: A Theological Encyclopedia of the Blessed Virgin Mary.</u> 63-66.

[9] Cf. Luigi Gambero, <u>Mary and the Fathers of the Church: The Blessed Virgin Mary in Patristic Thought</u>. S.M. trans. Thomas Buffer (San Francisco: Ignatius Press. 1999), 216-230.

[10] "The Secret of Mary" in: <u>God Alone: the Collected Writings of St. Louis Marie de Montfort</u> (Bay Shore, NY: Montfort Publications, 1999), 283.

[11] <u>True Devotion</u>. (Rockford, IL: TAN Books and Publishers, Inc. 1985), 7.; Also, "St. Eucherius" www.New Advent.org, 2005.

[12] <u>Rosarium Virginis Mariae</u>. Pope John Paul II, 2002, #21.

[13] <u>Marialis Cultus</u>, #26.

[14] Lumen Gentium, #62.

[15] Pope John Paul II "The Spirit's Special Presence in the Blessed Virgin Mary.". April 18, 1990 quoted in <u>The Holy Spirit in the Writings of Pope John Paul II</u>. Fr. Bill McCarthy, MSA. (Mckees Rocks, Pa: St. Andrew's Productions, 2001), 179.

[16] Pius IX, Ineffabilis Deus, 1854 quoted in Catechism of the Catholic Church #491

[17] Pope John Paul II "Mary's Presence in the Upper Room at Jerusalem in Preparation for the Coming of the Holy Spirit", , June 28,1989 quoted in McCarthy, 89-90.

[18] Patrick Gaffney, Editor in Chief. Jesus Living in Mary: Handbook of the Spirituality of St. Louis Marie de Montfort, (Bay Shore, NY: Montfort Publications, 1994), 233

[19] Luigi Gambero Mary in the Middle Ages: The Blessed Virgin Mary in the Thought of Medieval Latin Theologians. 131-141.

[20] St. Bernard, Theotokos, 75-76.

[21] "Bernardine of Siena," Mary in the Middle Ages. 290-299.

[22] "St. Bernardine of Siena," Theotokos. 77-78.

[23] CCC, #2089.

[24] Jesus Living in Mary, 595.

[25] "Francis Suarez" Theotokos. 334-335.

[26] "Justus Lipsius" in Catholic Encyclopedia http://www.newadvent.org/cathen/09280b.htm.

[27] "Ephrem the Syrian". Mary and the Fathers of The Church. 108-119.

[28] "Ephraem of Syria." Theotokos. 132-134.

[29] Pope John Paul II. Encyclical Letter Redemptoris Mater: On the Blessed Virgin Mary in the Life of the Pilgrim Church Vatican Translation (Boston: Daughters of St. Paul, 1987), #31.

[30] Cf. "Cyril of Jerusalem". in Theotokos. 114-115 and "Cyril of Jerusalem and the Jerusalem Catecheses" in Mary and the Fathers of the Church. 131-139

[31] Cf. "Germanus of Constantinople" in Theotokos, 156 and "Germanus of Constantinople" in Mary and the Fathers of the Church, 381-388.

[32] Cf. "John of Damascus, Doctor of the Church" in Theotokos 199-200 and "John Damascene" in Mary and the Fathers of the Church, 400-408.

[33] Cf. "Anselm Doctor of the Church in Theotokos, 33-34 and "Anselm of Canterbury" in Mary in the Middle Ages, 109-115.

[34] "Thomas Aquinas Doctor of the Church" in Theotokos, 343-344 and "Thomas Aquinas" in Mary in the Middle Ages, 234-240.

[35] "John Oecolampadius" Catholic Encyclopedia. http://www.newadvent.org/cathen/11213a.htm

[36] St. Louis Marie Grignion de Montfort."The Secret of the Rosary" in God Alone: The Collected Writings of St. Louis Marie de Montfort. (Bay Shore, NY: Montfort Publications, 1999), 203.

[37] "Coutances" in Catholic Encyclopedia htt://www.newadvent.org/cathen/0455b.htm and St. Louis Marie Grignion de Montfort Traité de la Vraie Dévotion à la Sainte Vierge (Paris: Editions du Soleil 1966), paragraph 57 no. 1.

[38] "Gaston Jean Baptiste de Renty" in Catholic Encyclopedia http://www.newadvent.org /cathen/12773a.htm

[39] "St. Vincent Ferrer" in <u>Catholic Encyclopedia</u>. http://www.newadvent.org/cathen/15437a.htm

[40] "Saints O'the Day October 9 Denis, Rusticus, And Eleutherius" http://www.saintpatrickdc.org/ss/1009lhtm. The reference to St Denis' letter to Paul is apocroyphal and not authentic. See Traité, #49, No. 1.

[41] Here I deviate from Father Faber's translation of "ses counseils diaboliques," which he translates as "his diabolical *councils*," in favor of "his diabolical *counsels*." Although the French can be translated into either "counsel" or "council", the primary meaning which ought to be maintained is the one of "bad advice from the devil."

Chapter Two

[1] <u>Catechism of the Catholic Church</u> #1264

[2] <u>Redemptoris Mater</u>, #38.

[3] Ibid., #21

[4] For further discussion see: Rev. Livoi Fanzaga <u>The Deceiver: Our Daily Struggle With Satan</u>. (Fort Collins, CO: Roman Catholic Books, 2000,) especially Chapter 10, "Temptations in Daily Life."

[5] See Fr. Reginald Garrigou-Lagrange, O.P <u>The Three Ages of The Interior Life: Prelude of Eternal Life</u>. (Rockford, IL: TAN Books and Publishers, Inc. 1947), 384.

[6] <u>CCC</u>, #2120

[7] Pope John Paul II <u>Ecclesia de Eucharistia</u>, ,(Vatican City: Italy, 2003), #36.

[8] See Adolphe Tanquerey, S.S.,D.D <u>The Spiritual Life</u>. (Westminster, MD: The Newman Press, 1930), #931.

[9] Garrigou-Lagrange, 385.

[10] <u>Lumen Gentium</u>, #65.

[11] Tanquerey, #1127-1131.

[12] <u>Redemptoris Mater</u>, #13.

[13] Tanquerey, #1057-1067.

[14] Ibid., #501-512 op cit..

[15] Ibid., #754-783 op. cit.

[16] Ibid., #1100-1107.

[17] <u>Lumen Gentium</u>, #61,62.

[18] Tanquerey, #1088-1090.

[19] Ibid., #1348-1351

[20] Pope John Paul II's "Reflections on the Gifts of the Holy Spirit." Address on April 9, 1989. Quoted in Fr. Bill McCarthy, MSA. <u>The Holy Spirit in theWritings of Pope John Paul II</u>. (Mckees Rocks, PA: St. Andrew's Productions, 2001), 378.

[21] Tanquerey, #1093-1094.

[22] Cf. "Dulia." <u>Catholic Encyclopedia</u>. www.newadvent.org

[23] "The Little Crown of the Blessed Virgin Mary." St. Louis de Montfort, www.newadvent.org

[24] Cf. Rev. Albert Power, S.J., M.A. Our Lady's Titles. (New York: Frederick Pustotet Co. Inc., 1932).

[25] "Paul de Barry" in Catholic Encyclpedia http://www.newadvent. org/cathen/02312b.htm. The original French title is Le paradis ouvert à Philagie par cent dévotions à la Mère de Dieu, aisées à pratiquer aux jours de ses fêtes et octaves qui se rencontrent à chaque mois de l'année.

[26] Letter of Pope John Paul II to the Religious of the Montfortian Congregations on the occasion of the 160th Anniversary of the publication of "True Devotion to the Blessed Virgin." December 8, 2003 www.montfort.org, 7.

[27] René Laurentin. Dieu Seul Est Ma Tendresse: La Vie et l'Expérience Spirituelle de L.M. Grignion de Montfort. (Paris: François-Xavier de Guibert, 1996).

Part Two
Chapter 1

[1] "Merit." Catholic Encyclopedia. www.newadvent.org,

[2] "Louis the Pious." en.wikipedia.org, 2005.

[3] Garrigou-Lagrange, 117-120.

[4] Paul Robert. Le Petit Robert: Alphabétique et Analogique de la Langue Française. (Paris: Société du Nouveau Littré, 1979).

[5] Abigail Ann Young "The Fourth Gospel In the Twelfth Century: Rupert of Deutz on the Gospel of John". www.chass.toronto.edu/~yount/text.hetml #part 1. 1998.

[6] Jordan Aumann, O.P Spiritual Theology. (Allen, Texas: Christian Classics, 1979), 263.

[7] Garrigou-Lagrange, 83-84.

[8] True Devotion, TAN, 134

[9] RM, #40.

[10] "Francis de Sales, Doctor of the Church" in Theotokos, 149-150.

[11] Fr. Reginald Garrigou-Lagrange, O.P Christian Perfection and Contemplation: According to St. Thomas Aquinas and St. John of the Cross. (Rockford, IL.:TAN Books and Publishers, Inc. 1937), 386-387.

[12] RM., #45.

[13] See Traité de la Vraie Dévotion à la Sainte Vierge St. Louis-Marie Grignion de Montfort. (Paris: Éditions du Seuil, 1966), #155, no. 5.

[14] See note NAB Jer. 31:22.

[15] Michael Miller "The Philosopher's Stone.". http://www.quackgrass.com, 1999.

[16] Cf. Traité de la Vraie Dévotion #159, no. 3 and "Henri-Marie Boudon" in Theotokos, 86.

[17] "Odilo of Cluny" in Theotokos, 271.